THE GUIDE

MANAGING DOUCHEBAGS, RECRUITING WINGMEN, AND

ATTRACTING WHO YOU WANT

DISCARD

Rosalind Wiseman
TO JACK

Published in the United States by Harmony Books, an
imprint of the Crown Publishing Group, a division of
Random House, Inc., New York.
www.crownpublishing.com

Harmony Books is a registered trademark and the
Harmony Books colophon is a trademark of Random
House, Inc.

Library of Congress Cataloging-in-Publication Data

[CIP data]

ISBN 978-1532966156

10 9 8 7 6 5 4 3 2 1

First Edition

TABLE OF CONTENTS

THE REAL BRO CODE

CHAPTER ONE

WHY THIS BOOK IS NOT A WASTE OF YOUR TIME

I have a friend who can't lose at anything. The last time we were playing COD, he got so mad he stood up and yelled, "Fuck this!" knocked over a chair, and stomped out of the house. It's ridiculous. The other guys in my group feel the same way, so we're starting to do things without him. But it's so stupid to drop a friendship over this. — Oliver, 17

I genuinely like playing hockey. It's part of who I am. But in high school you can't both be a jock and do anything else if you're a guy. So if you liked two kinds of activities and one made you a victim and one made you cool, can you honestly say you wouldn't pick the one that made you cool? —Jack, 16

My girlfriend just found out I cheated on her. She keeps asking me why I cheated, and I don't really want to tell her the reason . . . that it had nothing to do with her and I just wanted to. I know that sounds bad, but it's the truth. Now all of her friends hate me, and she broke up with me. Then she texts me. I'm so confused! —Kyle, 16

My friend's parents just accused me of taking something from their house. My friend defended me, but how can I hang out there again if that's what they're thinking about me? —Victor, 17

How do I get out of the Friend Zone?" —Every guy over the age of 12

I don't know you. I don't know if you can relate to any of these situations. I don't know where you live. I have no idea if you like school or can't wait to get out of there every day. If you have brothers or sisters, I don't know if they're incredibly irritating or you like hanging out with them. I have no idea if you sort of play sports, been obsessed since you were five (and hate it or love it) or think it's a huge waste of time. I don't know if you're into theatre, band, or you have no outside interests (no judgment) or what kind of video games you play or what music you like. The list of things I don't know is endless. But I do know this:

1. Guys are a lot smarter than most people realize.

2. Guys can have really complicated problems with their friends or families.

3. Guys sometimes say, "I'm fine, don't worry about it," when they're really feeling the complete opposite.

4. Some guys love death and destruction. This doesn't mean they're crazy or mean.

5. Some guys don't love death and destruction. This doesn't mean they're weak or weird.

Obviously, you have other people in your life. Hopefully, these people (parents, friends, family, friends' parents, teachers, school administrators, coaches, girls, guys on your team, kids in your neighborhood, school bus drivers, random kids, etc.) are generally fine—meaning, they don't go out of their way to annoy you or make your life miserable. But at some point you'll probably experience a situation with one of these people that's so irritating, unfair, frustrating, or stupid that you're tempted to punch something.

Except there's a problem. However good it may feel in the moment (before your hand is throbbing in pain), three things are inevitable:

1   You'll get in trouble.

2   At least one adult who has some power over you will be too mad at you to listen to your side of the story.

3   It won't solve the problem that made you lash out in the first place.

What you have in your hands right now is an operations manual to tell you what to do when you run into one of these intense situations. Of course, you can have other types of problems. Like the kind you ignore, even though down deep you know you're going to have to deal. This manual will show you what to do if another guy relentlessly annoys you or you're dealing with an adult who's freaking out on you. It'll give you a way to feel better when you've made a mistake and people won't let you forget it. It'll give you secrets to dealing with girl problems, like when they get mad at you and won't tell you why. It'll show you how to get someone to fall in love with you or how to break up with someone with minimum drama.

Why should you listen to me? Here's what you need to know so you can decide. I spend most of my time working with people your age. Any knowledge or advice I may have comes from listening to what young people tell me is going on in their lives. I believe teens deserve adults who admit the messed up things that happen in teens' lives and give them realistic advice that accurately reflects what's going on in their lives. I don't have all the answers, but I think what teens are going through is important and deserves respect.

A few years ago, I wrote a similar book about girls called *Queen Bees and Wannabes*. You may have heard of it, or of the movie based on it, called Mean Girls. I still work with teachers and parents, and for years I've thought about writing a book for guys like Queen Bees. But for some reason (like I was intimidated, didn't think I could do a good job, and didn't really want to expose myself to a potential huge failure), I kept putting it off.

I knew I couldn't write this book by myself. If it was going to have any chance of being good, guys were going to have to help. As soon as I started asking guys if they were interested in a project like this, I was amazed by the response. Over hundreds of guys from different backgrounds and schools said yes. Athletes, theater kids, loners, anarchists, they're all here. They answered my endless questions, read the chapters, and told me when I was wrong or what I needed to add. Why were they doing this? It wasn't like they were getting school credit for it. Here's what some of my guy editors said:

> *I feel that helping people in bad situations I've already been in is a duty. — Mathias, 16*

> *I want to be part of something bigger than myself that will make a difference for our gender and my "peers." But also because I feel like our "Guy World" is something that's been kept in the dark for too long. —Victor, 17*

I wrote this book so guys like you could be better prepared. So you could see problems on the horizon instead of when they come up from behind you and blindside you. Since you can't be prepared for everything, the book will also help you even if you get knocked down and it feels like someone wants to keep you there.

Here's how the book works. First, we're breaking down the basics of what the "Bro Code" actually is. Second, we move to friendships and conflicts among guys. Then we talk about girls, and finally we go into dealing with adults.

—

4

In every chapter, the editors chose tough scenarios to highlight for you, and then we (the editors and I) came up with the best strategies to handle them.

Throughout this book, when I touch on topics that are closely related to other sections of the book, I'll point it out so if you have a pressing issue, then you'll know exactly where to go and you won't waste time. If and when there's something going on in your life that's bothering you and you aren't sure what to do, this book may help you. Read it when you need it.

One thing to note: a lot of guys care about attracting girls, so part of this book is about helping with that. But obviously guys aren't just attracted to girls all the time so and they need and deserve the same level of advice and support, so I wrote the book with that in mind as well. Chapter fifteen is specifically written to address some of the issues gay guys deal with—especially with their straight friends, but the relationship advice in the other chapters applies to any guy regardless of who they're attracted to. To avoid confusion, I sometimes use the pronouns "she" and "her" based on the specific problem—but this isn't meant to imply that those sections are only intended to address straight guys. The reality is, no matter what, two things are true: 1) No matter who you're attracted to, things can get weird, and 2) Gay or straight, you're dealing with girls in some capacity, and that has its own set of particular complications.

Last thing, does your mom or dad or any other adult relentlessly ask you questions and you'd like them to stop? How about your parent refusing to believe you when you're telling the truth and then believing your brother or sister who lies to their face? Would it make your life better if someone told them what being a guy today is like without you having to tell them the private details of your life? Well, in addition to writing this book for guys, I also wrote a book for parents (and any adult who works with guys) called Masterminds and Wingmen that explains all of this to them. Those guy editors I described above also helped me with that book, so they told me exactly what parents needed to know. It tells parents when to back off and when and how to talk to their sons. So if you read any part of this book and think it's worthwhile, please tell your parents to read Masterminds and Wingmen. I'm trying to change the conversation about how adults talk about guys, and I need your help to do it.

CHAPTER TWO

THE UNWRITTEN RULE BOOK

I bet any amount of money that no one ever sat you down and said, "If you have a really big problem and you even think of admitting it and asking for help, you're a weak, pathetic excuse for a man." But somehow, without realizing it, most guys to some degree have this message wired into their brains. Where does this message come from? It's not like someone is beaming things into your brain all day since you were a little kid about when it's okay for a guy to ask for help.

Except, in a way, that's exactly what's going on. Think back to when you were five or six and what toys you liked to play with. You may have played with toys that looked a lot like this:

Now, I want you to imagine what this Batman[1] looks like when he's incredibly happy and excited. Imagine him in love. Now imagine him really sad or depressed. Does Batman ever look different? No. Batman's emotional range is always somewhere between serious, detached, sullen, and angry. No matter how physically hurt he is, Batman shakes it off. He never doubts that he can handle his own problems. If he's angry, he either clenches his jaw or exacts revenge with utter physical domination. If he really needs advice or he's being stubborn and making an ass of himself, Alfred is always there without Batman having to ask and always knows what to say.

It's awesome when you're a young boy and you're flying around the room with a Batman cape your grandma gave you. As Batman, you're the hero, you don't have to listen to anyone, you have unlimited power, and you can solve all your problems. Which, when you're five, is particularly cool because the reality is that you have very little control over your life. Someone else decides when you sleep and eat. They even decide what you wear.

It may seem like a big leap between pretending you're Batman at five and its possible effect on you now. But in many ways the adults around you can encourage you to have the emotional range of Batman, sometimes without realizing what they're doing or understanding its impact on you. Think back to your first memories of getting hurt, upset, or frightened. What do you remember the adults around you saying and doing?

Seriously. Stop reading and think about it. And feel free to stop and think at any point in this book. You don't have to rush.

---

[1] By the way, I love the current Batman movies. If you ever want to have a three hour conversation with me, ask me why.

Most adults, even adults who believe they want guys to be open with their feelings, will immediately respond to a boy being upset or hurt by saying something like, "You're a big boy! You're okay! Don't be upset! You're fine! Shake it off!"

Being independent, self-reliant, courageous and getting up after you've been knocked down are absolutely critical skills to have—and there's nothing wrong with wanting to be heroic. But when a guy is raised to believe that he isn't allowed to have feelings of uncertainty, fear, sadness, or insecurity, it can seriously mess him up. When that happens, a guy gets the message that adults believe something is fundamentally wrong with him, or any boy, who has these feelings. That's how so many guys learn to be ashamed for even having these "weak" feelings and they bury them deep inside.

It's not like these messages stop as you get older. They just get more intense and varied. You live in a world where people tell you in countless little ways what the unwritten "Guy World" rules are. These people come at you in a variety of ways. The ads you see. The movies you see. The video games you play. The books you read. How your parents, coaches, and teachers treat you. The list is endless and will change depending on your individual situation. But the message is always the same: you have to act, look, and even think in very specific ways or there's something wrong with you as a guy. These rules are often the invisible puppet strings controlling people's behavior. I'm not only talking about you. I'm talking about everyone, no matter how old they are.

Not every guy reacts to these rules in the same way. Some guys really drink the Kool-Aid. Others openly despise or rebel against the rules. Some guys are in the middle. But one thing is always true. In order to become your own man, you have to come to grips with how these messages exist inside your head and how they influence what you think, what you say, and what you do.

ARE YOU YOUR OWN MAN?

I often ask guys in my classes to bring in their favorite movie scenes or video game scenarios and then ask them if what they watch represents the way guys are supposed to act. Not surprisingly, the guys don't think it does—or if it does, not to any great extent. Then I ask these questions. "Describe a guy who can influence people or has high social status. This is a person everyone knows. If he has an opinion, everyone listens and agrees. What does he look like, and how does he act?"

We write their responses on the board like this, inside the box:

FUNNY	MONEY
STRONG/CUT	TALL
GETS GIRLS	RULE BREAKER & GETS AWAY WITH IT
ALWAYS RELAXED	CONFIDENT
INDEPENDENT	QUICK COMEBACKS
GOOD AT 'RIGHT' SPORTS	DETACHED
SLACKER ATTITUDE NO MATTER THE OUTCOME	

Then I ask them to describe a guy who doesn't have high social status. "This is someone who is likely to be teased, ridiculed, or ignored," I explain. "What does he look like? How does he act?"

We write their responses around the first set of answers like this, outside the box:

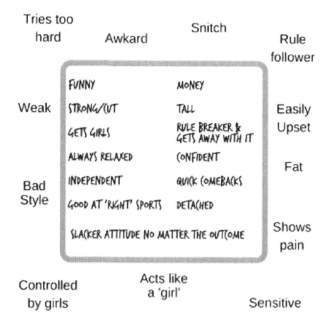

Tries too hard · Awkard · Snitch · Rule follower

Weak · Easily Upset

Bad Style · Fat

Controlled by girls · Acts like a 'girl' · Sensitive · Shows pain

Inside the box:

FUNNY

MONEY

STRONG/CUT

TALL

GETS GIRLS

RULE BREAKER & GETS AWAY WITH IT

ALWAYS RELAXED

CONFIDENT

INDEPENDENT

QUICK COMEBACKS

GOOD AT 'RIGHT' SPORTS

DETACHED

SLACKER ATTITUDE NO MATTER THE OUTCOME

I call this exercise "The Act-Like-a-Man Box" (abbreviated from now on as ALMB). After I've written down all these unwritten rules, guys can still have a hard time admitting how much control the ALMB has over their lives. Some get really angry about the unfairness of it. Like "money" is in the box. I agree that it's not fair, but it's still true that it's easier to have high status if you have more money. Then I ask them what they would do in the following situations.

- Four guys are friends. One guy in the group gets teased a lot and hates it but doesn't say anything.

- A star athlete wants to quit the team but feels he can't.

- A guy won't tell his friends that he got an A on his science test and that he studies really hard.

- A guy won't tell his friends that his girlfriend puts him down all the time.

- A guy is really struggling in school but doesn't want to admit to anyone how much it bothers him.

Then everyone in the room gets quiet because they can see how the box traps them. Doing the ALMB exercise isn't about where individual guys fit—either inside or outside the box. It isn't about the center of the box being better or worse than outside the box. It's also not about labeling the guys in the center of the box as the worst, most arrogant people you know. This exercise is about how we all get caught learning to value a person who has more "in-the-box" characteristics and devalue a person who doesn't. It's about understanding how these unwritten rules convince you and other guys that you can do some things but not others. It's about how adults actively put pressure on guys to fit and stay in the box. It's about what emotions you're allowed to have as a guy and how you're allowed to express them. And it can often train guys on exactly the ways to lash out at anyone they want to shut up.

Let me give you a somewhat ridiculous example. Even though I'm a straight woman, I'm regularly called a fag when I speak out about racism, homophobia or violence against women. Here are a few recent examples from my Twitter account:

@rosalindwiseman I bet she got raped by a whale cock and the jizz turned her into a fag.

Everyone tweet @rosalindwiseman is a fag
*@rosalindwiseman F****** fag*

So when I got those tweets it bothered me. No, I didn't freak out and obsess on them. People say mean stuff about me all the time and I can take it. But it does bother me. Why? Because I get the most hate when I am speak out against racism, sexism, homophobia and other forms of bigotry. It's ironic—because the people going after me with these words are making my point but another way of looking at it is these words are used to shut anyone up who is going against the ALMB. And, even with professional athletes coming out and a lot of people accepting gay marriage, it's still true that the knee-jerk reaction to dismiss anyone who acts outside the narrow range of the ALMB is to be called gay. Think back when you were younger and the first time you heard someone being called "gay" or any word like it. For most guys, at the latest, it's in fourth grade, and they instantly know that whatever they're doing that's getting this word put on them must be immediately stopped—like wearing fuzzy multicolored socks, liking the Disney Channel, getting upset when someone's mean, or defending someone who wears fuzzy socks or likes the Disney Channel. By high school, this dynamic can have an invisible yet viselike grip on guys that stops them from speaking out when other guys go after someone.

> *Last week ten close friends of mine were bullying this kid who is exactly like we've described him by not having high social status: fat, bad style, weak, etc. I told them to cut it out and that they should leave him alone, and while eight of them stopped,*

13

two told me to "stop being a fag." — Carl, 16

To equate speaking out about abuse of power and social injustice with being sexually attracted to other men makes no sense. If it did, straight guys would be defined as those who do nothing or who join in when someone's being abused. Then only gay men would have the courage to stand up. Not only is that inaccurate—gay men have challenges about speaking out just like everyone else's—but it's insulting to straight guys.
What's so frustrating and ironic is that homophobia stops guys from being courageous—not the courage to fight someone if challenged, but the moral courage to speak out.

> *I know many gay people and have many family friends who are gay, and I have to say, one of the most frustrating things about going to my school is how they use terms like "fag" and "gay." The even more aggravating part is how, if I imply that we shouldn't be derogatory to gay people, I'm somehow "gay." —Will, 15*

Thank you, Will. The same way someone who advocates animal rights

> *Isn't an animal, a person who advocates gay rights isn't necessarily gay. —Matt, 16*

Ultimately, the ALMB tries to keep you ignorant, clueless, compliant, and locked into blindly doing what is expected of you. Being ignorant and clueless is a completely unacceptable way to go through life. I want you to rebel against it. But you also have to look in the mirror and have the courage to ask how the ALMB influences you, your friends, and the adults in your life. Once you do both of these things, you'll have way more control over yourself and the problems you face.

POPULARITY IN GUY WORLD

One of the most common questions girls ask me is, "Why are the popular girls popular? People don't even like them." In girls' minds, a girl's popularity should be linked to people liking her because she's nice. In all the years I've taught, no boy has ever asked me that question. It's not because guys are unaware of the power of popularity and social status. It's because the definition of popularity is incredibly obvious to them. Popularity doesn't mean people like you. It means people know you have power and it's not worth confronting you in a conflict. It's like having shiny armor that gives you protection to do what you want—plus some girls (especially the ones who like shiny things) think you're hot. Of course, what armor also does is hide your weaknesses. Before you realize it, you're so dependent on it that you feel like you always have to wear it.

THE BREAKDOWN

Most guys I talk to believe there's a 10 percent who look like they fit into the ALMB the most, followed by the 75 percent who make up the general population, 10 percent who hang out at the bottom but have a strong group, and the last 5 percent—an outer perimeter of kids who either get how the system works and don't want any part of it or who have such poor social skills that they can't fit in anywhere. Every group has a corresponding girls' group to the point that some are entirely coed, but for the most part there's limited social interaction between these larger groups of guys.

There are a few notable exceptions when the groups tend to intermingle. The most common one is when people are using drugs or alcohol. The day after I sent this section to the editors, I got back this email:

> *I have proof of it from yesterday! In my school everybody stays within their own group. However,*

yesterday, my friend (slacker) was telling me before a party at night that he, along with 2 hipsters, 1 jock, 1 musician, 2 drug dealers, and another slacker, all got together to smoke pot. At first I was super-amazed to find out that some of these kids smoked pot, but also that the jock—who you'd think would be "too cool" to hang out with others who weren't from his group—was actually willing to hang out with the hipsters and vice versa. —Brian, 16

When you combine the ALMB, popularity, and the group breakdown, you're looking at something that spans generations. As in, the men you've grown up around can probably relate to all of this. (Whether they remember it or will admit it is another issue.) But your generation does have a unique relationship to this Guy World social structure. Being in the 10 percent of the ALMB doesn't always look the same as being in the 10 percent of the social hierarchy of a specific school. Being a musician, a skater, a hipster, or even a drug dealer—these are all paths to high social status. Especially in big diverse schools, there isn't one social hierarchy but an infinite number of them. But, here's the catch. No matter what a guy does or has that brings him high social status, that status can easily lead to being an asshole.

The simplest way to demonstrate this is with girls. A popular music hipster could be a more ruthless and arrogant womanizer than a star soccer or football player. Why? Because when you have social power, in whatever environment you find it, it can easily convince you that you have the right to be an asshole. So, if you're popular, it's your responsibility not to abuse it. Popularity and social power aren't necessarily bad (just like football and lacrosse aren't necessarily bad). Being an asshole is. Don't be an asshole.

THE 10 PERCENTERS

For the 10 percenters, conforming to the ALMB is law. If you're in this group, you aren't an individual, you're a piece of a machine.

There are four defining characteristics of this top 10 percent.

1. They look like they're good (as opposed to actually being good) in at least one Guy World sport—football, basketball, soccer, hockey, or even lacrosse or water polo (depending on your geographic location).

2. Their hair, clothes, walk, swagger, flow, and slang are the same. That look becomes their social uniform. (Think of how they all shave their heads before a game.)

3. Their parents can be so invested in their sons' status that they allow any "bad boy" behavior by supporting it outright, looking the other way, making excuses for it, or denying it all together.

4. Maybe most important, these guys have an intense desire to be in and remain in that 10 percent group.

Listen to what guys say:

> *They constantly put up a front, and they build it up in school. They walk around with this scowl and attitude of, I'm so cold and tired of everything. If I go up to a normal person and say, "Hey, what's up?" they'll say, "Hey, what's up?" back to me. But with*

the kids we're talking about, they don't mingle in the other groups because they think, Why should I? — Ethan, 16

It's like a cult. Every year a couple graduate, so they add a few. It's a continuous cycle. —Auguste, 18

At my school I'm in that 10 percent elite, but I honestly feel like I have to fight for it. I'm not the meathead jock who plays lacrosse and football and gets the praise handed down to them. To be up in the 10 percent elite, I have to be bold and make some moves that I personally wouldn't make but have to in order to fit in. We [the 10 percenters] are the ones with the parties and the booze, the hot girls, and I feel like if I wasn't fighting to be in this group I would just blend in with the rest of the crowd and high school would be pretty crappy. I wish I didn't care as much about my social standing, but no matter what any guy says, they truly care. —Cole, 17

THE MAJORITY

While the 10 percenters feel self-conscious about socializing outside of their tribe, the 75 percent of guys in "the Majority" usually feel that they can easily hang out with kids in other groups. The 75 percent is made up of different groups of about five to ten kids each. Of course, regardless of their social status, all guys are still subject to the pressure to live up to our culture's standards of masculinity, so the guys in the Majority can be self-conscious, but they aren't constantly thinking about their image in terms of the ALMB, the way 10 percent guys are. The only time a guy in the Majority intensely cares about his image is when he decides to fight his way into the 10 percent, but that's an exception, not the rule.

The 75 percent is much more open to change. I try to move around in the 75 percent group. What I've found is that it's a lot easier to be sitting at one table with one group in the 75 percent and go to another table the next day because they aren't as territorial as the upper 10 percent. —Will, 15

I'm in a pretty high group. Not the highest, but pretty high. This may sound weird, but honestly, what I'm about to say really meant something to me. In tenth grade I had gotten into theater, and one day the theater kids invited me to a party, and that felt incredible. Some people would say that those kids invited me because I'm in a higher group than they are, but that's not true. They're happy to keep to their group. When they did that, it was a huge feeling of acceptance. —Hunter, 17

THE BOTTOM RUNG

Adults often assume that guys on the bottom rung are miserable, lonely, and depressed. It's not true. Guys in this group know their low social position, know they can appear odd to others, and usually don't care as long as they have at least one strong friendship. Many of them believe that because they aren't even in the running for high social status, they have more dependable friends. That's debatable, but what is true is that the members of the group are usually very connected to each other and don't feel like they have to constantly prove themselves to anyone.

THE OUTER PERIMETER

The Outer Perimeter (OP) is made up guys who, in their peers' eyes, exist apart from the entire social system. It's populated with anarchists, pranksters, politicians, obsessed single-subject or single-sport high-achievers, and kids seriously lacking in social skills. Obviously, I'm grouping a lot of people in the OP who have very different characteristics and can be at the highest or lowest level of social status.

You can choose to be in the OP because you understand the ALMB (even though you may not exactly call it that), see no value in joining the social system, and have strong friendships outside of school. That means you'll also be exceptionally good at blending into the background. Other kids aren't going to think you're irritating; they just don't know what to make of you and sometimes don't know you're there.

There are also guys in the OP whose position is inflexible. If you're this guy, you can struggle with reading people, like trying to figure out what people mean versus what they say, or how to join a group of people and talk to them. Sometimes people can get irritated with you because you obsess on one topic or because you can't get the hint if they don't want to hang out with you.

> *With these guys, [playing] video games go beyond being a pastime, a distraction, or a way to blow off steam. It becomes an obsession, one that won't really help him make friends. It becomes the guy's sole method of interaction with others.* —Robert, 14

> *Since I am really bad at making friends, I have to keep any that I make. Right now I have one friend, but they don't want me making other friends. I don't know what to do. I'm stuck.* —Michael, 16

If you're on either side of this struggle, as a guy on the OP or someone dealing with a guy on the OP, it can be really frustrating.

THE MASTERMIND AND HIS MINIONS

Think about a group of guy friends. Most of these

groups are broken down as follows: a core group of friends and then an inner circle of five to eight guys. Within this group, each person plays a role or maybe more depending on his circumstances. What follows are descriptions of the roles that guys play in their group. If you can understand the role (or roles) you already are playing, you'll be better able to predict how conflicts are going to go down in your group and manage them better. If you can answer "yes" to the majority of items describing each role, you're probably identifying yourself.

Here are the different roles that guys can play:

Mastermind

Associate

Bouncer

Entertainer

Fly

Conscience

Punching Bag

Champion

In middle school the ALMB forces guys into one of these roles, which are obvious and constant as the guys interact with each other. In high school, some guys are trapped by their role as much as they were in middle school. But for most high school guys, the roles are not so rigid all the time. Think of it this way. Everyone, even the Mastermind with the highest social status, has moments in his life of being a Fly or a Punching Bag. In addition, when the roles really come out in high school is when there's conflict in the group. Instantly, each person's role comes out full force. The behavior behind these roles is your programming, and that programming is defined by the ALMB.

THE MASTERMIND

"The Mastermind" is charismatic and naturally good at figuring out people's weaknesses. He decides what's funny, stupid, cool, etc., and has the absolute right to dismiss any opposing viewpoint or opinion. This can apply to anything, from shoe color to real-world political issues. While he may not talk to girls a lot, he's good at getting and holding girls' attention without looking like he cares. He's excellent at arguing, and especially good at arguing with girls and making them feel stupid. If he looks like an ALMB guy, adults who love the ALMB love him or are easily intimidated by him.

Despite what we're calling him, Masterminds don't often look and act as calculating and intelligent as the name might imply, but their ability to influence others is what counts. It's hard to know how much of a deliberate Mastermind a guy is until the moment someone publicly and effectively threatens his authority. In that moment he instantly goes from having an "I could care less" attitude to becoming a self-righteous, crusading political operative.

> If the Mastermind talks badly about a less popular person, then all the other guys won't like him. But if the unpopular person talks badly about the Mastermind, it won't matter. —Ryan, 11

> He's excellent with the side comments. The ones you can't quite hear but you know are bad. —Max, 15

> He never looks like he doesn't know what to do. —Ryan, 14

What does the *Mastermind* gain? Power and control.

What does the *Mastermind* lose? It's hard to admit it, but the Mastermind can constantly feel pressure to maintain his position. He won't take risks that go against his image. He can't admit to anyone when he's in over his head. His relationships are weaker than he wants to admit because his friends' loyalty is based on fear or just not wanting to confront him because they don't think it's worth it.

THE ASSOCIATE

Although the Mastermind and "the Associate" can look similar, the Associate is much more social. He talks to and flirts with girls more often than the Mastermind. He's interested in other people's business and what advantages he can get from it.

> *He's the one the Mastermind respects the most. He can be honest with the Mastermind without having to worry about getting the shit kicked out of him. He's harder to tell by a simple glance, but if you watch the interactions within the group, he's the guy that the Mastermind will pay most attention to. —Ian, 17*

> *More people like him more than the Mastermind. Plus, he usually knows all the information. Like if a bunch of guys are hanging out, the Associate gets the texts about where people are hanging out. Then he tells the Mastermind what's going on, and then it just takes the Mastermind saying, "Yeah, let's go," and the group is going. —Keith, 14*

What does the *Associate* gain? Power by association.

What does the *Associate* lose? An identity separate from the Mastermind.

THE BOUNCER

"The Bouncer" is like the guy at a club: big, intimidating, and willing to sacrifice himself as part of his job responsibilities. He isn't good at verbally defending himself and can't read or understand people's motivations. Because he doesn't question people who have authority over him, he's likely to do stupid, dangerous things if dared or asked. Especially if he's encouraged by the Mastermind or the Associate, he loves to publicly binge-drink, be rude to guys who are outside their group, and say stupid things to girls because the Mastermind or Associate told him to. The girls in his social group don't like him, and he doesn't understand why. In situations with girls he's often the odd man out, or the guys set him up with someone who is similarly socially vulnerable.

> *The Bouncer has to be tall compared to everyone else. The Mastermind has to be physically strong, but he doesn't really have to use it. Sometimes I think the Bouncer isn't that smart. But he always acts like he doesn't care about school, so it's hard to know what's really going on. —Oliver, 16*

What does the Bouncer gain? Social status and power that he would never have without the Mastermind and Associate.

What does the Bouncer lose? Respect and the ability to have healthy social relationships. His blind loyalty stops him from seeing how he's being used by the Mastermind and Associate. It can be really hard for other kids to feel comfortable around him.

The Mastermind, the Associate, and the Bouncer have these characteristics in common:

- They don't like to lose. If they do, they make excuses and minimize the other person's achievement.

- They like to break rules in school in ways that make them look like they don't give a shit about what anyone thinks of them.

- When they do get in trouble, they make a point of undermining the adult who's disciplining them and telling everyone else how stupid the kids, parents, or teachers are who complained. In extreme cases, they will seek revenge against the adult and their original victim.

- They have little to no respect for female authority figures or adult men who don't fit into the ALMB.

THE ENTERTAINER

"The Entertainer" is willing to make fun of himself, especially when there's conflict or tension in the group. He loves debating but never takes it seriously or personally. He responds to the bragging and aggression by other members of his group by bragging in ways that are clearly absurd and untrue. Entertainers are aware of the ridiculousness of their group's behavior.

> *When he wants to be serious, people turn their heads and say, "Stop." They never take him seriously because they're always waiting for the laugh—Will, 18*

What does the Entertainer gain? A sense of inclusion, belonging, and security in the group because he's funny. He has membership in the group without having to act like an ass or feel desperate to be in.

What does the Entertainer lose? He always has to keep up the act=-. It's harder to be taken seriously about anything.

THE CONSCIENCE

"The Conscience" worries about the consequences and getting caught. Other guys can get annoyed at the Conscience because he's like having a chaperone around always telling you what could go wrong. If they have a lot of history with him, they'll put up with it. Because he wants to follow rules, he's much more likely to always do his schoolwork, follow the rules to the letter, and take care of his responsibilities, which leaves him vulnerable to both sharing and doing work for his friends and then being ridiculed for having done his work in the first place. Because he's trustworthy, he's used as a smokescreen when dealing with parents and authority figures. As in, "I'm so sorry, Officer. I know my friends were really loud. We'll keep the music down, I promise."

The Conscience usually gets a reputation for being the "nice guy," which he usually hates, whether it's girls describing him that way or his friends teasing him. Either way, he feels stripped of his masculinity. As a result, sometimes the Conscience has to prove he's not as nice and innocent as he appears, so he does something like hook up with a girl he knows another guy in his group likes.

What does the Conscience gain? Teachers, administrators, and parents consider him a good guy, giving him that extra layer of trust that the other guys might not have.

What does the Conscience lose? Sometimes he's excluded from what the other guys are doing because he might try to stop them from doing something mean, stupid, or dangerous. He's at risk of being seen as a snitch, which can damage his friendships.

THE PUNCHING BAG

In almost every group of guys, there's one guy who the other guys love but relentlessly ridicule. It's like when someone says, "No one beats up my little brother but me." If someone outside the group goes after the "Punching Bag," the other guys will defend him to the death. Whoever he dates, his friends will harass him for it[2]. Despite all of this, he hates conflict and just wants people to get along.

What does the Punching Bag gain: Not a lot. He has friends, but the price is high.

What does the Punching Bag lose: He has no choice but to accept his friends' behavior.

THE FLY[3]

"The Fly" is the kid who hovers outside the group, either the larger social group or an individual group of guys. He has no idea how annoying he is. If his parents have money, he'll try to build his friendships by bragging or buying. Guys can tolerate a Fly for a while, but usually the frustration builds and at some point the other guys have had enough and lash out. There's no guilt when excluding the Fly because he's seen as bringing it on himself.

What does the Fly gain? NOTHING. Don't be the Fly.

What does the Fly lose? A lot. Don't be the Fly.

THE CHAMPION

"The Champion" is a guy who isn't controlled by the

---

[2] The only exception being the impossible scenario of dating an undeniably hot girl with lots of guns; see: Jovovich, Milla.

[3] If you cross the Entertainer with the Fly, you get the Showboat. The more Fly characteristics he has, the more annoying he is— and therefore the more of a Showboat he is.

ALMB but has enough of its positive characteristics that people respect him. People like him. He can take criticism, doesn't make people choose friends, and doesn't blow off someone for a better offer. When people are harassed or demeaned, he intervenes but doesn't make everyone feel weird when he does it. He's comfortable hanging out with guys who are inside the box and guys who are outside the box. He holds his own opinions but still listens to others.

What does the Champion gain: People genuinely like and respect him.

What does the Champion lose: It can be lonely. People will sometimes turn on him for doing the right thing or not upholding the box. He can feel older and apart from his peers.

YOU DON'T HAVE TO BE BOXED IN

If you recognize yourself or other guys in these roles, that doesn't mean all of you have to stick with your roles. Masterminds can realize the price of their arrogance, Punching Bags can learn to stand up to their friends, and Flies can realize that people will like them if they stop trying so hard. What the roles give you is a way of looking at your decisions so you can make changes and act more in line with what you really want. At the same time, you have your own unique set of circumstances and friends. You may go to a school where everyone looks like you and basically has the same amount of money, a truly diverse school where twenty-five languages are spoken in the hallways, a tiny school where you've known every single person in the school since you were five, or a huge school where most people only know you by the school ID you wear around your neck.

Feelings of power and disempowerment, however, are universal, and it's common to struggle with friendships. There will always be a group with all the trappings of power. There will always be people in the middle. Everyone will have moments when they should confront people who have more power and whose voices have more influence. Everyone will have moments of seeing someone being trapped in the box or punished for not conforming to it, and not knowing what to do.

I think the worst thing about the group roles and the ALMB can be that you're forbidden to care about what happens to you and the people around you. But you have a right to care. You should fight back against people who want to box you in. No one can go through life being "fine" all the time. You have a right to feel passionate about changing the screwed-up things in your life for the better. You have a right to choose your path—whatever that happens to be—without any of this crap tricking you into thinking you don't.

CHAPTER THREE

THE LAWS OF BROTHERHOOD

I know it looks like we're insane and loud. We can be really rude, and our parents don't even hear how we usually talk to each other. But I'd do anything for my friends. I can't really explain the bond we have, but it's deep. —Auguste, 17

I love the guy. Stayed up all night walking around, talked the whole night. But we have gone through times when we've hated each other. One time we didn't talk for six months, but there's a bond there that isn't going to be broken . . .although he can be so stubborn when he thinks he's right. He's my hard truth friend. Just calls it out. Doesn't moderate his approach. That's why I call him "the Mule." ["The Mule," sitting next to him, smiles and nods in agreement.]. —Hunter, 17

They know me sometimes better than I know myself. They tell me things I don't want to hear, but since they want the best for me, I know I have to listen. — RJ, 16

Is there anyone you'd rather just sit on a couch and watch some stupid video on your phone or play games with than your friends? Is there anyone you've laughed harder with? Is there anyone who understands you better when something is seriously messed up in your life? Guy after guy I've talked to for this book agreed with me. But when guys admit how much they value their friends, they have to make fun of it by draping themselves over each other, pretend-hugging, and proclaiming, "I love you, man!" As Hunter says, "I know it's ridiculous, but we have to lisp when we say something emotional. We're just way too insecure with ourselves to show our feelings any other way."

Life is better—way better—with friends. For guys who don't have close friends (even if it looks like they have tons of friends), it can feel incredibly lonely. But friendships are complicated. Things aren't always going to go smoothly. And even though conflict is inevitable, even with your closest friends, the ALMB doesn't allow that. Guys are supposed to let everything roll off their backs or throw a few punches and then forget about it.

No disrespect, but that's stupid and unfair to you. You can't go through life thinking that the only two options you have when you're angry are squashing your feelings and punching people. Your life is way more complex. Think about it: Have you ever been really angry at someone, thought of the perfect thing to say to get your point across … but never actually confronted him? Or if you did say something, he turned your words around or did something else that made you regret bringing it up?

Let's take a moment and compare conflict between guys to how it goes with girls. You've probably seen how girls interact. From the outside, it looks incredibly intense. They're inseparable, they constantly analyze their friendships with each other, they fight about things that may make no sense to you, and then they hug in the hallway the next day. Some girls will even try to drag you into their conflicts (which is to be avoided at all costs, as I'll discuss in a later chapter).

Most guys' response is, "Girls are insane. I'll never understand them, and even if I did know what they're so intense/upset/angry about, I'm sure it's totally irrelevant or blown out of proportion." These experiences may give you the impression that girls' relationships and friendships with each other are more complicated and filled with conflict than yours. I disagree. Why?

Because one unwritten rule in Guy World is that a guy, even a close friend, can be as rude as possible and the other guy can't get upset. If he does get upset, then another unwritten rule is that he can be made fun of even more. If Guy World were a democracy—meaning, each guy had an equal right to go after the other guy—then things would be fine. But that's not what's usually going on. Instead, the combination of the ALMB and the roles we discussed in the last chapter combine to control who goes after whom. Now that you know what you're up against, you need to integrate that knowledge with a strategy to give you more control.

SEAL: CHANNELING YOUR ANGER EFFECTIVELY

I've never told my friends this, but I get so mad at their little comments. It's fine when it's just us hanging out, but a couple of them make a point of saying them around other people. They constantly mess with me about how short I am, how hairy I am, I'm gay—I'm not that good with the ladies. It's the usual stuff, and it's stupid, but I get really tired of it. Whenever I bring it up, they just laugh at me and get worse. Sometimes I want to explode, but they're my friends. What am I supposed to do? I feel like I just have to take it. Like part of having friends is that they just get to do this to you. —Sam, 15

I want you to remember a time when someone made you really angry or frustrated but you didn't feel like you could say or do anything about it. Remember what that felt like in your gut? Guys have described it to me like there's a huge rock on their chest, they want to explode, or they want to throw up. Or maybe you can relate to Will's description:

All you can think of is, Get me out of here. But you can't, so you fake it. You have to pretend that everything's okay until you get home. Then you just want to go up in your room and go to sleep.

No one wants to have these feelings. When you have them, it's only natural that you want to get rid them. The challenge is how. I'm going to show you a strategy for when that feeling hits your stomach. I'm going to show you how to think through exactly what's bothering you and decide how serious it is, how to approach the other person (or people) who's making you feel like this, and what your best chance is to get them to take you seriously. Right now, I'm talking about friends, but this strategy can be applied to anyone in your life who makes you lose your words or feel like you have to bury your feelings, including parents, teachers, coaches, and girls.

Think of it this way if it works for you. If you were about to go into a battle, you'd be nervous, uncertain about the outcome, adrenalized, and probably afraid. Of course you would be—those are totally understandable feelings to have under the circumstances. But if you allowed these feelings to guide your behavior, you'd act impulsively and increase your likelihood of failure on the battlefield.

The only way to channel your feelings into effective action is to prepare and strategize. You have to think about your approach, your resources, your weaknesses, and your strengths and then size up your opponent in the same way. When the moment comes to initiate your plan, you do your best, knowing it probably won't go exactly the way you wanted but feeling fairly sure that your preparation will allow you to adapt to changing circumstances. When the battle is over, the very fact that you have gone through the process and survived will enable you to do better next time.

This is the same approach I'm asking you to apply to seriously problematic social situations. It may seem strange to you to equate going into battle with social conflicts, but guys' feelings of anxiety, uncertainty, adrenaline, and fear are similar in those situations. Logically, if you want to have some control over how the situation goes down (and get that feeling out of your gut), you have to prepare the same way.

This is the strategy I want you to use when facing conflicts with anyone, from friends to enemies. You can use it when you're angry but also when you're worried. It's a four-step process that I call SEAL. It's not a warm and fuzzy "let's all be friends" thing. It's just a way to think through difficult situations. It stands for the following:

STOP and SETUP: Breath, look, listen, and think. Where should I confront this person? Do I confront him now in public, or later in private?
EXPLAIN: Tell the other person what happened that you don't like/want/are worried about and what you want instead. (Yes, the problem may seem obvious, but it doesn't matter—it needs to be stated.)

AFFIRM and ACKNOWLEDGE: Affirm your (or someone else's) right to be treated with dignity and acknowledge anything you did that may have contributed to the problem (which includes anything from sitting on your feelings to doing something deliberately crappy to the other person).
LOCK in (or lock out, or take a vacation): If you're in an ongoing relationship or friendship with this person, you need to decide if you want to continue the relationship, and if so, on what terms.

Let me be really clear. I am not telling you to go up to someone you're angry with and say something weird like, "Now I need to affirm my right to be treated with dignity." I am not telling you what to say or how to say it. Instead, this strategy works to frame how you want to approach a problem and organize your words and actions. Of course, it isn't going to be easy. You may start out feeling 100 percent miserable and stuck, and nothing I suggest, including SEAL, is going to get you down to 0 percent misery instantaneously. But by going through this process, I'm confident that you can decrease your 100 percent misery to maybe 80 percent. Once you're down to anything less than 100 percent misery, it gets easier to think more clearly, things don't seem so desperate, and your confidence increases.

Part of the SEAL process is to understand that people will probably react by getting defensive or trying to manipulate you into feeling bad, guilty, or regretting that you brought it up. This "push-back" is to be expected. SEAL involves always thinking about what the possible push-back could be, how it could distract you, and how you should respond to it.

Success in using SEAL isn't really about getting the other person to agree with you or making that person realize how wrong he is (or she is, by the way). SEAL is a way of putting into practice two things: being socially competent and doing so with a bedrock belief in treating yourself and other people with dignity (even when you think that's the last thing the other person deserves), with the ultimate goal of gaining the best control over yourself and the situation as possible.

If you don't use SEAL or some strategy like it, you'll be controlled by the Guy World "Rules of Anger." These are the unwritten rules that guide you—again, often without you even knowing it.

1. Tell yourself the problem doesn't matter and then walk around feeling weak.

2. Keep your anger bottled up until you explode over something that looks small.

3. Lash out at someone else who isn't going to put up a fight (meaning you're bullying them).

4. Use alcohol or drugs to ignore or dull your feelings.[4]

None of these ways of expressing your anger gives you a chance to get rid of your anger in a way that makes you

---

[4] On problems with drinking, refer to page 115

feel better or to truly address the problem that's making you angry.

GENERAL RULES FOR SEAL WITH FRIENDS NO MATTER WHAT THE PROBLEM IS

The Stop and Setup with friends is always the same. It should happen privately, like when you're playing a video game, walking back from practice, or just hanging out. The basic rule is that it's better to have intense, awkward conversations while you're doing something else so you don't have to look at the other person. That doesn't mean the conversation won't be weird, but it'll be less weird. Think of it as easing into the conversation and easing out. In less complicated situations, you'll always have to do the Setup and the Explaining, but you'll probably only have to do either the Affirming or the Lock. The whole thing shouldn't take more than two minutes.

If you really don't think you can do SEAL with the person, then you need to admit that your relationship isn't as tight as you think it is or want it to be.

FIRE-STARTING

Fire-starting is when a guy creates or increases conflict between two other guys by backstabbing, gossiping, or lying to drive them further apart. If you think this sounds like something only girls do, you couldn't be more wrong. Say two guys have been really good friends, but they get into a fight over something stupid and drift away from each other. It's not like they officially stopped speaking to each other, but they're giving each other lots of space. Meanwhile, the fire-starter comes in and starts lying to each of them about what the other guy said or did. When this happens to girls, the two girls usually end up confronting each other. That creates its own drama, but at the least, the girls know who was really behind their split. That doesn't happen with guys, because they won't talk to each other. They'll just stay away from each other indefinitely and never know that the fire-starter was behind their rift.

HUMOR: THE INVISIBLE WEAPON

Humor is the double-edged sword in Guy World. The good part of humor is that your social standing will be rock-solid if you're good with comebacks, can get people to laugh, make sarcastic, mocking comments under your breath, and can make fun of yourself. You can be short and terrible at sports, but if you're funny, people will still like you. Humor is often the great equalizer in the face of all the ALMB. It diffuses tense social situations. It teaches guys to get through the everyday annoyances of life without taking themselves or other people too seriously. All very good things. But even for the guys who use humor for good, there's a price to be paid when they feel that they're not permitted to take anything seriously ever, even when they have every reason to. Another bad part of humor is when it's used to initiate an attack against someone so they feel singled out and humiliated. For example, have you ever had to deal with another guy going out of his way to cause someone else maximum public humiliation while defending his actions by saying, "I'm just playing/messing with you?" It doesn't even have to be that extreme. Ever hang out with someone who makes little comments about you to make you self-conscious or embarrassed? If you have, you're not alone.

The problem can come from three types of guys: (1) a friend; (2) someone you have to associate with, like your families are friends, he's family, or he's on a team with you; or (3) some random guy who's decided that you're the one he's going to go after. Plus, different guys have different thresholds of what bothers them. If you get easily upset or irritated and have a harder time letting things roll off your back, you become an easy target. What it comes down to is this: a lot of guys get away with a lot of crappy behavior because "it's just a joke" and "we were just messing around." To stop that from happening, you have to be clear about how terms like "teasing," "messing around," and "joking around" are manipulated.

GOOD TEASING

Good teasing is one of the cornerstones of great friendships. Someone who cares about you, knows you well, and is comfortable with you can tease and joke around with you—"with" (not "at") being the operative word. With good teasing, there's no intention to put you down and the other person knows what's off-limits to tease you about. If you're on the receiving end, you know you can ask the other person to stop and he actually will.

Guys can "good–tease" each other by making incredibly rude comments about their mothers, how much sex they're getting (or not) and with who, things that if anyone else said them to you, you'd want to punch him in the face. Remember the democracy of put-downs: if it can go both ways, and if you tell the other guy he's over the line and he doesn't get defensive or blow you off, you're good.

IGNORANT TEASING

Have you ever been teased about something that really bothered you but the person teasing you didn't know that for some reason, even if it seemed incredibly obvious to you? It's always hard to tell someone you like that you're pissed off about something he said. But when the intent wasn't malicious (which isn't to say it couldn't have been insensitive), once the teaser understands the impact of his behavior, he'll get over his defensiveness and sincerely apologize because he recognizes that he went over the line.[5]

---

[5] If you're thinking instead, I'm dealing with someone who knows exactly what he's doing, go to page 45 with Rob about Malicious Teasing.

WHAT DO YOU DO IF YOUR FRIEND IS GOING AFTER YOU FOR THE WAY YOU LOOK, TAKING SHOTS AT YOUR HEIGHT, YOUR WEIGHT, YOUR ACNE, OR YOUR HAIR?

This is one of those situations that are often blown off. The unwritten rule is that guys can tease each other about specifically embarrassing things and the guy being teased should just take it and/or say something equally rude back. On the chance that it does bother you, here's an example of how you can handle it using SEAL. In this scenario, a friend is consistently teasing you for being fat, but the SEAL techniques shown here will also work if your friend is picking on you for something else.

Stop and Setup: Walking back from practice across a field.

YOU (Explain): Okay, sort of embarrassing to say this, but I need you to stop with the "moob" comments and flicking me.
FRIEND (Push-Back): What?? You're not serious. YOU (Explain again): Seriously, you need to stop.

FRIEND (Push-Back): Sure, if it bothers you that much. (laughs)

YOU (Affirm, in your head): Stay the course even though he's accusing you of being weak for letting him get to you. Don't back down or apologize for bringing it up.

YOU (Lock In, because you're easing back into regular territory): Thanks. Did you see who we're playing Saturday?

The message is communicated, it's not some weird hour-long conversation, you're in control of the conversation, and you return it to more normal ground in the end. Mission accomplished. If the kid doesn't stop making the "moob" comments, this becomes more than a problem of him teasing you. Instead, the problem becomes that he's deliberately disrespecting your friendship.

WHAT IF YOU'RE DEALING WITH A FRIEND WHO GIVES FAKE APOLOGIES?

True apologies have four characteristics:

1. The apologizer recognizes that each person has the right to see things the way he sees them. As in, no one has the right to say to anyone else, "You're overreacting. Don't be gay/retarded/such a pussy."

2. He speaks in a genuine tone of voice because he actually means what he say.

3. He knows what he did that hurt the other person and is willing to admit it.

4. He's willing to express his apology in action, not just words.

But people make fake apologies a lot. Basically, it comes down to a combination of arrogance, stupidity, and insincerity. Here's how you can tell if someone is making a fake apology:

1. His tone of voice is insincere and may be accompanied by sighing and rolling eyes.

2. He makes you feel weak for wanting the apology ("If you really feel that strongly about it, then fine, I'm sorry" or "I'm sorry if I offended you").

3. He apologizes to manipulate you into getting something he wants ("I'm sorry, can you please just drop it?").

How you deal with a fake apologizer really depends on how important that person is to you. If it's someone you don't know well or don't care about, then the fake apology is annoying, but you don't need to deal with it more than to remember that the person doesn't mean what he says. It's a different story when the fake apologizer is someone you deal with on an ongoing basis. If you're in a relationship (friends or more) with someone who consistently does what he wants and then apologizes later as a way to wriggle out of it, then at some point you need to address it with that person (remembering that being a good fake apologizer requires high social skills and intelligence, so you're probably dealing with a Mastermind or an Associate).

If you choose to call out a fake apologizer, here's how:

FAKE APOLOGIZER: Sorry! Now will you shut up?

YOU (Explain): The way you just apologized doesn't seem like you mean it. If I'm wrong, tell me.

FAKE APOLOGIZER (in a sarcastic tone): Seriously? No, I totally mean it.

YOU (Affirm): I don't want to make a big deal out of this. I just want you to say what you mean. Otherwise, don't say it.

HOW DO YOU SAY, "I WAS WRONG," IN GUY WORLD?

When I need to apologize, the next time we're

playing basketball I make a point of saying, "Nice shot," or, "Good game." I know I'm not actually saying, "I'm sorry," but my friend knows what I'm really saying—Rick, 16

We could be randomly walking in the hallway, and I'll say, "My bad," and he'll know what I'm talking about—Al, 16

You know how apologies are with you and your friends. Most of them are understated, or wordless, or about something else on the surface while on a deeper level you and your friend both know you're really saying, I'm sorry. A tight group of guys can deal with a lot of issues without any conversation involved at all. And that's fine.

But what if you really screw up and you know a quick "my bad" isn't going to cut it? Or you cross a line and feel like you need to make it clear that you didn't mean to? What should you say then? What separates a good and effective apology from a crappy apology?

If you want examples of the best and worst apologies, professional athletes set the standard. A great one happened a few years ago when Garrison Hearst of the San Francisco 49ers apologized after saying that he didn't want any "faggots" as teammates when he said, "First of all, I want to apologize for the comments that I made, and to the gay community. I didn't realize it would be so harmful. I want to direct it to my teammates for causing a disturbance among the team before this game. Being an African American, I know that discrimination is wrong, and I was wrong for saying what I said about anybody—any race, any religion. I want to apologize to the San Francisco 49ers organization, the city of San Francisco, for the comments that I made, and to my teammates for bringing this distraction upon us. I hope that everyone can accept my apology. Thank you."

Hearst's apology was good for the following reasons. He didn't excuse his behavior, and he showed that he learned something from the incident. He connected the discrimination he had experienced as an African American with discrimination against other people (i.e., he put himself in the other guy's shoes). He acknowledged that his actions had had negative consequences for other people, particularly people who depended on him. Lastly, he expressed the hope that people could accept his apology, but he made no demands.

An example of a bad apology? "I apologize if I offended you." Said by countless athletes and politicians after they've been caught.

What do you do when the other person won't apologize? As in he never apologizes for anything he does, and he mocks you for even trying to get him to admit what he's done?

Don't make a big deal out of it, but don't trust that person. He is incapable of taking responsibility of his actions. He will throw you under the bus whenever he feels threatened. And ironically this person usually has a pretty thin skin so that means he will freak out on you for pretty much the same thing he'd blow you off about. Person to be avoided.

FORGIVENESS

When someone apologizes to you, the best thing to do is say some version of "Thanks." I'd stay away from "Don't worry about it" or "It's okay," because those responses can come across like it wasn't important to you. You want to acknowledge the apology and move on. Have you ever heard a person ask for forgiveness right after he apologized? That's totally manipulative, because the person receiving the apology often feels like he has to say yes or he's being uptight and unforgiving. If another person says, "Do you forgive me?" and you aren't ready to say yes, you can say, "I'm not there yet, but thanks for the apology."

BLOOD BROTHER RULES
(BUT OBVIOUSLY APPLICABLE TO SISTERS TOO)

1. Don't let your brother take the fall for something you did.

2. Never rat your brother out (and you shouldn't have to if he follows rule number 1) … except when he's doing something to hurt himself or someone else. Unless immediate action is required, give him twenty-four hours to come clean himself.

3. Don't destroy anything your brother made or built.

4. Back up your brother when he's bullied or teased. What does that look like? Do not join in, and don't stay silent when other people do it—including your friends. If your brother starts the fight, you don't have to back him up, but you have to get him out unless he's determined to be in the fight.

5. You can tease your brother, but you can't humiliate him. If you can't figure this out, then go back to how I define teasing. Seriously, don't make your brother feel like shit. If you do, don't make excuses or blame it on someone else. And don't make someone else have to be constantly refereeing between you.

6. If your brother does well in anything, don't minimize it or put him down. Even though no one is going to admit it, getting a compliment from a brother, no matter how small, is huge. Likewise, put-downs are really deflating. If you feel awkward complimenting your brother, try wrapping it in humor. For example, "Hey, I saw you aced that calc test … so when you're a rich CEO down the line, it's cool if I just mooch off you, right?" or, "Dude, Ray Allen called. He wants his jump shot back."

7. Go to his game or performance. You don't have to go to every single one of them, and you don't have to tell him how great he was (but once in a while never hurts), but just showing up once in a while means a lot.

8. If you don't get along with your brother (either you never have or you think he's becoming a "lazy, egotistical, self-obsessed, jock, arrogant guy," as one of our editors put it), you can tell him once that he's over the line, but that's it. Your actions here are much more powerful than your words. Constantly pointing out his flaws doesn't work when your parents do it, and it's not going to work when you do it either.

9. Don't flirt with someone your brother likes or liked in the past. Not cool. Which means that everything beyond flirting is off-limits too. See what a "loyal friend" is on page 62

10. The world is hard enough without having your brother beat up on you. I'll never forget listening to a group of the guys helping me with this book argue about whether older brothers have the right to beat on their younger brothers. One guy was just adamant that it was his right and responsibility to "teach" his brother by being tough on him. And then one of the guys in the group said, "You're doing this to him, and he's going to take it out on someone else. You need to find a better way to teach."

CHAPTER FOUR

DOUCHEBAGS 101

He's my best friend, but sometimes I get so angry at him I want to punch him in the face. He's always pushing. He never stops. Always says things to people to make them feel like shit. But we're friends. How is it possible to hate your friend like this? —Bill, 16

MALICIOUS TEASING

Malicious teasing is done precisely to make you or some other guy feel inferior. The teasing highlights the difference between you and him and the other guys. The second you defend yourself, he puts you down again and he refuses to take responsibility for what he's doing ("Dude, I'm just messing with you," "What are you making such a big deal of this for? Don't be so gay/retarded, etc."). He can be so good at making you feel bad that you find yourself apologizing for speaking up.

Here's what's really annoying. If the malicious teaser claims ignorance, then how do you know when he's lying? And how can you effectively call him out? If you can't tell, then the malicious teaser will get away with what he's doing and make you look stupid in the process. Rob, 17 describes it perfectly here.

It's crucial that friends be willing to sacrifice a little bit for another friend with the assumption that anybody else in their group of friends would be willing to make that sacrifice for them. Whether it be loaning a friend some money for lunch and not expecting them to pay it back, revising an English paper for a friend, or talking to all your female-friends to try to find your buddy a date to the dance, these are all things that friends who are loyal are expected to do. Disloyal friends attack your loyalty by saying things like, "We've been guys for X years and now you're pulling this shit?" or "You've changed. The old John wouldn't have cared," or just a simple look could make you feel like an idiot for trying to oppose them.

In the grand scheme of things, there are worse problems than having a friend say things that annoy you. Why would it ever be necessary to bring it up? You do it for the following reasons: if your friend's comments embarrass you, if he makes you doubt yourself, or if you dread what he's going to do or say the next time you're with him. More than that, the definition of true friendship means being able to hang out with someone without that person making you feel terrible or stressing out about what he's going to do. "Friend" isn't a title. It's a bond.

There's another reason to call this guy out. These are exactly the kind of situations where one of two things happen: you explode over something small and then people think you're overreacting, or you never say anything and the other guy believes he can do whatever he wants to you, which usually means he's going to get worse.

BABYSITTING

> I want to confront him, but no matter what I say, he'll just blow me off. You don't understand how he is. He doesn't listen to anyone. —Ethan, 17

Ethan, the senior who said this to me (actually he was whispering while he looked over my shoulder to see if any of his friends noticed our conversation), was one of the most popular guys in the school. He'd approached me after I'd finished a seminar with all the school leaders— student council, peer leaders, and athletic captains. I was genuinely shocked that this kid said this to me. I remember thinking, Really? You're six-three, good-looking, people love you, you're the captain of your team—how could you be intimated by anyone?

But as soon as Ethan told me his story, I easily

understood his feelings. Ethan didn't want to confront some guy he hated. He wanted to confront one of his best friends — which made it way worse. This was a guy who thought he had the right to make people miserable for his own entertainment. During lunch, Ethan's friend (let's call him "Ryan") threw bread at the girls who he'd decided were anorexic, constantly harassed other players in the locker room, and mocked anyone who disagreed with him about anything.

Bystanders will often do everything they can to convince themselves that they shouldn't intervene when someone's behaving this way. They ignore it or distract themselves so they look clueless. They "stay neutral," which makes them look like either they're intimidated or they support the abuse. They laugh to convince themselves that what's going on isn't serious. Or they join in because it's safer to be on the side of the person with the most power. As Ryan's friend, Ethan knew that if Ryan listened to anyone, it would have to be someone in his inner circle. Ethan also knew he had a responsibility to do something because he was a leader in the school. He deeply felt that he was letting other people down, and he knew that people associated him with Ryan, which he was getting increasingly uncomfortable about. He also feared the cost of speaking out because Ryan would turn on him and make a big deal out of it. Up to that point, all of the good reasons for speaking out had been crushed against his rationalization that nothing he could do would ever change Ryan.

If you're ever in a situation even close to Ethan's, remember:

1. At some point you'll see someone do something really messed up to another person.

2. No one wakes up looking forward to telling a friend that he's being intolerable. It'll always be hard and uncomfortable. That doesn't mean that you stay silent, but it does mean that it's critical to acknowledge it's a hard situation.

3. It's common to get involved based on how much you like the individuals involved and on the power each one of them has. If you like the aggressor and/or he has high social power, you're more likely to excuse his behavior. If you think the kid he's targeting is annoying or doesn't have social power, then you'll more easily make excuses for what happened or blame him for somehow bringing it on himself. Ideally, however, all of that should be irrelevant. Getting involved should be based on facts, not on how much you like the people, how much social power they have, or how much your own social position may be threatened.

Depending on how messed up the situation is and how strong your personal sense of honor is, you can come up with all sorts of excuses for your actions. One of the most common is Ethan's: "Whatever I say won't make a difference." Ethan's response is mimicking the lessons he's learned from the ALMB. Ironically, most people think being in the box makes life easier, but it doesn't. In this situation, the box is trapping Ethan into being a weaker man than he wants to be.

LIKE IT OR NOT, YOU'RE JUDGED BY WHO YOU ASSOCIATE WITH.

If you're in Ethan's situation, when you walk across campus with someone like Ryan, eat lunch at the same table with him, or go to parties together, you need to admit that the people who aren't in your circle assume that you're like him and that you're always going to back him up. Equally important is that Ryan also thinks you agree with what he's doing. So do parents, teachers, and everyone else.

If you decide to approach any of Ryan's targets, it may seem very strange to that person that you're reaching out. Don't underestimate the power of voluntarily putting yourself in this position. Don't make excuses for Ryan. If you laughed or looked like you backed up his actions, own it. Here's how you SEAL it:

Setup: Email, text, or reaching out in person.

YOU (Explain): What Ryan did yesterday was messed up. I laughed, and it wasn't funny. I'm trying to figure out a way to get him to stop.

YOU (Affirm): At least know that I'm not going to back it up anymore.

Then there's actually talking to Ryan. After a lot of back-and-forth, Ethan and I came up with his ideal SEAL, which included all the push-back he thought he'd get:

Stop and Setup: At Ethan's house playing Madden

RYAN: Can you believe Jack made the team?

ETHAN: Do you really have to get on his case all the time?

RYAN: Yes. He totally deserves it.

ETHAN: You could let up a little.

RYAN: What the hell are you talking about? You laughed as hard as I did when he ran out of there.

ETHAN (Explain and Acknowledge): I laughed because I just didn't want to deal with it. But you have to stop. It's more than just this; it's throwing bread at the girls, it's starting fights when we go out. Think about it. That kid wants to quit. I'm the captain of the team, and you are really not helping.

RYAN: Do you need a tampon? This is possibly the gayest conversation I've ever had.

ETHAN (Lock In): Fine, you don't have to listen to me. But no one else is going to call you out on this, and I'm doing it because I actually care. Think about it.... (they go back to the game)

That was the ideal SEAL. Even in the ideal world, it was still messy, Ryan didn't automatically agree, and he still tried to make Ethan feel stupid for bringing it up. About a week later, when Ethan did get his courage up to talk to Ryan, did it happen just like we'd prepared? No. This is what happened instead:

Stop and Setup: Playing Madden.

RYAN: What is wrong with you lately?

ETHAN: Nothing.

RYAN: Whatever. You got up at lunch today because I was throwing shit at the girls—which they totally deserved. You know they were all going to the bathroom to throw up.

ETHAN (Stops, breathes, remembers our SEAL): Fine. Look, I'm going to tell you this because no one else will. The kid in the locker room, those girls, you have to stop.

RYAN (laughs): I'm sorry, what did you say?

ETHAN: You can blow me off. Laugh at me. I don't care. It's just too much.

RYAN: You're such a pussy.

ETHAN: Fine. I'm a pussy. Just think about it.

Like Ethan, you can't go into these things believing it's going to go down exactly as you practiced. That doesn't matter. The result does. Ryan couldn't agree with Ethan while they were talking because it was just too much for his ego to handle. But after their conversation, the bread-throwing stopped, that freshman kid could breathe a little easier, and Ethan handled the situation so that he could respect himself.

OTHER COMMON SEALS

What if you're being trashed by someone on online? The guy doesn't name you specifically, but it's obvious who he's talking about and he's come up with a rude nickname for you. Do you ...

... pretend it's not happening?

... ask someone to talk to him?
... start your own online war?

Ideal SEAL: Have a face-to-face conversation or send one email or FB message using SEAL that gets this basic message across:

I saw what you're writing on FB. I'm pretty confident that it's about me. But even if it's about someone else, it's still wrong. Obviously, I can't control what you do, but I'm asking you to stop. If you're having a problem with me, then I want to hear it to my face so I have a chance to actually discuss it with you.

What if someone's starting rumors about you? The common responses without SEAL would be:

- Disappear until graduation

- Immediately talk to whoever you can and check what people are saying

- Plot (possibly with someone else) about how to get back at the person who you think started it

- Say, "Whatever, it's not worth it," but really worry about it a lot

Here's how you can use SEAL to deal with a rumor:

Stop: Ask yourself, "Why does this person want to tell me? What's their motivation?" There are two possible answers. One is that he genuinely cares. The other is that he wants to create or increase conflict between you and the other person. You can figure out which one it is by how he tells you and his follow-up questions. If he's focused on how you're feeling or what you need, then he cares. If he's focused on what you want to "do" about it, then it's the second. While you're trying to figure this out, just say some version of, "Thanks for telling me. Please don't talk about this with others." Obviously, just because you say that doesn't mean he will, but it stops you from responding in a way that will increase the drama.

Now you need to turn your attention to the person who appears to be trying to bring you down to their drama level. So, either one-on-one or by text, here's how you'd do the rest of SEAL.

Explain: "I hear that you're talking (X) about me. I'm not asking you to tell me if it's true. I'm asking that, even if any part of it is true, you stop. I know I can't control that, but I'm showing the respect to come to you face-to-face to ask what's going on."

Push-back: "There's nothing going on. I have no idea what you're talking about."

Affirm and Acknowledge: "Okay, then I'd expect the things I'm hearing to end. But if I did something that upset you, I want to know."

Lock In (if appropriate): "We used to be good friends. If you ever want to talk about this, I'm here."

WHAT'S THE DIFFERENCE BETWEEN JOKING WITH YOUR FRIENDS AND BEING RACIST?

My friends all know how much I hate when people use the N-word, especially since they're white. Me and some of my friends were walking down the street, and we ran into another group of kids who I knew, and one of them (white boy) came up to me and said, "What's up, my nigga?" I was so furious, but my friends told me I was overreacting. —Wes, 17

Many of you go to truly diverse schools. (I don't mean schools that proudly proclaim their diversity because 10 percent of the student body is black and all their parents are doctors and 15 percent of the student body is from Hong Kong, Singapore, or South Korea.) You may hang out with people of different races and backgrounds, and everything is cool. You may proudly identify yourself as mixed-race, along with a lot of other people at school.

None of that makes it any less true that guys make

racist comments and jokes all the time. You and I both know that whenever this topic is raised guys tend to get defensive and insist that they're just being funny and the person they're talking about doesn't mind. Here's the deal. If you make these kinds of jokes, there's a really good chance that you're being a total ignorant ass. I'm just saying what other people won't. For your sake and the sake of the guys you hang out with, it's time to clarify what's over the line.[6]

NEVER FUNNY

Muslim and Sikh guys (whose religions are completely different): Calling them terrorists. Why? Because you're connecting them to a group of people who are consistently referred to as enemies of the "civilized world" and portrayed as violent, religious, crazy people.
Jewish guys: Throwing money at them or making jokes about ashes and ovens. Why? Because accusing Jews of greed and love of money is one of the main reasons they have been persecuted and killed throughout their history. Specifically joking about ovens makes it look like you think it's funny that children, mothers, and fathers were gassed to death and burnt in ovens in Nazi Germany.

Asian guys: Making comments about how they have small penises, don't need calculators or have parents who drive them 24/7 and beat them if they don't become music or math prodigies. Why? Even if the stereotype is technically "positive" (you're Asian, so you're smart), you're still trapping them in a stereotype.
Hispanic guys: Jokes about being deported or being uneducated or lazy. Why? Because you're telling that person he doesn't belong in this country and he's less intelligent and honorable than you.

---

[6] If you're making these jokes now, please proceed to the quiz on page 58

Black guys: Greeting your black friend by talking with forced, wannabe-"black" slang or using the N-word. Here's a good rule to follow: if you wouldn't use a certain word or talk a certain way to relate to a white friend, you shouldn't suddenly start using it to try to relate to a black friend. There's so much to talk about here that I've devoted a separate section to it. Keep reading.

Mixed-race guys: Referring to them as "whitewashed." Why? Because you're saying that they're trying to be white (i.e., something they're not) by talking "white," trying hard in school, or getting into a good college—as if only white people do those things.

Also never funny with the last three groups is any commentary on how they only got into your school or their future college (whether or not they're on scholarship) because they are a minority. Remarks like this only demonstrate your own insecurity.

Every time I've worked with guys who got caught being racist, they said they were just joking.[7] Some of those guys are being honest (ignorant teasing) and honestly feel terrible when they realize how their comments come across. These are the guys who learn this lesson once and never need to learn it again. Unfortunately, it takes some guys a lot longer to become decent human beings. So they lie (malicious teasing) and defend their right to be racist assholes.

These moments usually occur when there's an audience so they can entertain themselves by publicly humiliating someone.

When I ask guys about the stuff they say to each other and how they feel about it, the vast majority of them answer like this:

---

[7] If some of these insults haven't occurred to you before and you're reading this now and then using them to try to be funny, you have serious problems. Don't try that hard.

"It didn't really offend me, but ..." "It didn't really bother me, but..."

It's okay to admit that you were offended. It doesn't make you less of a man. Especially under these circumstances, admitting your feelings takes strength and intelligence. Fifteen-year-old Oliver shared his experience:

I'm not any minority, but I have a large nose and curly hair, so some of my friends call me a Jew. Sometimes I shrug it off like it's no big deal, but some people come up to me and say, "Sup, Jew." People call me a Jew and not my first name. They say I'm cheap, and some have even thrown pennies and coins at me. I don't really know what to say. I would hate being treated this way. I can't imagine how some actual Jewish kids deal with it. It actually opened my eyes on how some people are treated for just being different, and I try not to be racist or discriminate against others now because of it.

Now let's also go back to the examples of black, Latino, or mixed-race guys. There are white guys who think an excellent way to bond with a nonwhite friend is to greet him by mimicking the stereotypical slang associated with his race or ethnicity. If you're this guy, hate to tell you, but you're wrong. While your intention was good (you're trying to connect to someone), you're using racist stereotypes to do it. Your friend may never tell you how he feels. Why? Because when you're a minority, it's hard enough to feel comfortable in your environment without pointing out to people every time someone says something stupid to you about you. If you're with your friends, the pressure to not say anything is even more intense because those friends are the key to making you feel you belong at all.

If you're in a minority and are having this problem with a friend, here's how you SEAL it with this guy. Your first step is the Setup: figuring out where you're going to talk to him. If he's a friend, you can SEAL it while playing a video game or doing something else. Imagine you're sitting next to each other on the couch after school, playing COD, so you're both looking at the screen.

YOU (Explain): Seriously, dude, could you stop talking to me like that? IGNORANT FRIEND: Huh, what are you talking about?

YOU (Explain again): You know, when you [specific offensive thing he says], like you think it's how I talk. Just talk normally like you do with other people.

IGNORANT FRIEND: What?

YOU (Explain again, shaking your head about how stupid this is that you actually have to explain this): Because I don't talk like that, and I'm black so you sure as shit shouldn't.

IGNORANT FRIEND: Dude, this is crazy. You know I'm not racist!

YOU (Lock In): I know, that's why I'm telling you. I'm not stressing about it, I'm just telling you. (Go back to playing the game.)

Here's another example of what to do when someone is malicious:

> *I was hanging out with some of my junior friends by the lunch tables. I wasn't saying much, just hanging out; laughing at jokes, and this one kid named Nate said a funny joke. I laughed and said a smart-ass comment in reply, and he said to me, "Who let the niggas talk?" I almost fought him, but some of my friends held me back and told me to calm down. To be honest, I didn't know how to react. I tried getting my friends to set up a fight, but they didn't want to put the other kid in that situation. I have hated him ever since. I've wanted him to be punished in some*

way, whether it be by me or the school. — Wes, 17[8]

If you're one of Wes's white friends, you need to recognize how intense both situations are for him. First, don't tell him to calm down. Telling someone to calm down in this situation is patronizing and flat-out wrong because you don't get to tell him how he should feel. Don't let the one minority kid, whoever he happens be, stand by himself. It's up to you to stand by him in word and action. If you don't, then the other guy will dismiss your friend as "overreacting" and "out of control," which, in this case, reinforces the stereotype of black men being angry and seeing everything as a race issue. To say it mildly, this is unfair.

I asked Wes how he would have liked his friends to stand by him, and this was his response:

I'd want them to understand the meaning and the true hatred and disrespect that comes with the word, not to just say it and know it, but to truly understand it. I would have wanted them to feel the same rage as I did, but they are white and probably will never understand because they are privileged, blessed, and extremely pretentious, and they don't even know it.

Wes is right. The person in the majority is never going to know what it's like to be in the minority and attacked because of it. But what white guys (in this case) can do is demonstrate righteous power and transform the moment by standing by Wes and turning their back on the other guy.

If you're thinking I'm way uptight about race, I'm not. I'm uptight about people being stripped of their dignity. A lot of guys have friends of other races, and those guys tease each other based on race. Guess what? I do it too.

---

[8] If you're facing this situation, stop reading this chapter and read "Frontal Assault: The Right to Fight" on page 69

But only with people I'm really, really close to. With them, I know the nuances of what's within bounds and outside of bounds, and it's equal opportunity between us. They can make fun of me, I can make fun of them, and if one of us screws up, the other person speaks up, the offender says something like "Sorry about that," and it's truly over with.

One more thing: being a minority of anything doesn't guarantee that you'll apply your awareness to other minority kids. It's not like black kids don't make ignorant comments about Jewish kids or Jewish kids don't tease their black friends about being ghetto (which is highly ironic) or make comments about being a maid or being illegal to their Hispanic friends. People of the same race can make degrading comments to people within their race. Everyone can be ignorant. For all these reasons, if you're experiencing a pattern of behavior where someone makes racist comments and tells racist "jokes" to you, at some point you owe it to yourself to educate the other person about how they're coming across. You can't blow it off all the time or you'll explode.

A lot of people—and more and more of them every day—think of themselves as multiracial. These people also have strong opinions that they often aren't going to tell you. Sebastian does:

> I'm half Colombian, quarter Native American, quarter white, but my dominant appearance is of a white person. So while I don't face flat-out prejudice or racial slurs, what I have struggled with all my life is a different kind of ignorance. I'm very proud of my Latino and Indian identity, and I express it in many ways. I am fluent in Spanish (many people in my family don't speak English), and I am deeply connected to my tribe. (My uncle is the chief, and I visit tribal grounds frequently.) I am steeped in all three cultures. However, my skin is fair, I have blue eyes and light brown hair, and most of my friends are white. People (white, all) have on several occasions

loudly labeled me as "whitewashed" when I describe my identity, which I find deeply insulting. This shows a far more insidious racism: aggressively denying another's right to identify himself purely based on outward appearance. Worse yet, since the college admissions process, I have been discriminated against by many of my peers (all white or Asian), who have said the only reason I'd ever get into my top-choice schools is because of affirmative action (a measure many claim to support). Not only is this factually incorrect, but it's mostly hurtful, because it shows that they consider that I'm getting a leg up for no reason. In my opinion, this all stems from the same reasons high schoolers do things like throw money at Jewish kids or say Mexican kids should be deported: a desire to put people who aren't like them in boxes based on what they look like or where they come from. In my case, I'm violating the "rules" of what a Latino or Indian person should look or act like, so I'm treated with contempt when I assert my individual identity. — Sebastian, 17

This isn't about being multiracial, black, Latino, Jewish, etc. It's about being singled out, stereotyped, and degraded. If you're going to a school where there are only a few people who look like you, you only need one person to do the things Wes is talking about. It doesn't matter what race or ethnicity you are. You could be one of the few white students and run into similar problems. All of this comes down to one thing. I hear guys say all the time, "[X offensive word that this adult is telling me to stop saying] doesn't mean anything. It's just what we say." The only people who say this are the people who are in the majority who aren't on the receiving end of these jokes and comments. You'll never see a black/Hispanic/Jewish/Muslim/Sikh kid say, "Please make racist stereotypical comments at my expense. It just makes me feel so comfortable when you do it."

All of this comes down to probably the most important thing any guy has to have in his life to have a good life. Loyal friends. The definition of loyalty is "giving or showing firm and constant support or allegiance to a person." But what does support and allegiance really mean? It doesn't mean going along with a friend who's doing something stupid or unethical and who then plays the friend card to make you go along with him. That's called throwing someone under the bus. Here's how you tell the difference.

1. A loyal friend is happy when you do well. A disloyal friend reacts to your accomplishments by putting you down.

2. A loyal friend shows his loyalty by telling you things you don't want to hear. A disloyal friend may lie and tell you what you want to hear.

3. A loyal friend tells you things you don't want to hear in a way that doesn't make you feel stupid. A disloyal friend will go out of his way make you feel stupid.

4. A loyal friend never embarrasses you in public. A disloyal friend will embarrass you in public. He ignores your subtle communication that you want him to stop, which forces you to be more and more obvious and allows him to ridicule you even more.

5. If a loyal friend embarrasses you by accident, he owns up to it. A disloyal friend will blame someone else or make excuses.

6. A loyal friend genuinely apologizes. A disloyal friend apologizes in a way that makes you feel bad.

7. A loyal friend won't put you in situations that compromise your values. A disloyal friend will, and if you resist he will accuse you of being disloyal or weak.

8. A loyal friend will sacrifice something in order to help you out. A disloyal friend won't go out of his way to help you.

TAKE THE DOUCHEBAG QUIZ
Instructions:

- Be honest (or this won't work).*

- Select the answer that most often describes how you act.

- After you've answered all the questions, add up your score according to the table following the quiz.

*To increase accuracy, do the quiz with a friend and answer the questions for each other.

1. What is communication like between you and your friends?
A. I reach out to my friends regularly.
B. I don't usually reach out to my friends; they usually call/text me.

C. I always reach out to my friends, even just to be nice sometimes.

D. I rarely reach out to my friends (i.e., I call/text only when I need to communicate about a party or to get homework answers).

2. When someone you don't know says, "Hey, what's up?" how do you respond?

A. "Hey, I'm good. How are you?"

B. Nothing.

C. "Hey."

D. "Do I know you?"

2. What best describes your group of girl friends?

A. I don't have a group of girl friends, I just hook up with girls.

B. We're close, but I don't share anything too personal or embarrassing with them.

C. Very close with them — I use them as resources when I'm conflicted.

D. The group changes, but I generally hang out with the same group of girls.

3. What kind of jokes do you and your friends make?

E. We make fun of everyone, but never to their face and never anything over the top.

F. We'll make fun of anyone, even in front of them if that makes it funnier.

G. We usually just make fun of one another casually.

H. We usually focus on making fun of one or two of our friends.

4. How do you handle being in a position of authority/superiority/leadership?

A. I enjoy being seen as a role model and try to act accordingly.

B. I use it to my advantage when I need to and have things done for me, but not too frequently.

C. I don't make the younger kids do anything I wouldn't want to do.

D. I take advantage of being at the top. Why not? It's my turn to make fun of the younger kids and make them do things for me.

5. What is your approach to hooking up with girls?
A. I go for the hottest girls, usually when drunk at parties.
B. I try to at least know a girl or be familiar with her before going for it.
C. Slow and steady wins the race; it can take patience to succeed.
D. The younger the easier is my strategy.

7. How did you (or will you) pick your prom date?
A. Any date is fine as long as I have one.
B. The hotter the better.
C. One of my good friends/my girlfriend.
D. I need to know my prom date, who also needs to be attractive.

6. What did you do for the last birthday of a good friend?
A. Got him a gift and/or planned something for him.
B. Said "Happy Birthday" when I saw him on Facebook.
C. I forgot it was his birthday until someone told me.
D. When I realized I forgot, I told him he needed to buy me something for hanging out with him.

7. What do you think of team chemistry on the sports team or any other competitive team you're on?
A. It really doesn't matter as long as I'm performing well.
B. As long as we're not fighting, I'm okay.
C. It always matters, win or lose. We're a team.
D. It only matters if our team is doing well that

season.

11. When it comes to making fun of people you don't know, you …
    A. … do it whenever it's funny, especially in front of them.
    B. … do it occasionally, but I focus on my own friends for joking around.
    C. … just don't do it.
    D. … do it for fun, just not to their face.

If you answered …

	Questions 1, 4, 7	Questions 2, 5, 8, 10	Questions 3, 6, 9, 11
3 points	B	D	A
2 points	D	B	D
1 point	A	C	B
0 points	C	A	C

Maximum score: 36

Minimum score: 0

Scale:

1–9: No chance of being a douchebag.

10–18: You have your moments, but doesn't everyone?

19–27: You are not as awesome as you think you are.

28–36: People barely tolerate you.

You just took the Douchebag Quiz. If you didn't like your score, you're not alone. Will, the guy who created the quiz with me, didn't like the score he got. It was really funny to watch him tabulate his score and then reread his answers. He wouldn't tell me what his score was.

DOUCHEBAG: A HISTORY

Because the terms "douche" and "douchebag" are some of the most common words in the Guy World, it's important to know the original definition and how the terms are defined now. This is what an actual douche and its accompanying "bag" (the bottle-looking thing) look like.

To douche is to rinse some part of the body by putting water through it, but douching usually refers to the rinsing of the vagina. Now, let's look at one of the thousands of definitions of a "douchebag" in the Urban Dictionary:

> *[A douchebag] has an inflated sense of self-worth, compounded by a lack of social grace and self-awareness. He behaves inappropriately in public, yet is completely ignorant to how pathetic he appears to others. To everyone else, he is an annoying and arrogant phony who comes across as a wannabe overcompensating for his insecurities. .*

. . Often laughs at others' misfortunes regardless of its severity.

There are so many ways to be a douchebag. There's no one look, age, ethnicity, and environment where you will find them. They can happen anywhere at anytime; at work, at the gym, on your team, at school, at the mall, at a party, even in your own home. And there's a spectrum of douchiness from a moment to a way of life. To help you out, here is a picture.

For women, douching has actually been proven to be irritating—just like the douche's male counterparts. Now, while these pictures represent a particular type of douchebags, you know douchebags are a diverse group. What's important is the behavior that's tied to the word.

REHAB FOR DOUCHES

If your douchebag score indicates that you're exhibiting douchiness, what do you do about it? First, moving past your denial is key. If you're even having this conversation with yourself, you took the first step. Second, ask yourself how being like this is benefiting you. Seriously. If acting like this is making people not like you or not think you're a reliable person, you must be getting something important out of it. Otherwise you wouldn't be doing it.

One of the reasons why reasonable guys adopt this persona is because they want to hide their true self to get through high school. Jack, a junior, completely changed his personality just before his freshman year. For him, the douchebag personality was the armor I talked about in the first chapter.

I'll bet every second guy in every high school acts like me. Maybe it doesn't excuse it, but college is two years away. I guess I'll become that great guy then. In the meantime, my mom, my girlfriend, and my six-year-old sister are the only ones who can really know my dark secret—that I'm only like this half of the time.

Another reason for your douchiness could be that you're too invested in your association with a particular group. As a result, you look for opportunities to make everyone know your status and remind them that you belong to the group.

Believe me, it's not that I don't get why status and belonging are appealing. They often come with perks, like being in the "right" group, hanging out with girls, and getting into parties. But the truth is, toning down your douchiness won't lower your status, it will raise it. Nobody thinks, You know who I definitely want to invite to my party? The biggest douchebag I know. If you're less ouche, then everyone, including your friends, will be more relaxed around you, which means they'll like to hang out with you more. And you'll have more luck with girls. Seriously. Girls who are primarily attracted to douchebags are going through a phase of being so insecure that they do really stupid things.

Just remember, checking yourself to make sure you're not being a douche isn't something to do just for other people's sake. It is one of the most important things you can do to make your own life better.

TODAY'S SUPER-DOUCHES

I can't remember the precise moment that "laxbros"

came into my life. It just seemed that one day, a lot of guys were growing their hair longer and pretending it was effortlessly and perfectly layered while seeming to be completely oblivious to everyone else around them. Honestly, the way they acted reminded me of a group of eighth-grade mean girls who had suddenly been transformed into high school guys. I do remember the first time I went to a lacrosse game between two highly competitive teams on the East Coast and saw the parents. I distinctly remember a mom with fake breasts wearing a tight white T-shirt with her son's school name embroidered on it in madras pattern and a short khaki skirt, giggling like she was in high school. I remember the dads talking to each other about the "market." While these parents chatted, the coach was screaming at their sons about what useless little girls they were.

For some of you, especially those of you who live in some parts of the Northeast and go to private school (bonus if it's a boarding school), it may feel like laxbro culture has been around for as long as you've been going to school. If you live in the Midwest, it may seem like at some point in the last few years a certain segment of guys in your school all started playing lax and using words like "spoon," "laxho," "lax sesh," and "bra."

The easiest way to spot laxbros is how they apparently had a secret meeting one night and decided that they should all start wearing the same thing. The lax bro uniform includes (courtesy, of course, of the Urban Dictionary):

1. Headwear: Trucker hats, backwards college hats, visors, goofy winter hats, (i.e., puff balls and ear flaps)

2. Hair: The longer the better, the wavier the better (wavy lettuce out the backside of the helmet or cap)

3. Shirts: Bright-colored polos, youth league Ts, pinnies, or skins

4. Shorts: Plaid/madras, seersucker, team shorts

5. Footwear: Rainbow, Reefs, Sperry's, Turf shoes with high white socks

6. Accessories: Hemp bracelets/necklace, shooting string or sidewall lace bracelets, Ray-ban, Arnette, or Oakley shades, lax-themed tattoos (e.g., crossed sticks on calf)

Some other helpful descriptions from the Urban Dictionary:

> *Every Laxbro has a pseudonym like El Diablo or Sea Bass or something cool and lax like that. If you're not constantly holding your stick and getting woman to think your super hot just because you're a laxbro then your probably not a laxbro.*
>
> They get all the girls and can bang anyone they want.
>
> Bro: Yo come here let's bang
>
> Girl: Of course, you're a hot lax bro

If you're a high school guy in a middle-class or wealthy high school, you know that laxbros currently get the prize for being today's super-douches in Guy World. Somehow a really interesting and challenging sport became infected with a tribal culture of rampant entitlement, dismissal of all other opinions, using women, unapologetic hazing, and a belief in their own social importance in the overall social hierarchy—all while adamantly refusing to admit any of this is true. Plus, laxbro parents (as compared to parents whose sons play lacrosse) back up this crappy attitude and steadfastly believe that lax will be the key to getting their son into an elite college or a job in the financial sector after graduation so they can make huge amounts of money and have no life beyond being rich, super-stressed, and emotionally stunted.

This isn't to say that other sports can't have arrogant, obnoxious guys. For example, in the Midwest and North it's been hockey, in the South and Texas (and everywhere else), it's football. In cities and some areas of the Midwest, it's basketball. The guys who play these sports get high social status and are often treated better because of their participation in their sport. But there's never been a sport that has been so identified with being a white, rich, ignorant[9] asshole that's trying way too hard than today's generation of lacrosse players.

Lacrosse coaches and players will tell you that the best players don't like laxbro culture. While I promised the coaches and players that I wouldn't reveal their names, I did talk to many of them—including guys who attend Division I schools. Here's what one of them said:

> *These kids often do not represent the good players who play for the love of the game, but rather those who use the game as a social mechanism. These*

---

[9] For example, Warrior Sports, which makes the lacrosse gear worn by professional players, had a #Ninjaplease advertising campaign but claimed they had no idea what it meant. When Jovan Miller, one of only three black players in professional lacrosse, asked for an explanation and an apology, no one from Warrior Sports responded. Remember what I said about bad apologies? Miller didn't even get a bad one.

kids find false confidence in the simple fact that they play lacrosse and cast a bad shadow on others who play. It's not much different from football meatheads or any other popular sport. These douche athletes don't really get it and earn a free pass from those on their team because they're normal to them, while it's tough to see how exclusive the group can be to an outsider. Unfortunately, the upper-middle-class preppy rich kid stereotype has this same sense of exclusivity, and when combined with playing a sport comprised of many rich white kids, it can create a super-douche.

You can see the problem spelled out in this quote. Laxbros get a free pass from the non-douche lacrosse players on their team. But as soon as someone (including yourself) says, "It's normal, it's what we've always done," or, "It's tradition," you must have the courage to ask yourself this question: Why? Why is it normal and therefore acceptable that the laxbro guys on your team get to be douchebags? Even if you think they're stupid and you genuinely dislike these guys, when you say nothing, you are going along with whatever they do or say. People associate you with them, and they associate laxbros with a sport you love. You let them speak for you, and in many cases your feeling of loyalty to the guy because he's on your team (especially if you're on a winning team) justifies in your mind saying nothing when those people are dicks.

Again, that's no different than what happens in other sports. Players cover for other players. The only difference here is the preponderance of really rich white kids playing lacrosse. And really rich kids often have really rich parents who are used to getting their way and helping their children avoid the consequences they clearly deserve for their behavior.

If you play lacrosse, I'm asking you how you want to represent yourself. Do you want to be thought of as that guy? I'm not saying stop wearing the madras and your pinnies. If you think your lettuce looks good, then by all means don't cut your hair. But I am saying, have some pride and demand better from these guys and yourself.

CHAPTER FIVE

FRONTAL ASSAULT

Last Saturday night I went to a party with a friend. The party was located in a condominium building, so you had to go up these zigzagging stairs to get to the main floor. When we left, there was a group of approximately ten people, who were drunk and sitting at the end of one side of the zigzags. They called us "China in box" (which is a Chinese food chain where I live) several times, and they threw cigarette ashes, spat on us, and cursed at us. They were all about the age of 18 to 20, and we recognized one of them was a senior in our school (who played varsity soccer) and one was a recent graduate. They only stood and watched. We were two against ten, and we couldn't say anything or else we would've got beaten. My friend and I were bursting with anger. We sat outside of the building, and after five minutes they went down as well. It was like twenty minutes of stress, disgust, and somehow torture since we couldn't do anything. — Vince, 16

If you're in Vince's position, do you have any power in this scenario? Do you have to seethe in silence because there are so many of them and so few of you? What do you do at school when you run into that senior guy who did nothing while his friends went after you? Wouldn't you want to jack him up against the wall and beat the crap out of him? I would.

For all these reasons, if you're Vince, what should you do in the moment and how should you handle the aftermath? Or you may be facing a different but no less common scenario—what if there's a guy at school who is determined to be the biggest asshole to you? What if a guy just wants to get into a fight? He doesn't care with who or why. He just doesn't like you. You may have no idea why. He has anger he wants to vent and he wants to vent it on you. Or what if you have a friend who likes to go after people?

THE RIGHT TO FIGHT

I'm a teacher and someone who works to prevent violence, so it'd be fair to assume that I believe physical fighting is "never the answer." But that's not true. I don't feel that way personally, and I don't feel that way as a teacher. I know that guys are being told over and over again, by some combination of teachers, school administrators and parents, that fighting is wrong.

Meanwhile, another combination of people is telling guys that fighting is really the way to solve problems. At the same time, the culture is telling guys to fight. And when it comes down to it, we have the fundamental right not to be attacked, as do the people we care about and anyone else.

Under specific circumstances, you have the right to fight. That said, you have to answer for yourself two critical questions:

8. How willing am I to actually go through the experience of hurting another person?

9. No matter how righteous my position, am I prepared to accept the consequences from the institutions I'm a part of, like school and the justice system?

There are also ironclad rules:

*   You don't start the fight by your words or your actions.
*   You always match the level of your response to the level of the threat.
*   You need to stop the behavior, not the person.
*   You don't have the right to humiliate the person.

Having said all that, if getting into a fight is a realistic possibility, keep these things ront and center in your mind:

- It'll probably hurt—even if you have extensive training, or you're big and strong, or you have a good fighting instinct.
- The experience of fighting will go both slower and faster than you anticipated.
- There will always be something about the fight that you regret.
- You can physically lose the fight but win the battle of public opinion (i.e., people will respect the fact that you faced your opponent).
- You can physically win but lose the battle of public opinion (i.e., your actions reflect that you're being an aggressive dick who likes to pick fights and go after people out of the blue).
- Even if the fight doesn't happen at school where it can easily be recorded by school cameras, it's likely that your fight will be recorded and become public anyway. If that happens, adult involvement becomes likely and the consequences of the fight last longer.
- You can always walk away. Part of you may be angry with yourself if you do, but walking away in itself is a difficult decision. Give yourself credit for that.
- From the beginning, always have an exit strategy. You're going toward safety (an exit, a car, your group of friends), not away from the danger.

I look at the ethics of fighting this way: if someone threatens you, he's making a choice to accept the consequences of his actions, whatever those turn out to be. The decision you need to make is how you define the threat and what your best reaction should be. Your goal when faced with any kind of situation like this is to minimize your potential for getting injured or appearing weak and to maximize your ability to come across as physically and mentally powerful, with the ultimate goal that he'll leave you alone, now and in the future. That's what we're going to break down in this chapter.

If someone is threatening to beat you up, you're at least clear about the guy's intentions, and the probability of physically defending yourself becomes a real possibility. But Vince's situation was a lot more complicated. Technically, the guys didn't physically threaten Vince or his friend. The physical threat was implied because Vince and his friend were greatly outnumbered.

What are the options if you find yourself in a situation like this? You have three:

1. You can say nothing.

10. You can say something funny and depend on your social intelligence to get yourself out of the situation.

11. You can challenge the other guy to a fight; either hoping his friends won't back him or having decided you don't care because you're not letting them talk to you this way.

Logically, Vince decided to not say anything (which took a lot of self-control) because he believed that anything he did would give them the motivation to physically attack him.

WORDS DON'T HAVE TO BE NICE

Wes's situation (page 59) where someone said, "Who let the niggas talk?" is a great example of being absolutely justified in beating someone down. The difference is that Wes had more friends around him and he was at school, so the physical threat wasn't there like it was in Vince's situation in the apartment complex. To figure out the most effective response in this scenario, go back to the goal: to minimize personal injury and any display of weakness and to maximize your display of psychological strength.

Note that goals are different from desires. If someone is being an asshole to you, it's understandable if your desire is to punch him in the face. But will that stop the problem? Probably not, and it could end up causing you even more trouble. If you get lost trying to satisfy immediate desires, you won't accomplish your ultimate goals. If Wes punched the guy, would it stop him from being a racist dick or show his friends that they need to grow some? No. If Wes punches the guy, he'll get in trouble at school for fighting, and the guy will continue on as he always has. Wes needs to look past his immediate desire to deck the douchebag in the face and focus on his true goal: psychologically crushing the racist bully without getting into trouble with any clueless adults who may have authority here.

Therefore, it's way better for Wes to maintain his calm and say something like, "What exactly did you mean by that?" Or, "Surely you aren't calling a black man a nigger are you? Yes or no? I didn't think so. It's pathetic that you're so intimidated by me. Come on, guys, let's go." Since people almost always follow direct commands like "Come on, guys, let's go," even if they didn't have the courage to stand by Wes in the moment of confrontation, by following Wes's directions they look like they support him.

Sometimes using your words well and refusing to physically fight someone who's trying to humiliate you is more powerful. That doesn't mean your words are nice or that you're taking the softer approach. It means you're using the most effective strategy to neutralize a threat and accomplish your ultimate goal.

GOING FROM DEFENSE TO OFFENSE

Drew is a smart, big freshman who looks older than he

is. He plays football at his large public school in Virginia and loves to trick teachers into thinking he's not as smart as he actually is. Two weeks before school was over for the summer, Drew was walking down the hallway talking to a female friend when the girl's boyfriend jumped him from behind. The school cameras recorded the whole thing. In the moment after Drew was knocked down, he had to evaluate and measure the various risks that confronted him. Up for grabs was getting suspended, having the fight on his college transcript, getting into trouble with his parents, and defending himself now so he wouldn't have to fight later (which is a crapshoot because fighting hard can also escalate the intensity of future fights). All of these decisions had to be made in an instant.

Drew threw the guy against the wall and appropriately defended himself. So far so good: Drew wasn't getting into trouble with the principal. Then Drew took off his backpack and went after the guy again.

The boyfriend got a five-day suspension, and Drew got a two-day suspension. The principal didn't want to suspend Drew—she understood that Drew had to defend himself—but the moment he went from defense to offense was the moment she had to discipline him. It was the first suspension Drew had gotten all year—with only two more weeks of school to go. For Drew's dad, the suspension was unfair because Drew hadn't started the fight. For Drew, the suspension was worth it. It was a fair trade to show the guy who attacked him that he would fight back.

Like what happened in Drew's fight, there's usually an initial exchange of punches, and then there's a lull. It's in that lull that you have a decision to make. Do you reengage in the fight or do you stop? If you reengage, you'll probably get into trouble with adults. What kind of trouble really depends on what kind of school you go to, which is unfair but true. If you go to a private school, you'll probably get suspended, and maybe it'll go in your file, where a college admissions person will be able to see it. If you go to a public school, especially if you have a police officer assigned to the school, not only will you get suspended and have the fight recorded in your school records, but you'll probably be entered into the juvenile justice system in some form. So, yes, private school kids can do the same "bad" things as public school kids but get off way easier. (Not only with fighting, by the way, but with drugs as well.) It's totally unfair, but true.

If you were in Drew's situation, you might think it would be worth getting into trouble with the adults. Drew believed he had to go after the guy full-force to convince him to never go after him again. Using that line of reasoning, defense wasn't enough.

From Drew's perspective, his offense was part of his defense—for the future. That's the crux of Drew's problem. Drew understandably wants the future respect of the guy who attacked him so that he'll be left alone. But that desire for future respect among his peers screws him for his overall future right now: if he has a history of fighting, adults won't trust him. He becomes the problem. His future of doing well in school, going to college, and having adults in his life who can explain the fight to other adults becomes much less likely. To get the future respect of his peers, Drew is truly risking his overall future.

This is the way I want you to think about it if you find yourself in Drew's position—knowing that it's way easier to say this when you're not the person who has to do it. I think of the guy who jumped Drew as literally trying to stop him from having the future that Drew wants and deserves. Drew is academically and socially intelligent. He has what it takes to be successful. What will stop him is being brought down by other people and letting them dictate his behavior. Sometimes there are crossroads in life where you have to make decisions that impact the rest of your life. This is Drew's crossroads: will he take off his backpack the next time someone comes for him?

FIGHTING DRUNK OR HIGH

Don't do it. Don't convince yourself that drunk strength will win the fight. You're a liability to yourself, your friends, and your family.

WHAT DO YOU DO IF YOUR FRIEND PUNCHES YOU IN THE FACE?

There was a guy (let's call him John) who really liked this girl (let's call her Sue). John talked to Sue every day, and all of John's friends knew that he was really into Sue and that even if he was able to hook up with Sue, he wanted much more. One of John's friends (let's call him Bob) was really good at seducing girls. Because of that, John told Bob to stay away from Sue and not talk to her because John really wanted something with Sue. However, Bob didn't listen and began talking to her. Within weeks, Bob was able to close the deal and John was not. John got super-angry at Bob when he found out. Their fight began verbally and then extended into a physical one, but friends separated them before anyone got really hurt. The next few weeks were horrible between them; they couldn't be in the same room, they would not look at each other's face, etc., and this was from two guys who had been friends their whole lives.

Here's what happened. John wasn't angry only because Bob hooked up with a girl he liked. His anger ran much deeper. John was angry because it was more important to Bob to show off that he could get this girl even though he knew John really liked her. Bob had been doing things like this to John for a long time, but John had put up with it for the sake of the friendship. Meanwhile, John's resentment and anger grew, and with this incident he finally lashed out. The thing to remember here isn't that they were fighting over a girl, or that John couldn't take the fact that Bob could get her. Instead, it was really about violating the terms of friendship—obviously a way bigger deal.

Helpful hint: Saying, "What's your problem?" comes across as an accusation. Mostly because the person asking that question usually does think the other person is acting crazy.

More effective: "What's going on with you?" This question comes across as actually wanting to know why the person is upset or angry.

THE B-WORD

At no point did any of the guys I've discussed in this chapter define what they experienced as "bullying." I'm not surprised. Almost all guys I work with think "bullying" is an overused term that doesn't apply to their lives. Or if it does apply, they don't want to use it because it makes them seem weak and if adults find out they'll think they need to get involved.

However, occasionally it's a useful, appropriate word to use. One I'll use now. The official definition of bullying is someone using power and strength to make someone else feel worthless. It's usually defined as being one-way and repeated. As in, the perpetrator is relentlessly going after you to make you feel like shit. He (or she) could go after you physically or psychologically. Also important to keep in mind is that this person usually justifies his behavior for one of following three reasons:

1. He thinks it's funny to entertain himself by humiliating someone else.

2. The target needs/deserves to be put through a rite of passage in order to join the group

3. The target deserves to be attacked for something he's done. If the target defends himself, he's

threatened in some manner; either his physical or social existence or the end of his association with the group he's a part of (a group of friends, a team, a gang, a college frat, a band, etc.).

As you probably know, there are some people who are determined to assert their power and any resistance to that power has to be put down with an even greater display of power. All resistance must be crushed. Which is plenty of motivation to not stand up to the bully.

WHAT IF YOU HAVE NO POWER?

> *I'm a freshman, and a junior calls me "piglet," referring to the fact that I go to a school where everyone is uber-fit and I'm sensitive about my weight. I've asked him to stop, but he insists on continuing calling me "piglet." Knowing that he would not stop by me just asking, I attacked him and called him "geometry," because he's in geometry as a junior, which is really behind compared to the rest of the school. It doesn't seem to stop him, and tonight he hit me in the stomach, knocking the wind out of me. I'm afraid he's still going to call me "piglet," and if I talk back he might get more violent next time. — Jackson, 14*

Jackson doesn't need to fight the junior. A more intelligent strategy is to manipulate the social hierarchy of the school. He should use the same social hierarchy that justifies in the junior's mind his right to put Jackson in his place because he has to pay his dues as a freshman (i.e., be treated like crap and keep his mouth shut). To beclear: the argument of upperclassmen that "We showed proper respect when we were freshmen, and we put up with it," is stupid. Almost every senior class complains that the freshmen don't show the seniors the respect they deserve, while the vast majority of freshmen are completely intimidated.

When you're in Jackson's shoes, all of this is hard to see because it seems like you have no option but to let the harassment continue. But Jackson does have another option. He needs to find a junior or senior guy who has influence over the junior and is willing to tell him to lay off. That upperclassman can be a friend or teammate, but most importantly, it should be someone everyone respects. (A Mastermind, Associate, Entertainer, or Champion are your go-to guys here.)

If you have an older sibling who goes to the school or graduated from the school, use that connection to approach the upperclassman. If you don't have such a connection, you're going to have to talk to a guy who is intimidating in his own right and who you don't have any connection to beyond seeing him on campus. I know, incredibly awkward. But if you balance the one moment of awkwardness against weeks, months, or two years of enduring the bullying, it's worth it.

To make a good choice about who you think is best, take a few days to make your decision and then prepare what you want to say by using SEAL. Wait until you see the guy walking across campus or when he's by himself and catch up to him. I'd suggest saying something like this: "Hey, I know you don't know me (or you only know me because I'm Katie's brother), but I want to ask your advice. You know Todd, the junior? He's been calling me 'piglet' every day. Yesterday he punched me in the stomach. There's really nothing I can do about this but take it, so I was wondering if there's any possible way you could tell him to lay off?"

This strategy works well because it's a power play. You're demonstrating that you understand the power this kid has (some would call it kissing up, but whatever) and that you believe he's the only one who can stop the junior. It makes guys feel good to be recognized like this, even from a lowly freshman, and he can play the hero.[10] Then think of it from the junior's perspective. If a well-respected junior or senior tells him to back off, he has to. If he doesn't, he's now disrespecting someone who has more power than he does. Then it becomes a problem between the two of them, which the junior wants to avoid. The junior now has the incentive to back off, not because it's the right thing to do, but because his life will get more difficult if he doesn't.

WHAT IF A GUY HATES YOUR FACE?

I'm sure the guy who "hates your face" has a miserable home life and if you knew the details you'd feel sorry for him ... which doesn't matter at all when he's in your face trying to start something. This usually happens when you're out with your friends having a good time at a party, a concert, etc. The good thing is that this guy is usually with a group of friends who just want to have a good time. The bad thing is that they may be dumb enough to think they have to back him up no matter what stupid thing he does. The easiest thing to do is not be there, as in leave. Sure, you want to stay at the party, but if you're heading toward a fight, the night won't end well anyway. Fun doesn't include having your face smashed in.

You can also try de-escalation by saying something like, "I'm just sitting here," or distraction by using humor, but not at the bully's or anyone else's expense. If you start making fun of him, that's a surefire way to trigger a fight, and if you redirect by making fun of someone else, you're just contributing to douchebag behavior.
Just be prepared for the possibility that this guy's idea of a good time is getting into a fight and nothing you say is going to stop that. You either walk away toward safety or

---

[10] Remember the heroic opportunities I talked about in the beginning of the book? Here's what I'm talking about. It's not saving the world, but to this ninth-grader it is.

you stand your ground. If you're never going to see this guy again, you don't gain that much from standing your ground.

STANDING YOUR GROUND

There are times in life when you may have to fight, and it's going to go better if you prepare. By all means take a few martial arts classes, or even get way into it and make it a regular part of your life. Just do yourself a favor: don't take lessons from anyone who brags about how good he is or how many black belts he has. Instead, learn from someone who has the ALMB qualities (whether they're male or female) that truly reflect internal personal strength. These people are great to hang around anyway, even if you never get into a fight, so it's a win-win no matter what.

You may be wondering why I know so much about fighting and the nature of physical violence. I started studying martial arts in college. About five years later I received my second-degree black belt in Tang Soo Do karate. I saw time and time again that the best fighters didn't advertise how tough they were or ever went looking for fights. They avoided them if at all possible, but when it was called for, they knew how to stand their ground.

YOU'VE HAD IT

If someone's constantly going after you, you may get to the point where you refuse to be bullied anymore. When and if you come to that conclusion, this is serious, because ultimately no one will be able to defend you but you. Even if an older kid or adult is protecting you, they can't do it all the time and at some point the bully will find you alone. Remember the goal: maximize your projection of mental and physical strength.

With that in mind, it's better to choose when this will happen. I think one of the more effective responses to a bully is to say some version of, "You know where I'll be," because you're communicating a lot in these few words.

Between the lines you're saying, "I'm not going to put up with you anymore, and if you mess with me, I'm going to stand my ground or go down trying." The other message you're sending is, "We don't have to do this." This puts the choice in the bully's hands, but you're setting the terms. The bully risks either losing face by losing the fight or losing the battle of public opinion by so obviously creating a situation that doesn't need to happen. The bully's power is based on the illusion of the bully's power—an illusion that he needs to manage carefully.

One major thing you can do if you're going to confront a bully is to choose your location. As any general knows, favorable terrain is key to victory. In this case, "victory" doesn't have to mean winning a fight outright. What it does mean is settling the issue so that the problem stops, without putting yourself in a situation where you could get seriously injured with no help nearby. The best way to do this is by having a few friends with you when you have the confrontation—not that they need to jump in and help you beat the guy up. (In fact, jumping a guy is less likely to settle the issue than it is to make him want to seek revenge.) Rather, their presence will make your bully less likely to initiate a fight; your friends can also ensure that if a fight does happen, it stays fair and doesn't get out of hand. If having friends around isn't an option, at least try to make sure you're in a fairly public place with other people reasonably nearby. I'm not saying you should make your stand right in front of a teacher, but you don't want to be alone in a parking lot at night either.

Lastly, if you can at all help it, you definitely don't want to be outnumbered. The ideal situation is one with enough people or allies around that you're unlikely to get seriously hurt and one where you can win the battle of public opinion.

IT DOESN'T MATTER WHAT YOU CALL IT

Any of the situations described in this chapter could be

defined as bullying. But does it really matter? What counts is that all of these guys came up against an imbalance of power where they felt trapped. All of them had to interact with the individual perpetrators who started the conflict and with the guys who watched it happen and chose to minimize the event or do nothing. I'd be surprised if this hasn't happened to you too. This can weigh on any guy. If you have an experience like this, one where you're worrying a lot, dreading interaction with a person, or seeing your performance at school or on a team suffer, then it's okay to admit that this experience has affected you.

It's also okay to ask for help. The problem is that not asking for help is one of the strictest ALMB rules in Guy World. You have to know when and how to break that rule, and now I'm going to show you how.

REINFORCEMENTS

When I have a problem, I've always hated involving other people. I always tried to solve the problem on my own. Asking for help is a last resort. But this time I was in a pretty deep hole when I realized it wasn't a bad thing to need help. —Mathias,15

Most guys suck at asking for and getting the backup they need. Doesn't matter if they need help lifting a box, their friend has a serious drinking problem, or they're under way too much pressure at school or on a team, the most common guy response is to say, "It's fine. I can handle it." Why does it feel so impossible to ask for advice or help? Why are guys so screwed up about this? The ALMB gives you the answer: guys in the box are supposed to handle things. Check out the following examples. They represent the most common reasons guys give me for keeping their problems to themselves.

I overanalyze so much that I think of so many

*different possibilities. If no possibility looks good,
then I usually just shut down and don't talk to
anyone about it and try to avoid the situation. —
Andrew, 17*

*I prefer to avoid my problems because there's
always the chance that whatever it is will go away on
its own. —Sam, 16*

If you want to shut down and try to bury your feelings,
that's your right, but at some point you're going to
explode. Then you'll freak out the people around you and
it'll be that much harder for them to understand the
reasons why you were angry in the first place. Instead,
unless they really get guys, they'll focus on your explosion.
Then you'll understandably feel unfairly accused and get
even angrier and they'll assume you're an angry or even
violent guy.

*The reasons that guys don't usually ask for help is
because they think that the problem can be solved
without anyone's help and they'll usually only ask for
it when things get outta hand. —Dante, 16*

I have heard so many guys say the same thing as
Dante. But if you're waiting until things "get out of hand,"
that means it'll be 100 percent certain that the situation is
way worse than it was before. And when I've asked guys to
define "out of control," the usual answer is, "Someone is
about to die or get seriously hurt."

Seriously, that's too late. I know people worry about not
wanting to snitch and the "Bro Code." That Bro Code thing
in this situation is only a trick to keep your mouth shut
about some fucked-up thing someone's doing. Here's the
difference between snitching and reporting. People snitch
to get someone in trouble; people report to right a wrong.
When people get mad at the person who reported by
saying he snitched, they're blaming him for coming

forward. Which is ironic, because he never would have had to say anything if there wasn't a problem. Believe me, no one ever wakes up and says, "Today I want to tell an authority figure in my life about how someone I know did something, is doing something, or will do something really twisted and wrong." People know they aren't going to be thanked for coming forward. They know that life will get way more difficult before it has a chance of getting better. So why would you do it? Because your definition of what it means to be a man, for you, is not being silenced by others when you need to do what's right.

I'm not saying you should go running to someone every single time you have a problem. Like I've said before, it's really important to develop inner strength. And as you get older, you understandably want to manage your problems without adult interference. But there'll be some problems that you can't handle on your own. The only choice you have is whether you're going to be prepared to handle it effectively or have it blow up in your face. Because like it or not, sometimes taking care of a problem includes reaching out to someone else for guidance.

You need an ally. Someone you've already designated as your backup. Before you decide who this person is going to be, you need to decide what kind of person you need. While some adults know what to do when a guy asks them for guidance, some are average and some are worse than useless. The best ally has the following three characteristics:

1. Opinionated but not judgmental: You want an ally to tell you what he thinks without judging you.

2. Honest: He tells you when you're messing up, but doesn't make you feel stupid.

3. Reliable: When you need your ally, he's there. If he can't get to you right away, he tells you when he'll be there and he comes through.

Don't wait to figure out who this person is until the problem is blowing up in your face, because by that point you'll be so stressed that it'll be hard to think clearly and you'll make an impulsive decision. Knowing when and who to ask for help is a skill— one that competent people know when to use.

CHAPTER SIX

NO MAN'S LAND

I can't believe I just said that.

You look at the other person, and it's immediately obvious from the expression on his face. The air changes around you, and you'd do anything for a do-over. Maybe you try to fix it. Maybe you make a joke at your own expense and the atmosphere relaxes. Maybe you slink away and hope that what you said will be forgotten. Maybe you do something to make it worse and feel even more foolish.

Now imagine that in every social interaction, every time you open your mouth, you're probably going to make a mistake. When you see people in the school hallway, you just want to get it right. You remember all the things you want to say and how you want to say them. You've gone over this in your mind a hundred times. But then the doubt comes. What if the other person says something back that throws you off? What if you say something wrong? What if you say something that makes no sense? What if . . .there are a million what-ifs. You try to focus, but all the words crowd in your mind. There're so many words, how could they ever come out the right way? You have to try.
You walk up to some kids in your grade, hoping you're not doing anything that looks strange. You desperately want to get it right. Except that you don't know what you're doing that's so wrong to everyone else.

From the moment you were a baby, you took social cues from the people around you. By watching and interacting with them, you effortlessly learned how to act. You watched, you repeated, and then those actions became your own. You never had to consciously think about what you were doing. For example, when you were really little, you high-fived and your parents clapped and smiled, so you knew you were doing it right. You learned to blow kisses when your grandma left the room, and everyone loved it. By the time you were twelve, your hellos had changed. You knew to say, "Hi, Mom," to kiss your grandma on the cheek, and to greet your friends with your version of "Hey, what's up?" You also knew that you shouldn't stand really close to people when you talked or constantly interrupt them. By the time you are sixteen, you're doing the "Hey, what's up?" guy hug and communicating a huge amount of information to your friends by the precise way you raise your eyebrows.

So far I've been talking to you a lot about how the ALMB gives you all these unwritten rules that guide your behavior and frame how you value what you see and experience. What I'm talking about now is another set of unwritten rules—the rules we all use in our daily interactions with each other. To most of us these rules don't even seem like rules. They're just the way anyone conducts himself in any given situation. But the problem for some people is that these seemingly basic rules aren't obvious and in fact are really hard to follow. You may be reading this and know exactly what I'm talking about. Or you may be thinking right now something like, Is she talking about [insert name of really weird kid at your school here]?

There have always been "weird kids." People who think and act differently. There have always been shy kids, nervous kids, and kids who can't sit still. This isn't a bad thing or a good thing. It's just how people are. I see a lot of guys who have depression, social anxiety, dyslexia, panic attacks, or eating disorders. There're a lot of guys who convince everyone that they're fine and then have to excuse themselves to hyperventilate in the bathroom. In the last twenty years, many kids have been diagnosed with learning and social disabilities like autism, obsessive-compulsive disorder (OCD), or attention deficit/hyperactivity disorder (ADHD)—and the majority of these people are boys. I'm not going to get into the very real debates about why more people are being diagnosed or if they need medication. What matters for us is that the severity of these disabilities varies widely, and sometimes they aren't even visible. Even more important, kids with social disabilities are more likely to be mistreated, manipulated, disliked, ignored, or identified as aggressors at school. Let me give you a couple of examples that are typical for kids with autism and ADHD.

You're a sixteen-year-old guy. You go to a regular school, and you just seem weird and really nerdy to the other students. In science class, you're paired up with a girl. She's very nice to you as you do all the work. This goes on for a week. The homecoming dance is coming up, and you decide to ask her to go with you. When you ask her, she says, "Maybe." On Facebook that night, you ask her again and tell her all the things you're planning to make sure she has a great time. Two hours later, you post a message on her FB asking if she saw your earlier posts. You send that message three more times that night. You friend-request all her friends. The next day her parents file a complaint against you for stalking their daughter and you're told to stay away from her. You're completely confused. You thought this girl liked you.

You're a fifteen-year-old high-functioning kid with autism. Your history teacher can't control the class. The other students are always talking. You hate it. You can't think. The noise physically hurts you. You cover your ears even though your parents tell you not to do that when you're in public. A kid walks by your desk and knocks the papers off your desk. Last year another kid did that to you on purpose all the time. This kid must be doing it on purpose too. You jump up and yell at the kid who knocked off your papers and then yell at the other students to follow the rules. You're sent to the principal's office for being disruptive.

You're in ninth grade, and it's sixth period. You just had lunch. Everyone in class is messing around because the teacher hasn't shown up for class yet. All of a sudden the other kids are in their seats, but you just can't settle down.

You have to tell this joke to your friend. The teacher walks in to hear you say, "Pussy." The teacher asks you to repeat what you just said. All the kids laugh. You can't help yourself. "Pussy," you say again. She gives you Friday detention. Twenty minutes later, you can't keep your eyes open. You fall asleep at your desk. You wake up to the teacher making fun of you.

Some of these kids can be difficult to be around. The child in the wheelchair with spina bifida or cerebral palsy isn't going to do things to other children that look deliberately provocative. Sometimes kids with social disabilities will. It's way easier to ignore them. It's also easier to ignore the people who like to push these kids' buttons and get them in trouble. Adults do it all the time, and they're not accused of being mean or "told to be nice." This isn't about feeling sorry for these kids. It's about understanding how they're often screwed by the system.

FIRST, A FEW FACTS

When you read this, you may recognize some of the characteristics I'm describing in yourself or in people you know. That doesn't mean you or anyone else actually has ADHD, OCD, ASD, or depression. Lots of us have a little bit of these things. And really, don't get caught up in the labels put on people. Labels are starting places for greater understanding, but they don't define you or anyone else.

Autism affects the brain's normal development of social and communication skills. Current statistics indicate that 1 out of 88 children are diagnosed (and most are male), but since there's a range of severity, people use the term "autism spectrum disorder" (ASD). Asperger's syndrome is defined as a higher-functioning form of autism. People with Asperger's or higher-functioning autism want to interact with others, but the way they do it often alienates them from other people.

Attention deficit/hyperactivity disorder (ADHD) is an

inability to regulate one's activity level and manage impulses in multiple environments in developmentally appropriate ways. This means that while it's completely appropriate for ten-year-olds to have a hard time sitting for an hour, the child with ADHD struggles to focus wherever he is, including school, home, and after-school activities. The number of American children leaving a doctor's office with an ADHD diagnosis has risen 66 percent in ten years.[11]

Social anxiety is the extreme fear of being scrutinized and judged by others in social or performance situations. Social anxiety disorder can wreak havoc on the lives of those who suffer from it. This disorder is not simply shyness: People with social anxiety recognize that their fear is excessive and unreasonable, but feel powerless against their anxiety. They are terrified that they will humiliate or embarrass themselves.

Depression may include anxiety, anger, and avoidance of social interaction. Changes in thinking and sleep are common signs of depression in young people. Depression can also occur along with social anxiety or ADHD.

Obsessive-compulsive disorder (OCD) is an anxiety disorder in which people have unwanted and repeated thoughts, feelings, ideas, sensations, or behavior that make them feel driven to act in certain ways. They know their behavior is different than their peers and feel really self-conscious about it. For guys who like to make others miserable, the kid with OCD is the easiest target. It's victimhood on a platter.

SO WHAT DOES AUTISM SPECTRUM DISORDER LOOK LIKE?

I've given you the basic signs of some social disabilities and anxiety disorders, but the signs for autism spectrum disorder are so varied that I'm going to break them down

---

[11] Science Daily, "Diagnosis of ADHD on the Rise," March 19, 2012, available at: science.com

with more detail here. If there was ever a recipe for not getting along with other people and making school as difficult as possible, this is it.

Obsessive talk about subjects that others have no interest in: Since a kid with ASD can't read the social cues that the other person is bored or irritated, he keeps right on talking.

Interrupting others: Neurotypical boys talk over and interrupt each other all the time, but there's an art to it. Unless you're good at observing the specific details of how that happens, it'll be easy to miss these social rules, and that's precisely the skills these kids lack.

Little ability to compromise: There has to be a clear winner and loser. A person on the autism spectrum believes he knows all the rules better than anyone else, so it's wrong and unfair when one of the kids insists on having a do-over and all the other kids let him. The kid with ASD studied the rules, played by the rules, and now someone just won by cheating.

Literal-mindedness: A kid on the autism spectrum can't understand sarcasm or double meanings or tell the difference between little lies, lies people tell to be polite, and real lies. He also doesn't pick up on subtle polite rejections, so when he's rejected, he never sees it coming.

Poor physical agility: These kids often have difficulties learning athletic activities like riding a bicycle or catching a ball. So imagine what recess is like for these boys in elementary school, or PE class in middle school.

Repeated body movements. When a kid on the autism spectrum wants to concentrate or calm himself, he repeatedly rocks, flaps his hands, jumps, or rubs on something like the back of a chair. Yes, this looks really strange, but think about it a different way. Have you ever bounced your leg up and down really fast? Have you ever bitten your nails? Have you seen a girl twirl her hair? That's what's going on here.

Stilted speech patterns: These kids can't learn or mimic teen slang. Even if they're highly verbal and get social skills training, they can sound stilted, robotic, or oddly polite.

Inability to "code–switch": A kid with ASD doesn't change what he says depending on who he's with. For example, obviously guys use foul language all the time around each other but know better than to speak like that around teachers or parents. Guys with autism don't know the difference. As they get older, they can have difficulties code-switching about sex and may talk about sexual things (masturbation, etc.) no matter who's around.

Monitoring and snitching: Remember the scenario I described in the room where the kid flipped out because the teacher wasn't controlling the class? How much do you want to bet there was another boy in the class who deliberately did things to set this kid off? But the guy with autism has been so annoying to have in class that who's going to come to his defense?

Immature interests: Pokemon cards? Remember them? A lot of boys with autism still like them in high school. Mom as social adviser: Since kids with autism usually don't have a lot of friends they can get advice from, they talk to their parents, especially their moms, for advice about how to get along with other kids. Think about that. What if you had to depend on your mother to teach you the subtle social rules that exist with the kids you know?

THESE KIDS ARE SO EASY TO MANIPULATE.

> In eighth grade, the kids would say, "Go to the trash can." I optimistically went over to the trash can, and then people started laughing at me. I don't know what's happening, so I'm going to hope for the best. They'd tell me to do ten jumping jacks, and sometimes I would do it. They tried to follow this kid into the bathroom, and I said, "He doesn't need help in the bathroom." They were going in there to be mean to him. — Andrew, 17

Kids like Andrew are too easy to go after. If you're

standing there watching this happen, you can't go along with it. It's not a fair fight. At the least, distract the asshole from going after this kid. And I don't think it's too much to ask of you to say some version of "Leave it."

If it gets to the point where you see someone really struggling or panicking, it doesn't matter what label that person has. Ask him if he needs some help and what that help looks like, as in, who needs to be contacted?

ARE THEY ASKING FOR IT?

My freshman year I had a roommate who just had no social skills. He literally made other people hate him. When I tried to talk to him about it, he was completely unwilling to take other guys' advice to get along better with everybody else. —Ned, 16

There's this kid at my school who follows me around. I feel bad for him, so sometimes when he shows up at lunch I let him sit with me. But it's a no-win situation. If I'm nice to him, he follows me around more. It got to the point where I had to tell him to back off. I felt bad about it, but what else am I supposed to do? —Brandon, 14

These kids are called "provocative targets" because it looks like they're forcing other people to be mean to them. Who wants to be nice to the kid who's screaming at you to be quiet in class? Or who follows you around relentlessly asking you to pay attention to him? If you're nice to these kids, they follow you around even more and don't listen to your subtle rejections, so you're forced to be so direct with them that they get really angry at you. Who wants to put up with that?

You don't have to put up with someone else if that person is making you really uncomfortable. Period. At the same time, you're never justified in stripping someone of his dignity. So use SEAL to describe exactly what you don't like and what you want.

Remember that this kid wants to do it right. If he still doesn't listen, then tell him that you can't be around him if he isn't going to listen to you or respect what you need him to do.

ALWAYS CAUGHT, ALWAYS BLAMED

The line between target and aggressor can get very blurry. In the situation with the boy asking the girl to go to homecoming with him, was he truly harassing her? Can you harass someone unintentionally? If the girl felt unsafe, then of course she had every right to keep him away from her. But what if she knew he posed no threat? What if she complained about his "stalking" because she wanted to dissociate herself from him as much as possible and didn't want her friends knowing that this guy liked her? Who's the target in that case? And who's the bully?

One of the things I always tell teachers is, "You always see the second hit, not the first." That means that what adults see is the person who's reacting. We don't see the person who started it. If it's just common sense that the person who started it is a better bully or aggressor than the other kid, this is 100 percent true for kids with social disabilities. Especially if they have a combination of ASD and ADHD, which makes them substantially more likely to be aggressive, impulsive, and unable to see the consequences of their actions.[12]

Recently a young woman who had recently heard me speak sent me an email. She was upset about a video that was circulating in her community, and she asked me to watch it. I thanked the woman for her email and clicked on the YouTube link she'd attached. On it, a pretty high school girl was recording herself encouraging a male

---

[12] "According to researchers, adolescents with both ASD and ADHD are five times more likely to bully than neurotypical adolescents."

student with severe social and learning disabilities to yell that he wanted to have sex with other boys who were in the room. While he was delighted with her attention, the other boys (big guys, wearing football jackets) were not amused. As I watched this boy giggle in a desperate effort to please this girl, I was disgusted by the girl's callous use of him for her own entertainment and worried for his safety the moment she left the room. That wasn't the only video she posted. Another depicted her encouraging the same boy to headlock younger boys, "pretend–stab" them with pencils, and say obscene things to them as well. All of the videos took place at school—three of them within a teacher's direct sight.

As soon as I watched all of the videos, I called the principal of the school. Within twenty-four hours the videos were down, the parents were notified, and the teacher was held accountable. But here's the reality. I saw the videos because an adult in the community cared enough to contact me. The principal handled it correctly. But usually that's not what happens. Usually the adults never find out. When they do, it's because the "problem" exploded into the adult world. Like when those football guys beat the crap out of that boy.

Imagine you're a parent of one of those football guys and you hear that a boy had yelled, in public, that he wanted to rape your son. If you didn't know the context of how this happened, you'd at least think anyone who threatened to rape your son started the conflict. If you heard that this kid was doing the same thing to younger children, you might think that kid deserved to be beat up. Now imagine that the school administrator didn't understand the context and didn't have the common sense to wonder why any boy would be stupid enough to say those things. Typically in this kind of situation, a school administrator would give the football guys a short suspension, tell them to stay away from that kid (which they won't do), blame the boy because he's a violent, sexual deviant, and discipline him ineffectively. Meanwhile, the girl would never be held accountable.

I'd like to think that I'd have known that kid was severely impaired before I took the time to educate myself. But I don't know for sure. Even though I work with these kids all the time, I've never been trained. And you know who isn't trained either? Most of the school administrators, teachers, and coaches I know. The only relevant training they usually get is about restraining techniques, which should be the last thing you learn as an educator, not the first, and which certainly shouldn't be the only thing you learn when working with children who have social disabilities. The truth is that every day these educators are working with kids who are very likely to get into trouble for behavior that is directly linked to their disability, and most of them lack the proper training to recognize the disability and resolve the issue.

WHAT DO I DO?

Here's the hero's moment. I'm not joking. If you have a friend who likes to manipulate or get this kid to do his dirty work, go back to the bystander SEAL I described in chapter 3, "The Laws of Brotherhood." You also have to say something in the moment to stop your friend from abusing or encouraging the kid. I don't think this is something you can mess around with.

Imagine you're next to that girl. Take her phone and shut it off. Tell her she's not being cute. (I promise you, it'll work every time.) If the person abusing another kid is a guy who's more likely to push back, literally, call him out. If he doesn't stop after you say, "Leave it, don't be stupid, etc.," and fights back on it, distract the targeted kid, then stand your ground. Speaking out is always hard, no matter what you're speaking out against, but you have to choose some battles when a person's dignity is on the line.

Meet Brendon Ayanbadejo, a linebacker who most recently played for the Baltimore Ravens. Would you tell this man that he didn't have the right to speak his mind?

In August 2012, Maryland delegate Emmett C. Burns Jr. (the man pictured below) wrote to the Ravens' owner telling him to shut Ayanbadejo up because he publicly supported gay people's right to marry. This turned out to be a very stupid thing to do. Let's break down the reason why.

The National Football League epitomizes American masculinity and personifies the ALMB. Ripped? Check. Tall? Check. Handsome? Check. Straight? Check. Athletic? Check. What Burns didn't know was that Ayanbadejo didn't let the box trap him. In high school he was active in theater and politics and lived with his mom in an apartment on the campus of UC Santa Cruz, where he was surrounded by all different kinds of people. He also happened to play football.

In 2009, Brendon became one of the first athletes from

a major American professional sports team to speak out in support of same-sex marriage. It wasn't easy. "'If I was walking by, and they [the players] wanted to be immature and make comments, I'd keep walking,' said Ayanbadejo, who has a 4-year-old son and a 9-year-old daughter with his longtime girlfriend. 'If they wanted to be real men and have conversations, I would have, but no one did'" (New York Times, September 14, 2012).

Real men have conversations? Exactly. When Ayanbadejo heard gay slurs from his teammates, this is what he did: "I just drop a little something in their ear, and hopefully it lets them see a little bit wider that those words are harmful. They go, 'I didn't mean it like that.' I just tell them, 'If you didn't mean it like that, then don't say it'" (USA Today, September 12, 2012).

Ayanbadejo isn't a superstar, but he is a three-time Pro Bowler ('06, '07, and '08) and respected by his team for his conduct and ability. When Burns wrote his letter three years later, Ayanbadejo's actions had changed the Ravens' culture. After the Burns letter became public, "a bunch of my teammates were men about it," Ayanbadejo said, "and they had real, honest conversations with me. That had never happened before."

Then things got more interesting. When Kris Kluwe, a punter for the Minnesota Vikings, read Burns's letter, he responded publicly with a letter of his own that in no uncertain terms demonstrated that Burns, a U.S. congressional representative, was completely clueless about the U.S. Constitution and American history. But what Kluwe also did was show how effectively you can destroy someone with ruthless logic and humor. Here are some excerpts:

> *I would like to remind you that the very first, the VERY FIRST Amendment in this founding document deals with the freedom of speech, particularly the abridgment of said freedom. By using your position as an elected official (when referring to your*

constituents so as to implicitly threaten the Ravens organization) to state that the Ravens should "inhibit such expressions from your employees," more specifically Brendon Ayanbadejo, not only are you clearly violating the First Amendment, you also come across as a narcissistic fromunda stain. It baffles me that a man such as yourself, a man who relies on that same First Amendment to pursue your own religious studies without fear of persecution from the state, could somehow justify stifling another person's right to speech. To call that hypocritical would be to do a disservice to the word.

"Many of your fans are opposed to such a view and feel it has no place in a sport that is strictly for pride, entertainment, and excitement." . . . Did you seriously just say that? Have you not heard of Kenny Washington? Jackie Robinson? As recently as 1962 the NFL still had segregation, which was only done away with by brave athletes and coaches daring to speak their mind and do the right thing, and you're going to say that political views have "no place in a sport"?

This is the power of professional sports at its best. That these professional athletes—who participate in the most popular sport in the United States and whose size and strength embody male physical power (yes, I know one of them is a punter, but give me a break)—are the ones stepping forward to defend gay people is, in a word, stunning. In one moment they have shown that men who personify everything we glorify about masculinity can shatter the confining limitations of the ALMB by using its own power. Let's use this example in your school. Imagine a person getting up to announce the next meeting of the Gay Alliance or whatever cause people generally blow off or don't think applies to them. Is the person you're thinking of the political girl who almost everyone rolls their eyes at or tunes out when she speaks? Now imagine that, instead of her, it's one of the best athletes in the school making the announcement, a guy who looks like a high school version of Kris Kluwe or Brendon Ayanbadejo. Who would have more power to change public opinion?

If you have this kind of power within your community, just think for a moment about how you could reinvent yourself as someone who is truly transformational to the people around you—not just your peers, but adults as well. The power of sports to transform people's thinking can't be overstated. But people's personal experiences and the culture of athletics can be a lot messier and more disappointing. It really isn't about the sport itself but about the social entitlement and power we give the guys who play.

CHAPTER SEVEN
MAKING THE CUT

The moment you make the cut and you're on the team, you're joining an established culture with its own set of specific unwritten rules. It also makes perfect sense that as a new player you want to be part of the team, both on and off the field. The culture starts in varsity and trickles down to JV. Do the players respect the authority of the captain? Does the captain exercise this authority fairly? How seriously do players take practice? What happens if you don't want to shave your head before a game? Have you all signed a contract saying you won't drink but you drink anyway? All of the answers to these questions are already in place when you get there.

YOU MADE THE CUT AND NOW YOU'RE GETTING CRAP FOR IT.

I'm a freshman and made varsity baseball. The guys on my team were fine, but the other guys that are my age are giving me so much shit. It's incredibly annoying. — Sam, 15

Did you work really hard during the off-season? Did you grow four inches since last season? Did your body get more coordinated in the last few months? Any of these things can vault you onto the next level … and bring up another guy's raging insecurities and jealousy. It's annoying, but you can't let it stop you. The telltale signs of jealousy in this situation are unmistakable. The guy makes little comments to undermine your confidence, either in front of you or in front of your friends. He makes you doubt whether you deserve to be on the team, or he makes you feel guilty for making the team, as if somehow you don't deserve to be there. Remember, you made the team. You worked hard. You deserve to be there.

To handle this situation effectively, re-read the section on malicious teasing on page 46 because the strategy he's going to use to bring you down is identical to what is spelled out there. When you talk to him, you really don't want to have a long drawn-out conversation. He's going to make it hard because he'll do it in front of other people—maybe not in front of the whole team but with enough people around that he can reliably bank on you not calling him out. He'll most likely fake-compliment you ("Hey, Varsity," or, "What's up, first squad?") or minimize your accomplishments ("Anyone can make varsity by sucking up," "Special teams doesn't count," or, "If [name of a varsity player] didn't get hurt, you wouldn't be on the team").

Give him a pass the first two times he does this; maybe he just needs to work his jealousy out of his system. The third time, look at him and say, completely seriously, "Funny," or, "Are you finished?" and then go back to what you were doing. The fourth time you can say in a "light" way—as in, not sarcastic—"Talk to me about this when you make the team." The bottom line is that you don't want to appear weak by not saying anything about it, but you don't want to make it a power struggle between the two of you.

Michael had a different approach that's worth considering.

> *The part about the "talk to me when you make the team" is difficult to pull off nonsarcastically, and either way, I think the person would take it badly. Instead of saying that, you can say, "Do you need to talk about this?"—Michael, 16*

What I like about Michael's suggestion is that this question clearly communicates that the problem rests with the other guy but asking it doesn't publicly embarrass him.

YOU MADE THE TEAM, BUT YOUR FRIENDS DIDN'T, OR VICE VERSA.

However, this goes down, the result is often a realignment of friendships. Not making the team fractures the old roles and creates realignments and opportunities for a new identity and new friendships. Seriously, if you don't make the lax team and your friends do, you may have just avoided becoming a laxbro. Or maybe getting cut enables you to try out for another sport that's got a totally different group of kids. Change is difficult, but it's not necessarily bad.

WHAT IF YOU'RE REALLY GOOD?

If you're really good, so good that your talent clearly sets you apart, you have a responsibility that goes along with the social power inherent in your talent. I know you know that being better doesn't give you the right to treat other people like crap. But the reality is, being good at things, especially sports, often gives you an asshole pass. This is different than being an asshole because your association with the group makes you feel better and is important to you. This is about being an asshole when you're really good at something in the ALMB so people don't hold you accountable for bad behavior. The result is that you're encouraged and enabled to become an asshole.

The reality is that reaching the highest levels of athletics is about work ethic and intelligence. Lots of guys are talented. Even if you're the best in your school or league or state, there are most likely hundreds if not thousands of other kids who are better than you. However good you are, make it a point to show the kids coming up after you what the combination of talent and hard work looks like. You're good but that doesn't mean you have fallen into the trap of believing that your ability makes you above other people. You want the current and future guys on the team to look at you and want to work hard to be like you.

YOU MAKE VARSITY AS A FRESHMAN.

If you get on the team as a freshman, you've earned your place. But for most freshmen who make the varsity team, even if they're really good, they're not as good and not as big as the juniors and seniors. Even more importantly, they're not accustomed to the social situations that come along with being on varsity.

For example, the first time you get into a car with an upperclassman, let alone four upperclassmen, it's going to feel really different. All the guys pile in. Guys argue for shotgun and fight over the bitch seat. One of the guys may be hiding in the trunk because you're stopping by someone's house and parents may check how many guys are in the car. You're probably speeding, listening to music that you like, and it's loud. There are no parents telling you the music is inappropriate and turning the volume down. The world is suddenly much bigger, and you don't even have a license yet.

You're going to grow up faster, and it happens the moment you make the team.

TRIPS

If your team is going to a tournament where you'll be sleeping in dorms or hotels, it can be really fun . . . or a total shit storm. Outside of the school environment, the social power of the team's hierarchy gets more intense. If you have even just a few Masterminds, Associates, Flies, or Bouncers, you can have huge problems. If your coach isn't smart enough to assign rooms intelligently or can't hold his own with his players, try to choose which guy you room with. Try to room with someone who's in your year, who you practice with a lot, or who at least has a solid reputation. What you're looking for is trying to have one place during the trip where you can genuinely relax and be yourself.

When things do go wrong in these situations, it's

always possible in hindsight to point to a series of small events that led to the really messed-up situation. You need to see these small signs. Before you go on the trip, reread the roles section in chapter 2. Decide if any of the guys on the team fit these roles and what combination of the guys drives up the possibility of high levels of stupidity going down. Even one guy can jack things up and create serious problems. Three of them together can be a nightmare.

Here are small signs you're heading for a shit storm:
- When the players who are constantly riding other players make little inside jokes about what's going to happen to certain kids on the trip.
- When a Mastermind or Associate says, "Don't worry about it," but your gut is telling you something's wrong.

When someone says, "Wouldn't it be funny if we did (X) to Jake?" Or "Jake, you should totally do (X) . . . it'd be awesome." When Jake tries to get out of it, they increase the pressure.

I'm not saying you shouldn't have a lot of fun on these trips. Make the most of them. Make lots of noise, get into trouble in creative ways. If you cause destruction (property damage, etc.), don't lie or whine when you get caught. Pay for the damage. Clean up your mess. But the second the "fun" involves humiliating someone else, you're over the line. In that moment, ask yourself if you're prepared to take the consequences for where this will end—and those consequences include your ability to look yourself in the mirror.

PARTIES

When guys with more seniority invite you to their parties (whether they call it a party or just hanging out in someone's basement), they think they're doing you a favor. Especially for freshmen and sophomores, hanging out with older guys inevitably means hanging out with at least one insecure guy with a big ego and at least a few guys with much greater alcohol and drug tolerance than you have who think it's amazingly funny to get you wasted. Plus, older guys come with older girls. I know everyone thinks this is awesome, but older girls bring more complicated problems, like dealing with her friends, the older girl's ex-boyfriend hating you, the older girl's ex being on the team with you... Just think about it before you dive in.

NOTE TO THE OLDER GUYS

If you're an upperclassman and you have a younger or new member on the team, be careful. You or one of the other players may think it's hilarious to get this kid blindingly drunk. If you're in a position of leadership and you do this or let your friend do it, you've now compromised your authority among the guys. And what are you going to do with him after? Even if he sleeps over at your house, he's still going home hung-over. Ten seconds of laughing at the freshman reflects poorly on you for a lot longer. Freshmen also have rules like curfew that they have to abide by. Remember this. Encourage him to get home before his curfew. If he feels immature about it, tell him that you had one when you were a freshman. Give him permission to be the kid he still is. He may still break the rules, but it shouldn't be because you encouraged him.

YOU HATE YOUR COACH.

You have to learn to work with people you hate or don't respect, and sometimes that person might be your coach. You do become a stronger person by getting through this kind of situation. When do you know if you should stay or you should quit?

Annoying but Acceptable

- Not giving you enough playing time

- Being mean, but he's mean to everyone

- Making you practice so hard you feel miserable and occasionally throw up

- Yelling at you for not giving your best effort

Unacceptable

- Not being clear about his expectations and then blaming you when you don't meet those expectations

- Practicing without breaks and water, putting you and the other guys at risk

- Singling out a player or group of players for who they are (like their race, religion, ethnicity)

- "Encouraging" players by humiliating them. Especially singling out a player or a group of players by questioning their manhood, calling them girls, faggots, etc.

- Looking the other way when one of his players is violent or abusive to another person

- Excusing bad behavior in his star player because "he's such a good kid" but really because he wants him to play

One of the coaches would call us faggots and picked on this one kid all the time. Nobody did anything because they didn't want to be called a faggot

When you have a coach like this, it usually feels like there's absolutely nothing you can do about it but put up with it or quit. However, those aren't your only options.

YOU WANT TO QUIT.

Whatever it is, giving up something you've spent a lot of time and effort on (not to mention the sacrifices you and your parents have made) is incredibly stressful. Your emotions take over your ability to think clearly. It doesn't matter what it is—football, lacrosse, badminton, music, or theater.

Whenever you give something up that you've spent years dedicating yourself to, it can easily feel like you're losing part of your identity. That's why a lot of people in this situation take a long time to reach the conclusion that they want to quit. But staying with something that makes you unhappy will only make you more miserable, and it certainly won't make you better.

The tricky thing is that it's almost inevitable that you'll go through a phase when you want to give up but you should stick with it. On the other hand, sometimes you need to get the hell out. The only way you'll be able to figure out what's best for you is if you go through an intense process of self-reflection and assessment of the overall situation.

First, let's tackle the guilt. When you think of the miles your parents have driven, the dollars they've paid out, and the time they've spent sitting on those cold, uncomfortable bleachers, it can really make you feel like you'd rather keep playing than make them feel that their sacrifice was for nothing. But there are a lot of reasons why it's difficult to tell your parents. Quitting is often perceived as directly equated with poor character and mental and physical weakness. For parents, it can also feel like a reflection of their parenting. If you quit, they're bad parents. If you stay, they're good parents. This isn't true, but it's often what people believe.

What most parents don't know is that wanting to quit often has nothing to do with actually playing the sport. Guys don't quit over the extra drill or pushups. They quit because they give up on their coach. They quit because their parents put unbearable pressure on them. They quit because the guys on the team are horrible to each other or other people. It's perfectly reasonable to be sick of the crap that goes on in the locker room every day or to not want to share a locker with a date rapist.

If you don't tell them the truth, parents fall back on what they think they know and assume. I'm not saying this is easy. Who wants to say to his parents, "You make me insane. You live your life through me and I just want you to leave me alone?"

For your mental health, though, you have to do it. If you have an overbearing parent, my experience is that they react better if you stand up to them and say straight up why you want to quit. It's also a good strategy to be prepared to talk about something you want to do instead. As in, "Dad, one of the reasons I'm doing this is because I really want to concentrate on applying for this summer science internship." Also be prepared for them to have an emotional and defensive response when you break it to them. If you're not ready for that, you'll react defensively too, until your parents are yelling and you're closing down and retreating to your room or your friend's house. So if things get heated, tell them you want to talk, but only when you both can be calmer. This is turning the tables on your parents with the maturity thing, but sometimes it has to be done.

Another common reason guys want to quit a team is because something seriously wrong is going on but they're not sure what to do about it. Assuming you truly love the sport you play, before you talk to anyone, ask yourself these questions: Do I love the sport and hate the team? Is it worth transferring schools? Could I play at a lower level and be happy?

Once you make your decision about what you want to do, get your mom or dad alone so you can talk to them. Here's how it can go.

YOU: I don't know if I want to do this anymore. YOUR

MOM: What are you talking about? Why? YOU: It's just not working out.

YOUR MOM: Why? I'm not getting this.

YOU: Mom, it's not that big a deal. I'm just done.

YOUR MOM: You need to explain this beyond you feel like quitting. You have such potential.

YOU: Fine. Just forget I brought it up. (Silence in the car. You stare out the window and put your ear buds in. You're sitting there feeling so stupid that you thought it'd be a good idea to talk to your parents.)

YOUR MOM: What is going on with you?

You look at your mom and don't know what to say. You're torn between walking away and telling her everything. Partly because she'll feel so guilty if she knows the truth, but there's also this other little part of you that wants to tell her because she's your mom. You look away, struggling between the 90 percent of you that desperately wants to keep your mouth shut and the 10 percent that wants to tell her.

You can't keep it inside anymore. You tell her. Last Friday, after a solid month of being treated like shit, a guy on the team was held down after practice while four guys shaved his head because he "didn't have enough team spirit." One of the guys who held him down was you. You didn't want to, but you did. You'll never forget how the other guys laughed while the kid on his knees fought. You tell her that the coach knew it was going to happen and conveniently left the locker room right before the guy was forced down to the ground.

First and foremost, having your head shaved against your will is terrifying. You're being held down, so you're at the mercy of your tormentors, who have clearly communicated that they're determined to degrade you, and your neck is being exposed to a possibly sharp object that will instinctually make you have a flight-or-fight response. This isn't what "team spirit" is based on. It's what tyranny is based on.

There are three likely outcomes here when you tell your mom:

1. She is outraged and then insists on immediately calling the principal, the coach, or the shaved kid's parents.

2. She doesn't like what happened, but wants you to keep quiet and let it blow over.

3. She doesn't see why you're so upset because technically no one got hurt. If you have an ALMB dad, he may react by also accusing you of weakness or being too sensitive.

All three of these outcomes suck. If you're in this position and your parents force you to report an incident like this one, you're going to feel like you're snitching (or be accused of it). You're also going to have to admit that you participated, which also sucks. If your parents want you to keep quiet, you've now realized that they're too scared or passive to do the right thing. If your parents dismiss it as a prank or "guys will be guys," you'll have ample evidence that the ALMB controls them—which you probably knew already, but this will confirm it.

Here's what you do: You recognize that this is a

moment of true rebellion. You admit to yourself that this kid will never feel at ease on the team again (even if he's forced to say he is because he wants to show his "loyalty" to the ringleaders). You're going to remember the difference between snitching and reporting. People snitch to get someone in trouble; people report to right a wrong. And you're going to keep front and center in your mind that you're only in this situation because the guys did it and the coach permitted it by leaving.

No matter what kind of parent you have, you're going to report it to the person at school who you trust the most and who has the most power. You're going to write a letter using SEAL and email it to this person. Make sure you say where it happened, when it happened, who was there as a bystander, and who was there as a participant—including you. Describe the actions of the coach. If you're asked to meet in person with those who participated in the incident, do it, but bring your parents as backup. If you really can't rely on your parents, ask a teacher you trust to go with you instead. Don't go into this meeting alone because even with the most reliable principal, you want to cover your bases. You want the principal to know that another adult knows.

One more thing about adults. I chose the head-shaving incident because it's a common occurrence that's easily blown off by guys and adults as "guys being guys" or as "horseplay." But you also know that way worse things happen in locker rooms. It's not uncommon to hear about athletes (usually on the team with the most social status in the school and town) to assault another kid—a girl or a guy. At one of the schools I worked with several years ago, a varsity football player sexually assaulted another player in the locker room with a broomstick. While the perpetrator needed to be held accountable (and he was—he's now in jail), for years there had been a problem at this school with some guys believing they were above the law. The most powerful leaders of the school knew it, and they refused to address the issue effectively. As this story came out in the press, these leaders said that they "believed" this is the first time this has ever happened. Some of the parents said they were sure it was a "fluke." These things are never, ever a fluke. That guy would never have assaulted someone if he didn't think he'd get away with it. His experience at that school led him to believe that he could get away with bullying other students without interference by the adults in positions of power. Now, did the leader of the school know specifically that on that particular day that kid would assault another player with a broom handle? No. But these people are supposed to know kids and the culture of their own school, and they knew they had a problem on their hands. And the fallout almost always follows the same pattern. When it becomes public, the victim begins to minimize what happened to him because it's so humiliating to go to school with everyone knowing this about you. And as he does this and puts the incident behind him, the leaders of the school praise him for moving on because they just want to forget the whole thing ever happened—or more to the point, that it was discovered and made public.

Coaches and administrators are supposed to be your moral leaders. The same goes with any adult in your life. You're supposed to be able to depend on them. If you can, be grateful and make them your allies. But if they're hypocritical, if they lie, if they sacrifice their ethics and you in the process, don't let their moral cowardice infect you. Don't let them make you a weaker man, and don't let them bank on your silence to get away with their deceit. Admit the shitty hand you got, get angry at how ridiculously hypocritical some adults are, and then be the man you want them to be. Speak out. If you don't do this, you're going to carry this around with you. You're going to feel less of a man. The team will also suffer because true team cohesion and "spirit" can only be developed through trust and love.

Not all adults suck. In the book *Season of Life*, Joe Ehrman, a former NFL defensive lineman and volunteer high school coach, is described as he began the football season with his players.

> *"What is our job as coaches?" he asked.*
>
> *"To love us," the boys yelled back in unison.*
>
> *"What is your job?" Joe shot back.*
>
> *"To love each other," the boys responded.*

With Joe standing by his side, Biff, the six-foot-three, 300-pound head coach, gathered the guys around him and said:

> *I don't care if you're big or small, huge muscles or no muscles, never even played football or star of the team—I don't care about any of that stuff.... If you're here, then you're one of us, and we love you. Simple as that.... We're gonna go through this whole thing as a team.... A community. This is the only place probably in your whole life where you're gonna be together and work together with a group as diverse as this—racially, socially, economically, you name it. It's a beautiful thing to be together like this.... So enjoy it. Make the most of this. It's yours. The relationships you make here ... you will always have them ... for the rest of your life.*

This is what you deserve and what every guy deserves.

CHAPTER EIGHT
LEADERSHIP AND DIVIDED LOYALTIES

I'm really worried about this year because I'm in this leadership position that requires me to turn anyone in if I see them drinking or breaking another school rule. Even though I know I technically should, I'm not really sure I'm going to. Once adults get involved, things get so out of control. This kid could get kicked out of school—for something that maybe isn't that big a deal. I'm just hoping it's possible to go through the year without having this happen. —Jason, 17

If you've heard the term "Machiavellian," it's probably been when someone was describing another person's behavior as immoral and evil. The term comes from Niccolò Machiavelli, a fifteenth-century Florentine bureaucrat who lived when Italy was made up of city-states that were constantly at war with each other. When his government was overthrown, not only did he lose his job, but he was imprisoned, tortured, and then finally sent into exile. Dejected and angry, he retreated to his house in the country and wrote The Prince, one of the most important books on power and leadership ever written. Here are two pieces of advice from Machiavelli that Jason would do well to follow.

> *He who wishes to be obeyed must know how to command. It is not titles that honor men, but men that honor titles.*

There is nothing more difficult to take in hand, more perilous to conduct, or more uncertain in its success, than to take the lead in the introduction of a new order of things.

In my words . . . you don't accept a leadership position hoping that you're never going to face difficult problems.

Not only is that naive, but it also sets you up for failure. Instead, you go into leadership knowing that you will be challenged and your authority will be questioned. Even if you get to a point where you'd rather relinquish power, you signed up for it, so you have to face your problems.

TURNING SOMEONE IN

Everybody sees what you appear to be; few really know what you are. — Machiavelli

If you have accepted a position in school, like team captain, peer counselor, or student council, or in private school serving on the honor committee or discipline committee or as a dorm leader, prefect, etc., you have agreed to uphold the "law." That means: (1) your actions are consistent with the school rules, and (2) you won't play favorites, like looking the other way when your friends break the rules. I'm not saying this because it's ethical. That's important, but so is not losing credibility with your peers. If you abuse your position or inconsistently apply the rules, you'll come across as hypocritical and corrupt. You'll be a joke or a tyrant.

Of course, having these titles on your college application looks great, but know what you're getting yourself into. It's a reasonable conclusion to make that you may not want to be in these positions. But if you're already there, you have to accept the likelihood that you will have to turn someone in. It's never going to be easy, especially if it's a good friend. Good kids break the rules all the time, and it's hard to hold them accountable.

This will be a lot less stressful if you have a direct conversation with your friends as soon as your position takes effect. Here's my suggestion for what to say:

"Whether I like it or not, now that I have this position, if I see you drinking or doing drugs on campus or at school-related events, I'll have to report you. If I don't, not only will I get in trouble, but the other students will think I'm a joke or one of those kids who protects his friends but goes after everybody else. We both hated seeing that when we were underclassmen, so I need you to have my back."

For example, if you're the team captain and you all have signed a contract with the coach that you won't drink and people do, then they're giving you no choice but to report them. Some kids—even some of your friends—will deliberately break the rules in front of you to see how you handle the challenge. If you don't deal with them straight on, you will lose all authority immediately.

So what do you do when you find a kid or a group of kids breaking the rules? The moment you find out, think about their possible motivation. Let's take drinking and doing drugs. They either have a problem and need help (and maybe want to get caught so they can get help without technically admitting it), they believe the consequence is worth it, or they're taking advantage of their relationship with you and banking on you feeling so conflicted in your loyalty that you won't turn them in.

If you think they have a drinking or drug abuse problem, then use the SEAL in the drinking scenario on page 130. Whatever the reason they're in trouble, you need to give them limited options. Either they can tell an adult or you can. Give them a time deadline too—tell them they'll need to come forward in the next two days or you will.
If they believe the consequence is worth it, then they've already said by their actions that they can take whatever punishment they get. It's illogical to blame you for it. If they hadn't broken the rule, you wouldn't have been in the position to report them. Anyone who knowingly breaks school rules takes the chance of getting into trouble for it. If they think they're going to get immunity and you help them, then you're being used.[13]

---

[13] Remember the difference between snitching and reporting. You aren't snitching here. You're reporting.

CONTRACTS

For years sports teams have had oral or written contracts to mandate players' behavior. I'd like to take it one step further and suggest that if you're in any leadership position, one of the first things you do with your peer group is write down a specific code of conduct that you all agree to abide by. People's word should be enough, but don't rely on it. What you absolutely can't do is be a leader who is enforcing rules on other students but not abiding by those same rules himself. Say it and do it or don't do it.

Even if you don't have an official written contract, everyone in your specific group has agreed to abide by the rules associated with your position. If you see people in your group breaking those rules, remember that it's your responsibility to hold them accountable. Say you go to a school with some kind of dress code and you're a member of a leadership group, like the student council or a peer leadership group, and one of the girls in your group is always wearing skirts that are way too short—and so are some of the freshman girls. I know the typical thing most people think about a guy in your position is that there's nothing that makes you happier than being around girls with skimpy clothes on. But for a lot of guys in leadership positions, the girls' hypocrisy and the realization that her actions make him look bad is more annoying than the benefits of looking at a girl's legs or chest.

> *The other problem is, I can't say anything to the freshman girl because I'm a senior and that's just awkward. I need the senior girl to say something because I can't. But she's doing the same thing.* — Rick, 18

You have to call the senior girl out. At the least, you have to talk to the other senior girls who aren't being so hypocritical and get them to talk to her. I know I'm repeating myself, but if you don't do what's right, you look either weak or just as fake as every other politician or person in a leadership position who gets power and doesn't hold himself to the same standard he's holding everyone else to.

THE POPULAR VOTE

Lots of guys are voted into leadership positions because they're funny and popular, but they have little intention of working hard once they're there. Meanwhile, people with more substance who would have worked much harder in the job don't get elected. If you're the popular guy who won the election, it's not your fault that enough of the student body voted for superficial humor over substance. But once you have the job, get off your ass and honor the commitment you signed up for.

What does that mean? If you're elected to student government, it's your responsibility to represent your constituency: the entire student body. Seek out the people you don't know well and who aren't in your social circles and ask them what they'd like from you this year. Ask students and faculty what previous incumbents in the position did well or poorly. Look for ways to bring different people forward and make them more visible in the school. Don't make your speeches during assemblies only about how great the school is, don't make inside jokes that only your friends get, and don't make fun of any event that you have to announce. Promise to work on things that matter to the whole school and make sure all the students know they can talk to you, especially if they disagree with you. All schools have serious issues that can be effectively addressed by a competent student government. Don't be a lapdog to anybody.

WHAT IF YOU LOSE?

It probably won't bother you too much if you lose to someone you think is capable. But it's incredibly frustrating if you lose to someone who's funnier than you but has shown no interest in actually taking the job seriously. Don't sit there and wallow in anger. Be angry for a few days, but then demonstrate your strength of character by showing that you're not going to be stopped by one loss. Plus, other opportunities that may be smaller in scope but more meaningful may come up. It may not be as public as student body president, but look for positions where you can accomplish an agenda you set out.

There really is a silver lining here if you can find one of those smaller positions. As the student body president, you can't usually call student assemblies, and it can be really challenging to get the entire student community mobilized for a common purpose. As the head of a team, the student newspaper, or a club, it is much easier to accomplish what you want to do.

GIVING THE POSITION THE GRAVITAS IT DESERVES

Ethical leadership comes down to one of three choices:

1. Supporting everyone's right to be treated with dignity.

2. Taking a neutral position that will appear to others as siding with the person who has more power.

3. Overtly backing up the person with more power.

Unfortunately, you have grown up in a time when you've seen leaders touted as upstanding and honorable either take the neutral position or outright support their peers who abuse power. It's also true that the more unquestioned public power a leader has, the more likely he is to sacrifice people's dignity to maintain his institution's appearance of greatness. True greatness only comes from having the courage to constantly examine how power and leadership are exercised. Aspire to greatness.

CHAPTER NINE

WASTELAND

By far, the scariest part of my job is being introduced before a high school assembly. Put yourself in my shoes. You're standing next to a teacher in front of eight hundred students. There are the junior guys in the front row who are determined to laugh at you. There are the freshman girls a few rows back who are desperately hoping one of the older guys will say hello to them. Off to the side, either in the very front or the very back, are the scary senior girls. All of them believe that they're about to be bored to death. Then the teacher, who usually means well, introduces you like this, "Guys and girls, we have such a treat today. Rosalind is a national expert on bullying, cliques (pronouncing it cleeques), friendships, cyberbullying, and the problems you guys get into. She really gets teens, and I'm sure listening to her will be a very rewarding experience, and please show her what a respectful audience is like."

Or it could be worse. Instead of a well-meaning but out-of-touch teacher, I can have a patronizing blowhard introduce me. Like the principal who warmed up the student audience for me by lecturing them: "The problem with you all is that you abuuuuse technology with all that texting and the Facebook. Adults uuuuse technology. You abuuuuse it. Do you know that? You abuuuuse it." You have no idea how much I wanted to push that guy off the stage. Either way, I'm thinking, Kill me now, while forcing a smile and taking the mike from this person who just made it a million times harder for me to convince these kids I know what I'm talking about.

I recently experienced the challenge of the well-meaning teacher destroying my credibility with a group of really smart and cynical students, which meant that for the next forty-five minutes I had to bust my ass so they wouldn't think the assembly was a complete waste of time. Up to that point, I'd only mentioned in passing that you could use SEAL when you were worried about someone. So I was shocked when one of those guys in the front raised his hand and asked me how he would use SEAL with a close friend who had a drinking problem. The room fell silent. These kids were each other's families. They knew what was going on in each other's lives like no one else did. It was absolutely clear that many in the room could relate.

Here was a guy who looked like nothing ever bothered him, he had his life under control, and he always knew what to do, but he was publicly admitting that he needed help. After I answered him, the questions poured out. All related to helping friends. That Q&A session lasted way over what the school had scheduled, but I stayed as long as the kids had questions.

After the presentation, I realized that I needed to think more deeply about the answer I gave that front-row student that night and then share it with other people in similar situations. Here's what I've come up with.

No matter what the problem is, when you're worried about someone and you're getting ready to tell them how you feel, this is a high-stress situation for both of you. When people are stressed, they tend to fall back on what's comfortable to them. For example, if you confront the Entertainer, he'll push back with jokes, if you confront the Punching Bag or the Fly, they'll push back by agreeing with you (but won't change their behavior), and the Mastermind will push back by making you doubt yourself. The Bouncer will get angry. Part of your SEAL here is assessing what you know about this person and how he'll most likely react.

HOW DO I KNOW THERE'S A PROBLEM?

When you're worried that someone you know may have a drinking/drug problem, the first thing that happens seems pretty basic—the people around the guy have concluded that he has a drinking/drug problem. But it's not as easy as it seems. When you think about who makes this decision, you naturally think of the guy's friends, his girlfriend, his parents, or a coach. But all of these people define "a drinking problem" very differently, because the bar for that definition will be lowest for the adults, a bit higher for the girls, and extremely high for the guy's friends.

For example, some parents—at least the ones who don't buy alcohol for their kids—will think there's a problem if they find the guy drunk or high more than once. Most girls think there's a problem if the guy is drinking every weekend until he throws up or blacks out. But the guy's inner circle, the ones most likely to know how much he's actually using certainly wouldn't agree with the adult assessment and probably wouldn't agree with the girls because they themselves are probably using about the same amount. For example, throwing up or blacking out may be identified among the guys as a normal result of drinking too much on any particular night. It's the body's way of saying it has had enough.

All of this comes down to a simple point: the actual amount a guy drinks/drugs may not be enough for his friends to think there's a problem they have to do something about. For guys to believe their friend has a problem, it has to have a serious impact on other aspects of his life. Like not showing up, being drunk or hung-over for meetings or practice, or performing significantly worse at games or other events. Another indicator could be getting super-aggressive and starting fights or insisting on driving. Or bombing a test, or not going to school.

My brother and his friends went to a party, and one of their friends blacked out, so they took him home. But when they went back to the party, the kid showed up a little later because he had driven himself there but had no recollection of how he did it. That was a clear indication. —Will, 20

Here's an easy rule for you to follow. Since your bar is so high, the second it occurs to you that your friend has a problem, this in itself proves he has a problem. If you start talking about it with your other friends, he definitely has a problem. Seriously, the fact that you all are talking about it is all the proof you need.

Once you've had your realization, what do you do? Part of your Stop and Setup is to think about who is going to tell him. If you do it one-on-one, it'll be easier for him to blow you off. If you do it in a group, it'll be easier for you to stand your ground, but it'll be overwhelming for him. The ideal situation is to have the guy he's closest to speak to him, with one or two other guys he respects along for backup. To state the obvious: this isn't like one of those intervention shows you see on TV. You choose a time and place where he feels comfortable and there's no chance of other people interrupting you. All of the guys agree that if he attacks or blows off the person who states the problem, the other guys will back him up. You all have to agree not to capitulate or say, "I don't know, dude, I didn't really want to be here."

The other big challenge here is that there's no way to prepare the guy for the conversation. It's not possible to say, "Hey, dude, two days from now I'm going to tell you that you're an alcoholic and need to get help."

The timing of this SEAL is critical too. Don't do it when anyone is drunk, high or hung-over the next morning (including you). For example, if he binges on Saturday night, your window to have the talk is between Sunday afternoon and Tuesday night. It's also likely that this SEAL will take two conversations: one when you initially tell him, and then a follow-up to check in with him once he's had time to think about what you said.

PART 1

YOU (Explain): I feel weird saying this, but I really think that you have a drinking problem.

FRIEND (Push-back): No way. Fuck off.

YOU (Explain): Seriously, I'm worried about you.

FRIEND (Push-back): What the fuck? You drink just as much as I do.

YOU (Acknowledge): I've been thinking about that. Recently, I've been cutting back because I didn't want to bring this up without checking myself.

FRIEND (Push-back): This is insane.

YOU (Lock In): I know this sounds weird, but I really care about you, and I'm worried. Like, if you were a girl, I'd be hugging you right now. I know I can't force you to talk to someone, but I really think you need help.

FRIEND (Push-back): Fine. Now can we just drop this?

YOU (Lock In): Sure.

PART 2 (A COUPLE OF DAYS LATER)

YOU (Explain): How's it going with the thing we talked about?

FRIEND (Push-back): What do you mean?
YOU: (Explain): You know what I'm talking about. Did you talk to anyone?

FRIEND (Push-back): I don't know.

YOU (Affirm): I know I can't force you, but I'd go with you if you wanted. I could just hang outside.

FRIEND (Push-back): I'm not going to some psychiatrist or drug counselor.

YOU (Lock In): I'm not saying that. What about Coach Smith or the counselor you liked last year? Just consider it.

Unfortunately, most high school guys will have a friend who needs help with drugs or alcohol. It's one of those moments when you need to think about the times you've said, "I love you man, I love my guys, I'd do anything for my friends," and realize that these are more than things you say. It's what you do when it's hard. When you'd rather do anything else but face this guy and tell him the truth. It's in these moments that he desperately needs your support, even if he has no idea how to ask for it.

OKAY, BUT NOT ALL OF MY FRIENDS ARE ALCOHOLICS OR DRUG ABUSERS.

Let's dial it back a little, because this is a somewhat extreme scenario (although common of course), but it's probable that, if you haven't already, you'll experience people running off the rails without you having to confront them for being an alcoholic or having a drug problem. They're just being a huge drunk/high pain in the ass at the moment.

THE DRUNK GIRL

If you're in the 10 percent, your chances of interacting with the Drunk Girl go way up. By the end of sophomore year, you can reliably count on her making an appearance every weekend. But even if you're not in the 10 percent, as soon as you start going to parties the Drunk Girl has a way of running into most guys (sometimes literally), regardless of social position. Although she usually appears harmless, she's a walking train wreck, and it can be easy to get run over.

Here are Drunk Girl indicators:

- Loud
- Belligerent
- Thinks she's funny
- Squinty eyes
- Cries a lot
- Hooks up with people and then cries about it
- Sloppy, falls over, falls down, laughs
- Overly flirty

I know it seems like the Drunk Girl behaves in unpredictable ways, but she really doesn't. She's either going to be very happy, very flirty, very sad, or very angry, all in the most public way possible. What feels out of control is how and when she bounces back and forth between any and/or all of these states.

Under no circumstances (which includes that she's ridiculously hot) should you hook up with this girl. I assume you know that, but it needs to be emphasized. Like when you see her, think of the worst STD picture you've ever seen, look up the STD you're thinking of on your phone, imagine she has the biggest, scariest boyfriend, anything it takes to remind you that it's a bad idea.

But the real question is to what extent are you obligated to manage the Drunk Girl? If she's a friend of yours, then you owe it to her and everyone around her to get her under control. That means, if she's throwing herself on anyone or getting in anyone's face, distract her by saying, "Hey, come here for a second," and then take her to the kitchen and get her some water (and Ibuprofen if it's handy). While you're watching her drink the water, say, "I'm a little worried about you. Can you just take a break?" You must do this in private. Don't say, "You're embarrassing yourself. You're getting sloppy ...," or belligerent, or anything else that will make her defensive. Give her clear directions about where you think she needs to go to rest and get sober. If she doesn't listen to you (and chances are good she won't), at least you've given her the chance to settle down and you've done right by her as a friend.

If the Drunk Girl is your girlfriend, this is very tricky, because she's likely to do something really stupid and expect you to back her up. For example, if she's in the belligerent phase, she could start a fight with some guy and then expect you to defend her. If this happens, put your girlfriend behind you and say to the guy, "Sorry, my girlfriend's drunk, hope you understand." If possible, don't do this in front of your girlfriend because you want to avoid arguing with her about how drunk she is. If the guy's a dick about it and says something about what a bitch she is, joke about it like, "Right now, totally agree, but I have to take her home now." When she gets mad at you for not defending her honor, don't back down. If she's going to start fights, that's on her.

If you don't know her well and she's making someone miserable, go up to one of her friends and ask them to get her a drink of water. The reason I'm focused on the water is because you want to stay away from saying anything like, "You need to get your friend under control." Plus, the earlier she starts rehydrating the better it'll be for everyon

THE DRUNK GUY

If the Drunk Guy is not your friend, stay away from him.

THE DRUNK GUY WHO'S YOUR FRIEND

Like the Drunk Girl, there's a pattern here that makes him entirely predictable:

- When he's sober, he's wound tight and is always proving his masculinity. This means he's likely to be a Bouncer, a Mastermind, or a Showboat.

- You all start drinking (and/or whatever else) in the afternoon and keep at it through the day and night.

- There are more guys than girls in the group you're hanging out with.

- Small conflicts have been simmering between the Drunk Guy and someone else.

If you have at least three out of these four conditions, I guarantee you the Drunk Guy is going to explode. What do you do? The first thing is to ask yourself if there's any way you are this guy. If you are, or even think it's a possibility, you have to realize that this is a setup for you. It's probable that the things that make you blow up when you're drunk are things that you're keeping inside and letting fester when you're sober. Being the Drunk Guy is a loss of control—which people excuse because you're drunk, but it's still a loss of control. You're still letting your anger control you. It's your choice if you want that to be the way you express yourself. I do know that if you do it often enough, people either deliberately provoke you or want to keep you at arm's length because they don't want to clean up after you.

If you're the friend of the Drunk Guy, you don't have that much control over what he does. If he's heading down the path, you can say, "If you get wasted and belligerent, I'm not cleaning up after you." If, a few hours later, he's becoming a problem, you can say, "Hey, come here for a second," take him into the bathroom, and give him some water. Ask him: "Can you just take a break? We can leave if you want." Again, privacy is key. Don't say, "You're embarrassing yourself. I told you this was going to happen." Again, if he doesn't listen to you (and chances are good that he won't), at least you've done right by him as a friend.

SEXPECTATIONS

CHAPTER TEN

WHAT ARE GIRLS REALLY THINKING?

How do you argue with a girl who's either delusional, unwilling to listen, or always thinks she's right? — Victor, 17

For better or worse, there's no getting around the fact that you live in a world with girls. Even if you go to an all-guys school, at some point you have to study with girls, work with them, argue with them, and compete against them. They can be your friends, your enemies, or your girlfriends.

Your high school experience (and your whole life) will go better if girls like you. I don't mean liking you because they all want to hook up with you, or liking you because you do everything they say or take their side against guys. I mean, if you project internal strength and treat girls with respect, I guarantee the non–drama queen, hot girls will find you attractive. Let me give you a very specific example that I'm sure you can picture easily.

There are always guys who love to point out to girls how boring women's basketball is. These guys are missing the point. If you want to have hot, cool girls like you and want to hang out with you, sit on those bleachers and support the team. Girls hate the debate about what a joke women's basketball is (or any other women's sport). This hatred isn't based on the merits of the argument. It's based on the indisputable fact that the guys who insist on "winning" this argument do it because they get off on putting women down. The only girls who don't hate this guy are insecure and not worth your time.

You want to be the guy who projects confidence (you can even be cocky) but doesn't put girls down. If you do that, girls will have your back and more. Believe me, I know the power of girls when they decide they hate a guy. You don't want to be that guy. There'll be a time in high school when it's very handy to have girls on your side.

Along with the guy editors, I've brought in girls to help me with all the chapters on girls. You'll see their commentary throughout. You'll also see separate boxes in the chapters where guys ask girls questions, girls give their answers, and I add to that answer where needed (meaning when I don't think the answer is entirely honest). Then I do the same where girls ask guys questions and guys answer.

I'm going to give you specific advice about what to say to girls—but keep in mind that these are guidelines. They're based on SEAL, but don't quote me word for word because you want to sound like it's really coming from you.

To begin, here's what I want you to remember about girls:

1. Girls can be very confusing to guys. Guys can be just as confusing to girls.

2. You'll probably get into a situation with a girl where you'll become incredibly frustrated, if not extremely angry. Remember, if you can't manage your mind, you can't manage your mouth. This is when you can get into trouble.

3. You have hormones. This can complicate your friendships with girls.

4. By the way, girls have hormones too.

5. Sometimes hormones get in the way of your friendships.

6. Whether you're gay or straight, you could still have every problem I listed above.

GIRLS AS FRIENDS

Yes, it's possible to be friends with girls. It's also possible (not 100 percent certain, but possible) that one of you will want more than friendship and then you'll enter into the Friend Zone. There's more about that later in the chapter. Here I'll explain why it's key to be able to have a close platonic friendship with a girl.

1. She can explain the girl perspective.

2. You don't have to worry about what you say. (If you do, you've either just become friends or you like her as more than a friend.)

3. It can be easier to admit things to a close girl friend than to even your closest guy friends. Why? Because guys can hide their feeling even with their closest friends. Rather than subjecting yourself to their ridicule, being "serious" with a girl (talking about a problem that's really bothering you) can be a safer choice.

4. She can tell you when you're being a jackass, but in a way that doesn't make you feel stupid.

5. If you're gay and you go to a school with a lot of ALMB guys, being friends with a powerful popular girl is your best protection from them because they don't want to get on her bad side.

   Girls have helped me tweak my personality a bit in terms of being more sensitive because I usually say things as I see them. I have no filter. —Matt, 17

THE ACT-LIKE-A-GIRL BOX

In chapter 2, I talked about the unwritten rules for guys. Of course there's an unwritten rule-book for girls that has just as much influence on their behavior. I'm not going to spend a lot of time on this (if you really want to get into it, read Queen Bees and Wannabes), but you need to know enough to give you a foundation. Once you know the basic rules for girls, understanding girls will be way easier.

Just like I asked you to think about the emotions that Batman is allowed to have, now I want you to look at Mattel's Monster High toys—one of the most aggressively marketed toys for seven- to ten-year-old girls. People have been freaking out for a really long time about Barbie and the bad messages that doll sends to girls, but this is worse in one very specific way. Barbie is clearly a woman. Monster High Girls are girls. When girls play with Barbie, they're playing with a doll that embodies what they'll look like when they grow up. That's a problem, but way worse is a doll like the Monster High Girl, because it's telling girls what they're supposed to act like and look like now.

There are a lot of unwritten rules here. No matter what, girls always keep that sexy doll expression. If they're upset, if they're happy, if they're depressed, they always keep that look on their face. Even if they're dead or a monster, they have to look anorexic, they have to have long straight hair (no matter what their race—the girl on the right is Mattel's version of a black or Latina girl), they have to keep up with the latest fashion (as do all their friends), and they have to have a boyfriend. In this case, there are written rules: here are three descriptions of Cleo taken from the Mattel website.

> *Cleo does her best to look fabulous and she wants everyone to know it.*
>
> *She is very competitive and like all competitive people this can cause its problems.*
>
> *Cleo tends to have much more disrupted relationships with other characters, perhaps because she has such a strong character.*

Read the second sentence again. Would anyone ever tell guys that "competition causes problems"? Hell no. Can you see why this would mess little girls up and then impact their behavior as they got older? There are other, better characters for girls in the media. In fact, they get a wider range of heroes to look up to than you do. (Like they get Katniss. She's still beautiful, but she gets to be a total badass.) However, it's just overwhelmingly the case that girls are still given messages to hide their competitiveness and their competence and focus on conforming to the perfectly skinny, just enough curves, always cute, never uptight girl that everyone loves. Why does this affect your interaction with girls? Because the ALWB plays head games with girls just like the ALMB can play head games with you. And whether you're gay or straight, understanding girls will only make your life easier.

PAY ATTENTION!

You know those girls who don't have a lot of girl friends because they hate girl drama? Those girls usually depend on their male friends. Recognize how important you are to them. They can handle things fine on their own, but your support goes a long way.

DOES SHE THINK YOU'RE FUNNY?

You may have noticed that girls and guys can have very different ideas of what's funny. Here's the deal. In general, a girl friend likes when you tell disgusting or dirty jokes because she knows it means you truly feel comfortable with her and your friendship is real. It also makes a girl feel like she's considered "one of the guys," which is also good (but only to a certain degree because then she's also being Friend-Zoned by the group of guys).

> *When I'm friends with a guy and have no sexual relationship with him, I act more casually around him because there's not really any pressure to be a perfect "lady." I don't feel the need to impress him, so I can be immature around him. —Emily, 16*

> *My best friend is a guy, and I think it works out way better. Girls have too much drama. He can tell me disgusting jokes, and I really don't mind. But if they do get annoying, I can tell him to stop and he will. —Hannah, 16*

Read the last line of Hannah's quote again. Remember what I said about real friendships in chapter 2? Real friends are the people who, when you tell them they're over the line, they stop. It doesn't matter if we're talking about guys or girls. It's always true.

However, you can't count on all of your girlfriends being as clear and direct as Hannah. The best way to know if a girl genuinely thinks you're funny is the speed and naturalness with which she responds. If you say something disgusting to her and she reacts by immediately saying something just as disgusting back, then you know you're good. If she rolls her eyes and laughs simultaneously, that's also good. If she weakly laughs, gets quiet, or says something like, "That's so sick," or, "That's so wrong," then you know you're over the line and it's time to stop.

It all depends on the individual girl and her personal boundaries. Here's a situation where it could go either way.

> *Two of my best friends who are girls freaked out on me because they thought I was somewhat of a man-whore. After I'd broken up with my girlfriend, I went on a bit of a spree, and word may have gotten around, and they weren't too proud of me, to say the least. I offered them spots 7 and 8, but they didn't think my joke was too funny.* —John, 16

John's friends didn't appreciate his offer to add them to his hook-up waiting list. However, some of the girl editors reading John's quote did think it was funny. None of these girls are wrong; each has her own opinion. Just keep in mind that, like with guys, group dynamics kick in when girls are with their friends. Just like the Mastermind decides what's funny in a group of guys, the Queen Bee decides in this case if the boy is funny. Picture a Bouncer or Fly making a joke around the Queen Bee. Would she think he was funny? No, she'd probably roll her eyes. But what if a Mastermind or Associate made the same joke? Exactly. She'd laugh. In a group, whether something is offensive, stupid, or funny tends to be decided by the most powerful person in the group.

However, there are some standard guidelines with girls and humor that usually apply. Most girls aren't going to like you constantly making perverted jokes. Sometimes is fine. All the time is annoying. A girl, like anyone else, really doesn't like when you consistently point out her flaws or weaknesses—especially in front of other people—and then tell her she's being uptight or laugh when she tells you to stop. This doesn't mean you can't joke around or even pick on her, but it can't be all the time, and it can't be in public. If she tells you to stop, just shut up.

Girls ask: Why can't guys ever be serious?

Guys say: Girls take things too seriously.

I say: "Serious" means different things to girls depending on whether the situation is private or public. If it's public, and the girl says, "Can't you be serious??????" she wants the guy to stop doing whatever stupid, loud, obnoxious, perverted thing he's doing. If it's private, the girl wants the guy to actually respond to her question in a way that accurately reflects what he thinks and feels about what she's asking.

What complicates this situation is when a girl is offended but won't straight up tell you and fake-smiles or fake-laughs.[14] I know it's understandable to be frustrated at someone who doesn't like what you're doing but won't tell you. But be honest—guys do it too. As Mary points out, for girls it feels like a no-win situation:

> Girls feel that guys don't really care if girls are upset. In order for a guy to understand what he's doing or saying isn't funny, then you have to get really serious, and then it gets awkward all around, so it's easier to just brush it off. —Mary, 15

Here's an actual situation that will help you picture the

---

[14] When someone smiles genuinely, their cheeks move upward and the skin around their eyes wrinkles. When someone fake--- smiles, the eyes don't wrinkle like that, and usually only one part of the mouth moves (like when people are smirking). Also, genuine smiles last longer (between half a second and four seconds) than fake ones.

problem more easily.

> *This weekend I went to a party and read your email to a couple of friends. I asked the girls what were some of the top things that guys said that would get them mad, and they said when guys would make them feel dumb or stupid. One of the guys constantly kept putting down some of the girls there, but that was because we are all very deep friends and they knew it's a joke. So yes, they do feel bad, but they take it as a joke. — Brian, 16*

Check out what's going on here. When directly asked, the girls told Brian what they really felt about the put-downs: they don't like them. They pretend to take them as a joke because it's the price they think they have to pay to be with their friends.

Why wouldn't Brian's girlfriends admit they're mad? Haven't you been in a situation where a friend does something over the line but you don't say anything? Or you laugh along because he says he's joking, you don't want to make a big deal out of it, or you think you're going to sound annoying? That's exactly the same thing that's happening with girls.

WHAT DO I DO WHEN GIRLS FREAK OUT AT ME?

Girls get angry in fairly predictable ways. Some of these ways can be very confusing, like this . . .

> *For no reason, this girl stops talking to me, so I ask if she's mad at me, and she says, "No." So I think she's not mad at me. Then her friends tell me she hates me. And I still don't know what I did. —Seth, 14*

. . . or frightening, like this:

When girls are mad, it's all about the numbers. What numbers? The number of other girls they bring with them to destroy you. —Alan, 14

Girls get into a group and then get mad at one guy, and then they corner him and attack him. If a group of guys did that to a girl, everyone would hate them. —Jacob, 13

From a guy's perspective, when a girl gets angry at him, it usually feels like one moment everything is fine and then the next, completely out of the blue, the girl freaks out at him. This is because most of the time he's probably oblivious to a sequence of actions he did that pissed her off and he's not paying attention to what she thinks are her obvious signs of frustration and anger.

Sometimes you know what you did that pissed her off and all you can say to yourself is, What was I thinking? And then other times it's like, What? I don't get it. Why? —Tyler, 15

Either way, when you're in a fight with a girl, you're going for the same goal: getting your point across and vice versa without anyone being made to feel stupid or having the whole thing blow up in your face.

WHAT IF A GIRL IS ANGRY WITH ME AND EXPECTS ME TO READ HER MIND?

I get how annoying it is when a girl is mad at you, you have no idea what you did, and she won't tell you. The mere act of asking her is held up as evidence of your guilt. The classic girl response here is, "You should know. If you don't, then I'm not going to tell you." There are two possible explanations for this strange behavior. Either she's manipulating you and she wants you to run after her, trying to guess what you did, or she has been conditioned to think that this is how she should communicate her anger to guys . . . and she wants you to run after her, trying to guess what you did.

Without making excuses for girls, sometimes they do this without realizing what they're doing. It's part of their Girl World wiring. If you ask a girl if she's mad at you and she denies it, look at her body language. If she's saying, "No, I'm fine, why would I be mad at you?" while raising her eyebrows, shaking her head, and speaking in a flat or sarcastic tone, she's angry with you. Then your response is, "If you're mad at me, you need to tell me directly. I can't read your mind."

If she responds with some version of "If you really valued our friendship, then you should know what you did to make me mad," that may indicate that you've done something repeatedly that's annoyed her, like fake-apologizing. If that's the case, admit it and genuinely make the attempt to stop what she's talking about. If she's saying this as a way to communicate, "If you really cared, you'd be able to read my mind," you say, "I do value our friendship, which is why I want you to tell me what the problem is. You have to tell me what the problem is for me to have a chance of fixing it."

ATTACKED BY THE PACK

I was having lunch, and this group of girls came screaming at me because of something I apparently said about their friend. The girls were saying things like "You're such an ass, why would you say those things about [name of girl]? What's the matter with you, you freak?" In the end, I figured out they were mad at me because of something my friend said but they thought it was me. —Carson, 16

Girls love to get together and go after a boy they're angry with in public. Yes, I'm saying that girls do this as a calculated strategy to embarrass guys. If you were in Carson's position, it'd be totally understandable to think these girls are crazy, annoying, too involved in other people's business (to which a girl would say, "My friends are my business"), and behaving like drama queens. Are girls only ganging up on guys like this to be evil?

They don't think so. Girls believe they have a higher purpose: they're righting a wrong. But there's another reason girls attack as a group, one they don't like to admit. If the girls know Carson is good at arguing (aka a Mastermind or Associate), they could be too intimidated to approach him alone (again, they won't want to admit this), so they come together to reinforce each other. Since, from Carson's perspective, this seems like a group of girls ganging up on him, he believes he's justified in being as rude as possible back at them.

What should Carson do? If he wants the drama to escalate even higher, he can tell the girls they're crazy and should mind their own business, or he should obviously ignore them while saying something nasty about them to his friends so they can hear him. If he wants the drama to deescalate, he can SEAL it by recognizing the public environment they're all in and saying something like, "If [name of girl] wants to talk to me, then she should, but you coming up to me like this isn't the way to solve the problem." Then he can go back to talking to whoever he was speaking with before they approached him, or calmly get up and take his tray in. He should make it short and fast. Then later, Carson should communicate with the girl directly to find out what the problem is.

What if Carson was guilty? What if he did say rude things about the girl? Or what if he didn't exactly say what the girls are accusing him of, but he still did or said something wrong? He still doesn't want to have a long, drawn-out conversation with these girls, but he does need to address their concerns by saying, "You're right, and I'm going to take care of it. But it's still between me and her. I'll tell her I'm sorry." What he wants is to stop the girls from having ammunition against him. If you've found yourself in a similar situation, reread the apologies section to figure out how to proceed. And keep Tyler's advice in mind:

Never confront a girl in front of her friends. It becomes the whole group's problem, and then it's the whole school's problem, and then you're done.

WHEN GIRLS WANT TO KILL YOU

Guys can be amazingly good at pissing girls off. When I asked girls to list the most common phrases guys use that make girls want to punch them, this is what they told me:

- "Relax."

- "Don't worry about it."

- "Calm down."

- "Settle down."

- "You wouldn't understand. You wouldn't get it."

- "Okay, okay, fine, whatever you say."

- "Why are you in such a bad mood?"

- "I'm sorry" (but he has no idea what he's saying he's sorry about, and it's really obvious he's just saying it because he wants her to stop fighting with him).

- "You're being totally irrational."

- "Talk to me when you aren't having your period."

- "Why do you have to be such a bitch?" (It's like the N-word rule: girls shouldn't say "bitch" either, but it's way worse when it's coming from a guy.)

- "Make me a sandwich" (or any comment regarding women's traditional domestic role).

If the goal is to get a girl to calm down, none of these responses will work. They just make her angrier. Let's be honest. There are five possible reasons why a guy would use these phrases:

1. When he doesn't care about the girl or what she thinks about him

2. When he's in an argument and he wants a quick, easy way to put a girl down, shut her up, or distract her

3. Because he has no respect for women and thinks it's funny to remind them of that

4. Because he knows he's lost an argument

5. Because he realizes he's wrong and so he says these things as a way to "save" himself

   If a guy says, "Make me a sandwich," in an argument, you may as well say good-bye to his manhood. —Harris, 18

If a guy needs to resort to saying something so blatantly sexist, then he doesn't have the real power to confront the girl on the merits of what they're arguing about in the first place. When guys say things like this in front of an audience (like their friends), it's more about humiliating and infuriating the girl. Here are some examples.

   We do know that saying these things make girls mad. Either the guy has no intention of resolving the

conflict and only wants people to think that he's making an effort, or he just hasn't dealt with girls enough, making him completely clueless about how girls work. There's also a possibility that if the conversation happens in public, the guy will want to seem either in control or careless about the whole thing, leading to comments such as "Make me a sandwich," or, "Talk to me when you aren't on your period." By extension, this could also be a way to make the girl go away because of the humiliation, but this is a simple quick-fix, as down the road the problem will be much, much bigger, because so will her anger. —Matt, 17

I have a guy friend who makes sexist comments and always puts girls down, and I know he's kidding, but he says it all the time, so I wonder if maybe he isn't kidding. So I asked him if he was, and he said, "No, well, sort of." —Molly, 16

There's no such thing as "sort of kidding." Either you're kidding or you're not. Molly is struggling because this guy "sort of" doesn't have a baseline of respect for girls, and Molly happens to be one. That's a tough thing to admit to yourself, never mind bring up with a friend, who'll probably respond with even more put-downs.

This is another situation where girls keep their anger inside and then blow up about something small. One comment, a comment the guy has made a hundred times before, is just one comment too many and the girl explodes. To the guy, his behavior isn't any different from anything he's done before. Here's the moment when a guy needs to stop himself from automatically blowing off the girl for "overreacting." He needs to realize that she is actually getting her courage up to say how she feels and for that reason alone needs to be respected. If he can control himself and really hear her, it can go from either or both of them feeling like this is a no-win situation to one where he gets serious credit for trying.

Remember, if girls like you, your life will be better in many ways.

Girls ask: Why is it that when you win against a girl you make it a really big deal, but when you lose you blow it off and act like it was nothing?

Guys say: We're always supposed to win, but if we lose we have to keep it quiet because losing (especially to a girl) is unacceptable.

I say: Guys who are insecure about their masculinity are the most determined to appear the most masculine. It's ironic, because the guys who are the most outspoken about girls not being real competition are the same guys who gloat the most about their victories.

While we are on the subject of girls and games ... it's so beyond obvious that any guy gamer who feels the need to insult a girl gamer by saying she's a slut, fat, needs to be raped, or needs to get back to the kitchen is ridiculously insecure. It's a clear indication that competing against girls is so frightening that he wants to make the virtual environment so hostile to her that she won't want to play. If you have a friend (in RL or online) who's doing this crap, you need to call him on it. This isn't a question of loyalty. It's a question of whether he has the ability to compete on a level playing field.

CHAPTER ELEVEN

WHEN GIRLS DRIVE YOU CRAZY...IN A BAD WAY

I'll admit that girls can do things that are incredibly annoying to guys. Like, no matter what you say, you're wrong. They are holding you to a higher standard than they are holding themselves to. They're manipulating you and denying it. Making you crazy and denying it. You'll probably have additional ways they drive you crazy, but these seem to be the most common.

GIRLS CONSTANTLY PUTTING THEMSELVES DOWN

Do you think it's irritating when girls constantly say things like, "I'm so stupid," or, "I'm so fat," or, "I'm so ugly"? You know what? It is irritating. But there's an understandable reason why girls complain about their appearance. On average, girls see over six thousand advertisements a day that are created to make them feel insecure and anxious about their bodies.[15]

If girls don't have people in their lives who consistently teach them that their self-worth doesn't depend on fitting this physical ideal (and no one does, since almost all the women in the ads are Photoshopped[16]), girls will absorb these messages. These messages then become part of their internal language—and that's what you're hearing when girls talk about how ugly and fat they are.

But no matter what the reason, you're probably

---

[15] See "The Lost Art of Un-Photoshopping," posted by Bianca, July 12, 2012, available at: coversations.nokia.com

[16] Which means the pictures of women you see are "enhanced" as well, and giving you an unrealistic idea of what beautiful women are supposed to look like.

wondering, What am I supposed to say to her? I've already told her a hundred times she's not fat. Nothing I say makes a difference. Well, for one thing, don't say, "Okay, you're right. Your arms look like sausages. You should really do something about that." You may also be tempted to be brutally honest by saying something like, "If you feel this way after I've told you countless times that you're not fat, then this entire conversation is a waste of time." That also won't work. Listen to this girl sum it up for you.

A girl can understand objectively that she's pretty, guys can tell her all the time that she's attractive, but at the end of the day, none of that is enough. At the end of the day, the voices in the back of her head that say, "Your thighs touch," "Your stomach is flabby," "Your boobs aren't big enough," etc., are so much louder than all the tangible voices. They overpower the rational and convince her that she needs to try harder and be prettier.

It extends beyond looks too. A girl can know in her logical brain that she's smart, she can do well in school and at work, but that's insufficient too. The same voices that tell her she isn't pretty tell her, "You're not smart enough," "You're good at this, but why can't you be good at this other thing too," "What you just said was really stupid," etc. It's just never enough.

> Because those negative voices crush everything
> else, people need to be careful about how they tease
> and criticize girls. It's easy to say, "Oh well, you'll
> hate yourself anyways, so it doesn't matter what I
> say," but that's painfully wrong. The voices in her
> head are constant, but the outside messages can
> change. So if you criticize a girl a lot, even if it's in
> jest, her voices are that much more powerful, and
> they can make her feel that much shittier about
> herself. But if you're nice to her, she's probably still
> not going to like herself, but you're giving her
> enough armor against the voices that she can live
> with herself. I'm not advocating lying to spare a girl's

feelings, but sometimes a joking "you're fat" has a lot more gravity than one would think. —Maureen, 18

Neither Maureen nor I believe you can save a girl from these feelings of inadequacy, but as Maureen says, you can be part of her armor. Here's a sample conversation you can have with a girl friend who has just complained that she's fat for the five-hundredth time. Remember—put this in your own words!

YOU (Explain): You keep putting yourself down, and it's really frustrating because I feel like nothing I say makes a difference.

GIRL FRIEND (Push-Back): I know, I'm sorry. I'll stop.

YOU (Lock In): Don't apologize. I just want you to realize that you're better than this. You're measuring yourself by a perfect ideal that doesn't exist anyway.[17]

Here's what the girls would think if you said something like this.

A response like that would be incredible. It really shows he cares and understands how difficult body image is for a girl. If a guy said that to me, I would appreciate and respect him so much more. —Emily M., 16

When I'm in a bad mood and I call myself fat, he

---

[17] Make sure you have this conversation away from your male friends so they don't make fun of you during and after you say this to the girl.

doesn't just say I'm not fat, he tells me why I shouldn't be calling myself fat. It really makes me feel a lot better. —Emily C., 16

You're not kissing up to girls if you say things like this. You're not automatically going to be labeled as the nice guy who never gets any. You can still play hard to get and say bad jokes. Promise.

A GIRL WANTS TO HANG OUT WITH ME AND MY FRIENDS AND THEN GETS MAD AT ME FOR NOT GIVING HER ENOUGH ATTENTION OR NOT BACKING HER UP WHEN MY GUYS SAY OBNOXIOUS THINGS TO HER.

Girls always feel uninvited or unwelcome with the bros. I don't know how to solve this problem, but it's a big one. —Josh, 16

I'm not referring to the situation where one or more girl friends come over in a larger group of friends to hang out. Instead, I'm referring to two likely scenarios:

1. She's getting attention, but not the attention she wants—or that anyone would want—because the guys are making fun of her.

2. She's not getting any attention and then starts to complain about it.

For the first problem, you need to stop seeing this as girls versus guys. You're not five years old. You tell your friends to shut the fuck up. A similar situation can occur when a group of girls and guys are hanging out and one of the girls wants to play whatever game you're playing. If one of your friends makes comments about how bad the girl is, say something short and to the point. If you don't, it brings the whole atmosphere down. "Don't be an ass, just let her play," should be enough. You may get some shit from your friends, but you should be strong enough to deal with that, right?

On to the second problem. In this situation, your girl friend wants to hang out with you because she likes you or because the two of you are already together. If she feels left out, she's going to express her anger by dropping small, medium, and possibly large hints about how she's feeling that will come across to you as incredibly annoying. From your perspective, her complaints probably comes across as completely unrealistic because what did she think was going to happen? You have to head this off at the pass by clearly communicating your expectations and listening to any of hers. I'd explain to her before you meet up, "There's going to be six of us over here. If you're coming over just to see me, now maybe isn't the best time. But if you want to come over and do what we're doing, then that's good." If she does hang out with you all, she's being cool, and the guys are still obnoxious to her, don't ignore it or laugh along. If she's conducting herself according to your mutual agreement, then the least you can do is have her back. If she's not acting according to your agreement, you lie and say, "Hey, I'm going to get a Coke. Megan, can you come with me?" Hopefully, if you have any, your smart friends will know what you're doing and not say anything stupid as you two walk out of the room. When you're in the kitchen, say to her, "Hey, I can see you're unhappy, but we agreed about how this was going to go. I want to hang out with my friends." This is also your chance to offer to see her the next day and then follow through with it.

A girl asks: Why are you such a jerk in front of your friends and totally nice to me when we're alone?

The guy says: You want too much when my friends and I are together, and it gets on my nerves.

I say: Guys can't look like they're controlled by a girl in front of their friends or they risk having their friends talk behind their back or to their face about how weak they are. They'd rather bet on the girl tolerating their being a jerk and then apologize to her later than actually change what they do.

GIRLS GET MAD AT ME FOR CALLING THEM "SLUT," "BITCH," OR "WHORE," BUT THEY CALL EACH OTHER THE SAME THING ALL THE TIME.

The girls at my school are incredible. They're such hypocrites. They call each other "sluts," "whores," and "bitches" all the time, but the minute a guy does it they freak out. I'm not going to just take that. Someone needs to tell them how full of it they are. Someone needs to be honest. —Sam, 17

The short answer is, Sam's right. It's hypocritical for girls to call each other these words and then get angry with guys when they do it. But just because that's true doesn't make it right for guys to do it. It just gives you an easy excuse. Girls also believe that when guys use these words, it's way more disrespectful and degrading than it is coming from a girl.

Since we're talking about sluts and whores, let's take a moment to address the "It's just what we say, it doesn't matter" defense that both guys and girls use. I'm not asking people to never say, "bitch," "slut," or "whore." But words have power, and using them a lot doesn't change that.

The word "slut" (or any word like it) has long been used to refer to a woman who's only valued for sex and has no right to an opinion. The word "bitch" has been used against women for being too opinionated. Both words are about denying women the right to speak. Both words are particularly powerful against girls because of two characteristics: (1) they quickly shut a girl down, and (2) they make her feel either terrible about herself or incredibly angry. Basically, they're both trigger words, and they influence girls' behavior in many ways.

For example, you know how some girls can take forever to get ready, constantly changing clothes but never satisfied with how they look? It's easy to assume that these moments prove that girls are obsessed with their looks because they're superficial. That's not what's going on. Instead, girls are trying to figure out a complex equation: how to look sexy without coming off as slutty— i.e., being and feeling attractive while avoiding being trashed by other girls for being too slutty. So they're trying to achieve the impossible by pleasing both girls and straight guys, two groups with competing agendas.

> *We dress to catch one person's attention, but as a result make everyone else notice and flip a shit. I don't think the balance is just hard to strike; I think it's impossible. —Maureen, 18*

Guys ask: Why do girls wear tight clothing if they don't want the attention?

Girls say: We have the right to wear what we want, when we want.

I say: Many girls do want guys' attention, but there's a big difference between appreciating an attractive girl and treating her like she's stupid and/or a slab of meat. When girls wear revealing clothes, don't make the assumption that they want to have sex. Wanting to feel sexy is not the same as wanting to have sex with you

---

GIRLS TAKE ADVANTAGE OF THE DOUBLE STANDARD BY VERBALLY OR PHYSICALLY ATTACKING GUYS AND WE CAN'T DO ANYTHING ABOUT IT.

When girls scream at me and push me, I just bottle up my anger. My dad always says I can't hit girls, but it's so wrong that they just get to do whatever they want to me and I just have to take it. A week ago, when I was walking back after a football game, this girl got right up into my face. I just kept walking, but she wouldn't stop yelling at me. I didn't say this, but what I really wanted to do was say, "Just leave me alone, bitch." But I can't do that because then she'll really freak out, I'll get into trouble, and nothing will happen to her. I just smile and try to get away from her as fast as possible, but it makes me so mad. — Aaron, 16

No guy should have to put up with a girl taking advantage of him like this. Here's what I want you to do when you're in a situation like Aaron's. Stop walking, face her, and as calmly as you can say, "Stop. What you're doing isn't cute and doesn't make me want to listen to anything you have to say. It actually makes me never want to talk to you again. When you can handle yourself better, try again." Then calmly leave.

GIRLS ARE COMPLETELY EVIL.

I had a class with a girl. We'd been sort of messing with each other, but nothing flirty. Before class one day she took a soda I had in my backpack and drank it. So I took some papers out of her binder—stupid stuff. But the next day, before class, she went into my backpack again and got my soda. But this time she poured it on my head. I was so surprised that I jumped up, and when I did that I accidentally pushed her to the ground. All of the sudden, she's attacking me with two other guys (one was her brother, who was also in the class). They're holding me down and punching me. I had to go to the hospital to get stitches in my head. They were suspended for five days, and the school pressed the harshest charges they could on my behalf. I didn't really want them to do that, but I guess there wasn't any choice.

The worst was that she posted on Facebook that I had punched her in the face for no reason. For two days it seemed like everyone in my town believed it. Until my friends and the other kids in the class were able to convince people what really happened, it was really bad. If people thought this about me, in every school in the surrounding area, where was I supposed to go? Those days right after the fight were pretty bad. —Ian, 17

What I want you to take away from Ian's story is that there are people, both males and females, who are determined to set you up and bring you down. That girl deliberately created a situation where she could start a fight, look innocent, and then get guys to back her up. As I said in the *Frontal Assault* chapter, when you're under attack, you have the right to defend yourself. You match your response to the level of threat.

But more than that, when the school administrators disciplined the girl who attacked Ian and pressed charges, they showed that they weren't being manipulated by her "I'm a helpless girl" strategy. That's when she tried to use Facebook to get her peers on her side. It would have worked too, if not for Ian's friends and the other students in his class coming to his defense.

GIRLS TRY TO TRAP GUYS WHEN THEY ARGUE.

I usually see guys argue with girls in three different ways. One, she dominates the conversation by overwhelming the guy with the sheer amount of words coming out of her mouth and her ability to remember small details about who said what. Two, he dominates the conversation in the same way the girl can. Three (I think the smallest percentage), both people are truly trying to figure out how to work through the problem based on the actual situation and the individuals involved.

If you're up against a dominator, I know it seems easiest to shut down, withdraw, and just stop talking to her. Believe me, I get it. But you have the right to be heard in the argument, and just because she can remember every detail of her side of the story doesn't take away from the fact that your experience and perspective matter. If she's running over you with words, or you feel like she's trying to trap you into a mistake, say this:

"Look, you have the right to see things your way, but you can't tell me I'm wrong for having a different opinion. I'm not going to counter every example you're bringing up with another one of my own. If you want to solve the problem, you have to be willing to listen to me and respect my opinion like I'm trying to do with you. If you can't, there's no point in us talking right now."

No doubt, a dominator is tough to deal with, so you need to focus on the goal, which isn't getting her to agree with you. Even if she did, she might not be able to admit it. Instead, the goal is communicating directly, not letting your anger get the best of you by leading you to either try to dominate back or shut down, and feeling that you handled a difficult situation in a way that you can be proud of.

If you're the one who has the tendency to dominate, the same rules apply. If you've ever had the experience of arguing with a girl and you're confident in your debating abilities, you may have come across as dismissive. Listening is about being able and willing to be changed by what you hear. Anything else is just doing what adults mostly do: dominating each other until one of them gives up or makes a mistake in their logic.

For example, if the girl makes a good point in an argument, most guys will only acknowledge this by shrugging and saying, "Whatever." Saying "Whatever" doesn't communicate that you believe the other person made a valid point. I was arguing this exact situation with Erik, a sophomore whose opinion I respect and who is clearly intelligent. His argument was, "There's no point in debating girls. To be honest, I'm right." I asked Erik if he'd ever had the experience of arguing with someone who just wouldn't admit to ever being wrong. He thought for a few moments, and then his eyes widened and nodded his head.

I have an older brother who constantly argues with me. I could say 2 + 2 = 4, and he'd say, "No, it's five." It really doesn't matter what I say—that's what he's going to do. It's incredibly frustrating. Oh . . . okay, now I get it. When the girls are arguing with me, it's like that.

For all of us it can be hard to see how we're coming across to another person.

WHAT DO I DO IF I'M ARGUING WITH HER AND SHE SAYS, "STOP ATTACKING ME!"

You stop yourself from immediately telling her that you aren't yelling or attacking her or any other statement indicating that you think she's irrational. If you're doing this because she's entitled to her opinion, that's great. The other reason you say this is, if you don't, you'll make it worse for yourself. Take the strategy that decreases the drama. Say, "I'm trying to tell you what I think about what you're telling me." If she continues accusing you of going after her, tell her that you want to talk to her later when both of you are calmer and then walk away. (Please note that I didn't say you can tell her to "calm down" or "relax.")

APOLOGIES AND GIRLS

How you give and accept apologies shouldn't change depending on the sex of the people involved. Remember, true apologies have four characteristics:

1. You recognize that every person has the right to their feelings and perspective and no one has the right to say to anyone else, "You're completely irrational."

2. You have a genuine tone of voice because you actually mean what you say. You're not a hypocrite.

3. You know what you did that hurt the other person and are willing to admit it.

4. You're willing to make amends, to show your apology in action not just in words.

Both guys and girls can apologize and not mean it. Just remember that both of you have an equal right to disagree with each other, to see things differently, and to be mad about it. What neither of you has the right to do is make the other person feel stupid and overdramatic in the process.

One more thing about apologies and girls. If you don't know what you're apologizing for, don't apologize just so she'll stop talking or crying. I have listened to countless guys tell me that they have apologized for this reason. It'll come back to haunt you because you'll inevitably do the same thing again but then you'll look stupid.
Here are examples of bad apologies to girls.

> *"I'm sorry those comments were said." "You know I didn't mean any of that." "Things got of hand."*
>
> *"If you really need me to say I'm sorry, than I'm sorry."*
>
> *Here are examples of good apologies to girls:*
>
> *"I'm deeply sorry I said those things."*

"I was really out of line, and I didn't think about how what I did would embarrass you."

"If you want me to tell people that I said those things about you, I will."

When a girl needs to apologize to you, don't blow her off with, "It's okay." Remember, it doesn't make you less of a man to say, "Thanks." If the girl apologizes and then immediately asks you if you forgive her, don't say you do if you don't. If she gets angry with you because you won't go along with forgiving her, she's manipulating you. Forgiveness can take time.

CRYING

Crying is an expression of any kind of intense feelings. I often cry when I'm laughing my ass off. In general, girls cry because Girl World gives them permission to do it. Since crying is something girls are accustomed to, it can mean less to them than it does to you. For example, if you cried, chances are really good that something truly terrible has happened to you. For girls, that's not necessarily true. Or, girls can feel something deeply, cry, and then let it go. But no matter what, girls can think and talk while they cry. Girls aren't having mental breakdowns and they aren't forever emotionally devastated just because they're crying.
Of course, it's true that some girls cry to manipulate people into feeling sorry for them so they can get their way. It's also true that you can feel forced to comfort someone like this. You can say, "I'm sorry that happened to you," and then leave it at that.

But don't make the assumption that all girls cry easily or cry to manipulate you. A lot of girls are smart enough to realize that while they have the right to cry more easily than you, or they can trick you into feeling sorry for them, it comes at a high cost— looking weak.

When I do cry about guys, it's not because that boy is particularly great, it's just because every time something goes wrong it makes me feel more and more insecure. When it comes to crying to get what you want, a lot of girls did that when they were younger, but now that we're more mature, I think it is severely frowned upon. At this age, it's definitely seen as manipulative. —Kate, 16

For me, crying is something that I normally do when I'm alone. I hate crying in front of other people, especially guys. There are certain girls who cry too much, so I try to monitor how much I cry. But it can definitely help when you are feeling stressed or alone. —Dana, 16

WHY DO GIRLS ACT LESS INTELLIGENT THAN THEY ACTUALLY ARE?

When I was twelve, I remember wondering why girls had to act so fake around guys. They would stand around in clusters and scream and giggle and shoot looks over at some guy. Maybe one of their friends would come over and give you a message. If they act like that now, I would think they were trying to hook up. It's obvious. No one acts like that much of a moron unless they want to hook up. —Patrick, 16

Have you ever heard a girl sneeze in a way that sounds like she's a small cat? Seen a girl you know is really smart get around a specific guy and laugh or giggle at everything he's saying, even if it's not funny? When a girl acts like this, I call her behavior "Fruit Cup Girl," after a sixth-grade girl I taught many years ago who pretended during lunch that she couldn't open the top of a fruit cup so she could ask the guy she liked to do it for her.[18]

The reason Fruit Cup Girl can be attractive to a guy is that she provides him with an opportunity to fulfill the hero role, even if it's as small as opening a fruit cup. But FCG is also an excellent example of why things between guys and girls are so confusing. I wouldn't blame you in the least for being frustrated at girls who say they want you to respect them and then act like Fruit Cup Girl.

> *I think guys are partly responsible, because somehow girls understand or believe that guys tend to like dumb girls, and girls want guys to like them, so it makes us want to slip back into the Fruit Cup persona.* —Emily G. 15

It's not like that sixth-grade girl had someone sit her down and explain that she should act incompetently to get the boy's attention. She just knew because of those unwritten rules of Girl World. In the short term, it can feel like there are real benefits to being Fruit Cup Girl. Girls have a "script" that makes it easy to get a boy's attention. But there are also some serious negatives; guys won't take FCG seriously, and the other girls will judge her for being stupid or slutty. The reason girls do this is because the FCG can make them really uncomfortable. On the one hand, they're jealous of the attention FCG is getting. On the other hand, they know guys don't respect her (which of course doesn't stop some of them from hooking up with her), and they can hate her for making all girls look stupid and shallow.

As girls get older, they usually believe it's too immature to act like Fruit Cup Girl, so they need an excuse. That's where drinking and drugs come in. As long as a girl has a

---

[18] Yet another one of those heroic moments I was talking about. Got to take it where you can get it, right?

drink in her hand, she has an excuse to be FCG. The metamorphosis from Fruit Cup Girl to Solo Cup Girl sets the stage for girls to use alcohol and drugs as justification for being sexy stupid.

Before you criticize girls for doing this, remember that guys do it too. Haven't you seen an otherwise reasonable guy showing off, bragging, taking off his shirt for no reason (even using it for his FB profile pic), or getting really loud around girls? It's the same thing as Fruit Cup Girl. You just call him "That Guy."

THE FRIEND ZONE

According to the Urban Dictionary, the "Friend Zone" is: *A state of being where a male inadvertently becomes a "platonic friend" of an attractive female who he was trying to initiate a romantic relationship [with]. Females have been rumored to arrive in the Friend Zone, but reports are unsubstantiated.*

One of the first groups I met with for this book was at Louisville Collegiate School in Louisville, Kentucky. Over the year I met with several groups at the school: seventh- and eighth-graders, tenth-graders, and eleventh- and twelfth-graders. While the younger guys were perfectly fine discussing other topics, the older guys only wanted to talk about the girl problems. As I listened to them, it was clear to me that these guys were at least partially delusional as they assured me that girls were the ones who made no sense. So I asked them, "What are you delusional about?"

Immediately one of them answered (and I can't remember exactly who because everyone was talking at once): "Getting out of the Friend Zone. I go to bed every night thinking tomorrow will be the day I get out of the Zone." All the guys laughed in recognition.

Then Jordan raised his hand, and all the other guys fell silent. All of a sudden, it felt we were in a confessional.

I'm so deep inside the Friend Zone, it's not even

funny. Let me explain this girl.... She is very ...
attractive. (All the other guys nodded, and a few
shook their heads in sympathy and muttered
dejectedly, "So hot.") We've been friends forever.
We live near each other, so I go over to her house all
the time, and do you know what she does?... This is
so painful.... I'll be talking to her in her room, and
she'll change her shirt in front of me. (At this point
one of the other guys put his hand on Jordan's
shoulder and patted him on the back for support.)
You can't get more in the Friend Zone than that.

Fast-forward a few months later, and I was back in
Louisville, meeting with the same guys, and the
conversation still revolved entirely around girls. But this
time the focus was on prom. Jordan raised his hand.
Should he go for it and ask his Friend Zone girl to the
prom?

Immediately, the group erupted in a heated debate.
Ultimately, we decided that once in a while a guy should
throw caution to the wind and put his heart on the line.
Once that was settled, we moved on to an equally
important issue: Jordan's entrance and exit strategy. We
decided that he would text her to ask if he could come
over after school for a few minutes (the entrance), but
would also tell her that he could only stay for a few minutes
because he had to go over to another guy's house right
after (the exit).

Here's what happened, as emailed to me immediately
after. I'm including my advice and commentary.

JORDAN: Tonight I was at Debby's house (Friend
Zone girl). As I was leaving, I said, "Do you ever think
about us maybe being more than friends?" I was
going to ask her to prom depending on the answer.
The response I got was: "You're not serious. Shut
up," to which I replied, "I'm dead serious." She said,
"Shut up, no you're not," and walked inside. I'm a

wee bit lost.

ME: Don't be confused. Either she's mulling it over because she hasn't thought about it and she's a little freaked, or she's freaked because she doesn't want a relationship but really wants to keep the friendship and doesn't know how to say it. Either way, you were as clear as you need to be. You manned up and took the risk.

JORDAN: Thanks for the advice. Do I ask someone else to prom now?

ME: Yes.

After the prom, I checked in with Jordan. Here's what ended up happening: "It was awkward for a while with her, but we're cool now. Plus, it worked out in my favor, 'cause I'm now with the girl I asked to prom instead, and I really like her, so it's all good!"

HOW DID I END UP IN THE FRIEND ZONE ANYWAY?

It's not always going to work out like what happened with Jordan: you take the risk, you fail, but you emerge victorious with another girl. Your experience could be worse or it could be better. But sometimes you have to try. The big question for any guy in the Friend Zone is whether he should take the chance to admit his feelings. If you admit your non-friend feelings and she doesn't feel the same way, then your relationship, which you truly value, could become so awkward that your friendship is ruined. But if you can break out of the Friend Zone, you'll be with someone who you truly care about and are physically attracted to.

Is it worth it? First, let me explain how you got into the Friend Zone in the first place. If you're in the Friend Zone, there's about a 99 percent chance that the girl knows how you really feel. The problem is that she doesn't want to admit it to anyone, including herself. Even if it's incredibly obvious that you're crazy about her, she'll deny it. I know this sounds strange, but you have to trust me on this. Girls often are in deep denial that guys want more than a friendship from them. Why? The answer actually explains a lot about girls.

Most girls have a hard time believing that they can say what they really feel to guys they're sexually attracted to because they're afraid they'll come across as needy, uptight, or too demanding. Girls get the message from a lot of places (the media, their parents, their friends, their peers, other guys) that they can't make any demands on a guy or else he'll reject her.

These Girl World messages are powerful and pervasive, and most of the time the girl may not even be consciously aware of them. This is why girls say one thing but really mean another. Why do girls say they don't want a commitment when they do? Because they don't want to seem too demanding. Why do girls say they aren't mad when they are? Because then they seem uptight. Girls believe that guys only like girls who aren't just physically attractive but who are relaxed too—as in, they make no demands.

What does this have to do the Friend Zone? Because when a guy is in a girl's Friend Zone, none of these rules apply. She can be herself with you in a way that she can never be with a boy she's in a sexually intimate relationship with. It may be small consolation to know this about a girl you're secretly dying over, but it's the truth.

Once any kind of hooking up is involved, it gets even worse. Most girls have a really hard time communicating what they really want, need, and feel because they're terrified of coming off as too demanding and needy. Frankly, the girls have a point. How many times have you seen a guy walk away from a relationship because it just seemed like too much to deal with? Girls who have a sexual relationship with a guy aren't going to truly share their doubts and insecurities the way they will with a guy who's their best friend. There's just too much pressure on girls to hide what they really want and are really feeling with guys like that. End result? You get her heart and mind, but you don't get her body. Yes, it's unfair.

SHOULD I TELL HER HOW I FEEL?

I'll tell you when you shouldn't. When you're drunk, it's a bad idea. Period.

I know it's tempting to drink to give yourself courage. Plus, you can always use the "I was drunk" excuse to deny that you were serious after she turns you down. I get it, but really, it's not worth it. You'll be sloppy. If she turns you down, you'll do something you'll regret, like hooking up instead with her friend, or the girl right in front of her, or someone she hates.

> *If you do get into a serious conversation when drunk and feelings come up, end the conversation by talking about what you're going to do tomorrow. Or, ask her, "Will we be able to talk about this tomorrow?" Or something like that, to ensure that it isn't just brushed off the next day.* —Will, 20

THE UNCERTAIN ZONE

If she wants to keep you in the Friend Zone, she'll probably act like your conversation never happened. That's because she wants your friendship to go back to the way it was before, and that's the best way to go about smoothing over any residual awkwardness. Now, there's a chance that after she has the opportunity to think about it, she'll decide that she wants you out of the Friend Zone. You'll know this if she brings it up again in some way, usually within the first couple of weeks after you told her. If she doesn't bring it up again, don't wait for her to change her mind. Realize that you aren't getting out of the Friend Zone anytime soon and focus your attention on other people.

What if she dates douchebags after you tell her how you feel (or at any time)? Well … you'll be torn between hating her, hating him, and being sick with jealousy and resentment. Obviously, you like this girl as much for her personality as for what's physically attractive about her. It can be enraging that this girl you like so much is being weak or superficial.

Don't act out your jealousy and frustration by being resentful and sarcastic. If you're feeling the resentment and hate taking over, say something like this to her: "Obviously, you can date whoever you want, but it's hard to be as close friends with you when you're hanging out with a guy who goes out of his way to be a dick to people." (Or whatever he's doing that you don't like. Be specific and keep it short.) She may not agree with you and dump the guy immediately, but at least you're treating your friendship with the respect it deserves.

If you're stuck in the Friend Zone and it's genuinely making you unhappy, then it may help to expand your social horizons. Think about it: if you spend most of your time hanging out with one girl who's both your friend and your crush, and she's dating other guys while you're stuck playing confidant and crying shoulder, then of course you're going to end up doubting yourself and wondering what "those guys" have that you don't. But if you're seeing other people and/or hanging out with a broader group of people, then even if part of you still wishes that one girl saw you as more than a friend, it's going to be easier to deal with because you'll be able to keep things in perspective.

One important thing to remember, though: there's a difference between expanding your horizons and just mindlessly hooking up with other people. Asking someone else out or spending more time with another set of friends can help a lot. Hooking up with random people won't. Even if it feels good in the moment, once it's over, you haven't actually done anything to make your life better. Usually, you just end up feeling worse about yourself or dealing with the consequences of the random hookup.

All of these decisions about hooking up (or not) bring us to the very messy, sometimes incredibly complicated aspects of dating, being exclusive, wanting something more, falling in love, or relationships. If any of that is a possibility, you need to prepare.

CHAPTER TWELVE

THE WINGMAN'S CODE

Girls are risky business. You put yourself out there and you're rewarded with rejection. Or maybe you have other problems, like you and your friend like the same person, or you're coming to the conclusion that no one's ever going to like you, or your friends don't like your girlfriend and she thinks they're slackers, or you just found out you got cheated on, or you aren't really interested in girls sexually but you have friends who are. This chapter is about these kinds of problems. And just as a reminder—like I said in my intro, this material on dating and relationships is meant for both straight guys and gay guys because it doesn't matter who the person is on the other side of the equation—things can get complicated.

Bottom line is, when you like someone, you need a good approach, a strategy to get them interested, and a strategy to keep them interested until you can mutually figure out how much you really like each other. But doing that can be really confusing and nerve-racking, so remember:

1. Whatever interest you have in girls is completely fine, now and forever. That means you could be girl-crazy, sometimes interested, fall for only one girl hard, not interested right now, or never interested. Whatever you feel, no matter what pressure you get from parents, friends, or whoever, it's all good.

2. The same goes for your friends and every guy you know.

3. It's easy to convince yourself that everyone else is way more comfortable with this entire subject than

you are. This isn't true. No matter what guys say, every guy has moments of feeling insecure, unsure, afraid of rejection, and terrified about expressing what he feels to the person he likes. There's just no way most guys are going to admit it.

4. You will have your heart broken. It will suck.

5. Everyone has different "sexpectations," and they need to be respected. Just because you grew up in Guy World doesn't mean you have to want as much sexual attention and interaction as you can get whenever you can get it. The same thing goes for every person you have any kind of sexual interaction with.

Why are so many girls attracted to arrogant guys who treat them like crap? It's one of the most common questions guys have. It's an excellent question and certainly worthy of your frustration. The quick answer is that people tend to be attracted to confidence. I'll answer the question more fully here, and many others, but first we need to start at the moment when you decide you like someone and you want to figure out: (1) how to tell her without exposing yourself to massive embarrassment, and (2) whether she likes you back.

HOW TO TELL A GIRL YOU LIKE HER

The Subtle Approach

- Text her about safe topics like homework.

- Specifically compliment something about her that isn't sexual, like how she played in her last game, a question she asked in class, or an art project you know she did.

- Pay attention to her when she's talking.

- Be there for her as a friend when she's going through problems.

- Be helpful to her on day-to-day stuff.

- Find out her interests and talk to her about them casually.

Pros of the subtle approach: If she doesn't like you back, you haven't exposed yourself to awkwardness.

Cons of the subtle approach: She may misinterpret your behavior as just being nice and may like a guy who's more direct.

The Direct Approach

- Text her that you want to hang out with her.

- Pay her specific, direct compliments that don't make you come across as a pervert.

- Put your arm around her shoulder.

- Hug her (but not too long, because then it's creepy).

Helpful hint: At the discovery stage of a relationship (i.e., when you're figuring out if you like each other), be careful about physical contact. A simple arm around the shoulder will suffice.

Pros of the direct approach: Your actions won't be misinterpreted.

Cons of the direct approach: You run the risk of being humiliated or rejected if she doesn't like you back.

> *Can you tell the guys to briefly explain why you like her so she believes you and knows you actually care?* —*Kylie, 15*

Kylie brings up an excellent point. Beyond being physically attracted to someone, why do you like this person? Take a minute to think about it, because it's way more complicated and annoying to realize you don't like someone after you've gotten into some kind of relationship. Just list three things beyond "she's hot."

HOW TO TELL WHEN A GIRL LIKES YOU

- She initiates any kind of physical contact, like hugs or shoulder massages.

- She smiles at you and then looks down or away.

- She blushes when you're around or talking to her. If she's fair-skinned, especially if she's redheaded, she may be prone to developing red splotches on her neck and face. If this happens, even if you don't like her, please have sympathy for her.

- She takes advantage of opportunities to show you she's paying attention to you.

- She repeatedly tries to have a conversation with you.

- She repeatedly initiates text conversations.

If a girl goes out of her way to touch your arm or hug you way more than usual, then she's usually interested. If she smiles at you and then looks down or blushes a lot around you, she definitely likes you. If all else fails, ask her best friend. Scary, I know, but if she doesn't like you, the BF will give you a funny look and say something like, "I don't think so," or, "No, she's taking a break from guys right now" (trying to let you off easy). But if she says something like, "I don't know, maybe you should go ask her/talk to her," or if she smiles and says, "Go for it," and then runs away, then obviously you should go for it because there're all these bright neon lights that say: SHE LIKES YOU! —Kimber, 15

STALKING

A guy needs to tell a girl he likes her in person, but he can't make it stalkery by just blurting out, "I like you." —Sydney, 15

Stalking used to only apply when someone was obsessed with another person they didn't know or only barely knew. There was no mistaking it—stalkers were scary and to be avoided at all costs. Now the word is commonly used as a way for a girl or a guy to negatively label another person who's attracted to them but they don't like back. Here's how some of our editors describe stalking.

When you say no and the person continues to text/call/email/Facebook you regularly. —Austin, 17

Someone who's a stalker is constantly texting you and checking up on you, as compared to a friend that's just wondering how you're doing. Everyone likes their space, and if a guy is texting a girl every hour, the girl is going to get annoyed pretty quickly.

Usually, when a guy straight-up says he likes the girl, he has some reason to believe that she might say she likes him back. If this is true, there has been mutual flirting going on between the two. But if the conversations seem somewhat one-sided, or the guy is the one who is always asking the girl to hang out and the girl always seems less than enthusiastic, that's usually a clear sign that she isn't into you. So, if the girl doesn't seem into the guy, and the guy tells her he likes her, it can come off as a bit creepy or weird. — Emily M., 16

Are you being a stalker? Here's a quick checklist:

- Everywhere she turns, you're there.
- You stare at her a lot.
- You stalk what she's doing and who she's doing it with on FB.
- You post or send more than two unsolicited and/or not-responded-to messages to her on any social networking platform.
- You continuously check her status updates.
- You're not getting clued in that she isn't attracted to you.
- Post-breakup: you find excuses to run into her.
- Post-breakup: you insist on rehashing the reason you broke up.

Guys ask: How do I know if a girl who's flirting with me is really interested in me or not?
Girls and I say: You can tell if a girl likes you if she keeps trying to continue the conversation. If she's flirting with you as much as she is with other guys around you, she's

probably just seeking attention. If she's laughing
leaning toward you
looking you in the eye or at your lips—nicely done. She's
most likely specifically flirting with you.

PICKUP LINES

Ninety-nine percent of the time, pickup lines don't work
… and when they do "work," it's generally because the guy
using them is confident, funny, and self-aware enough to
only use them as a joke. In other words, it isn't the line
that's bringing him success, but his confident demeanor
and willingness to make himself look ridiculous on the
chance that she'll talk to him. If you're tempted to say
something like, "I lost my teddy bear, can I sleep with
you?" or, "Is that a mirror in your back pocket? Because I
can see me in your pants," don't. Just don't. Lines like
these seem cheesy at best, and downright creepy at worst.

Girls ask: When a boy talks to you, why does he look at
your chest?

Guys say: Because we can't help it, especially when
girls wear things that make it impossible to look
anywhere else.

I say: Women's and girls' breasts are actually pretty
distracting to most guys.

FLIRTEXTING

Texting can be a good tool for flirting and gauging
someone's interest, but text overuse and dependence can
result in failure. Sarcasm and some kinds of humorous
flirting really don't work with texts because you can't
identify tone. Texting can also make you paranoid because

you might dwell on what you think the text really meant. Think of texting as the initial strategy to test a person's interest in you without having to be in front of her if she isn't interested. But just as it's safer for you to keep your feelings and intentions a little gray, the same can be said for someone who likes you. Then it's your turn to figure out what she means between the lines.

Don't wallow in confusion. When you're texting to flirt, do it once. If she doesn't answer, do something in person and bank on her response in person to confirm her feelings for you. If she texts a lot but ignores you in public, there's only so much of that you should put up with, because that means she's either embarrassed to talk to you or too worried about what her friends think.

What does it mean if you get a text that says, "Do you want to hang out?" Depending on the person, it could vary from wanting to hang out with you as a friend, to liking you but wanting to get to know you better before hooking up, to definitely wanting to hook up. A quick heads-up on girls and emoticons. Don't jump to conclusions. Don't assume that, if you get the winking emoticon, she definitely wants to hook up. Some girls are flirting with you when they send the wink. The smile emoticon is definitely less flirty but may be more than just a friendly gesture—it may be more. A heart doesn't have anything to do with hooking up. Sending a heart emoticon is like sending a picture of a puppy. Cute and harmless. If you get an emoticon, take it under advisement, but don't jump to any conclusions.

If you're hanging out in any way and texting to ask about or confirm logistics, you can continue texting until you get the answer. If she isn't answering you, or is consistently vague, she isn't interested.

However, no matter what, don't fight by text (or Twitter, FB, or Instagram for that matter). It won't go well. You're not in sixth grade anymore, and it'll blow up in your face no matter how old you are. Any rational person knows this. The thing that messes people up is that they get so angry or anxious that they respond before they have control over their emotions. The only way to resolve conflict is to talk in person. (If this is happening to you, go straight to "Arguing in Relationships" on page 241.

READING BETWEEN THE LINES OF "I'LL TELL YOU IF YOU TELL ME..."

Speaking of sixth grade, if you're engaged in "I'll tell you if you tell me ..." with the person you like, there's nothing to be embarrassed about...okay, there's a little bit to be embarrassed about. But more important, you need to know how to interpret what the other person is saying so you don't unnecessarily make an ass of yourself.

If the person you like says, "I'll tell you who I like, and then you tell me," she's offering to admit who she likes first for three possible reasons. One (least likely to be true, but possible), she really likes you and has gotten to the point where she has to get it off her chest. Two (more likely), she likes someone else and wants to talk about it with you. Or three, she's avoiding conflict and awkwardness with you by making a preemptive strike and telling you who she likes (not you) before you can admit you like her (and she either knows this or thinks she knows this). If you like her, you can either take the chance of rejection or keep quiet.

If she says, "You tell me who you like first, and then I'll tell you," that means she's nervous about telling you who she likes. Why would she be nervous? Because you are the person she likes and she wants to see if you feel the same way. If you like her, you can take the chance to tell her how you feel directly rather than hedging. If you don't like her and like someone else instead, you can tell her. Just don't torture her by going into detail about how you feel about this other person. If you don't like someone else, don't make someone up.

HOW DO I GET THROUGH THE "I LIKE YOU AS A FRIEND" RESPONSE?

Immediately say, "That's cool," and then run away.

Just kidding. Well, sort of. Take a deep breath, because the more oxygen you get to your head and therefore the calmer you are, the less likely you are to blush and stammer. Remember, it's a little weird for both of you. Say something like, "It's cool, don't worry about it." Even if you're dying inside, just say it. Stick around for at least a few minutes, and then tell her you have to get home for some reason. The next time you see her you may feel awkward, so as soon as you see her, get it over with and say hi and be moderately friendly. No matter how awkward it is, do it. Then you can pay attention to something or someone else. The more you wait to find that perfect time to talk to her, the weirder it's going to get, and then you'll convince yourself not to talk to her at all. From there it's just a spiral down into a bigger and bigger awkwardness. So just get it over with.

BEING SET UP: SHOULD YOU GO FOR IT?

A girl kept coming up to me and saying I should ask this girl, so I did, and the next day she broke up with me. —John, 15

There are three reasons why you'd get set up:

Scenario 1: The double date is the most common reason for getting set up. You have a friend who wants to go out with someone and wants you to come along. Don't believe any of the things he says about how great it's going to be. If sparks fly with the person you're set up with, that's an extra bonus. If not, just have a good time and limit your expectations. The night is not about you, so don't complain if it's not a wildly exciting night. See "Wingman's Rules" on page 193. for further clarification.

Scenario 2: You have a friend who believes that you should go out with a specific person he's determined is right for you. This is the least common reason to be set up, and pretty much too good to be true. First, ask your friend why he thinks this person is so right for you, and then you can judge. If you don't want to go, then don't. Just don't say no out of fear, because really, what do you have to lose?

Scenario 3: You're set up by someone who loves being in people's business and setting people up is a great way to do that. Proceed with caution! If you know and like the person you're set up with, then go ahead. Otherwise, I'd say no. You aren't your matchmaking friend's entertainment.

Guys ask: Why do girls always go to the bathroom together?

The girls and I say: It's a big-time bonding opportunity. Girls check in with each other, gossip, and do reconnaissance. They'll talk about whether they're into the guy or want to escape. (If it's escape, the bathroom is the best place to strategize how.)

A GIRL LIKES ME, BUT I DON'T LIKE HER BACK.

Some people are good at reading social cues. Some aren't. Most people will get the message if you don't answer their texts or you keep your comments general. Don't embarrass a girl in public by being rude in front of your friends or her friends. If she continues to follow you, privately explain in person or by text that you aren't interested.

Ideally, the least awkward way to tell someone you aren't interested is to have a mutual friend tell her how you feel.[19]

---

[19] This is a completely different situation from breaking up with someone you have any kind of relationship with. Dumping someone by text is extremely bad form.

If you have to do it yourself, you can text it or say it in person. Keep it short and to the point, as in, "This is hard for me to say but I don't like you as more than a friend."

I HAVE A HUGE CRUSH ON A GIRL, AND I CAN'T SHAKE IT.

It's not like you can turn off some switch in your head so you can stop obsessing on someone. If you're having a heart-stopping, can't breathe, feel sick to your stomach, unrequited crush, don't beat yourself up about it. Crushes happen. Actually, they're sort of awesome and a huge adrenaline rush. Either way, just accept it.

If the girl doesn't like you back, allow yourself to be bummed out about it for a few days, maybe a week, and then do your best to distract yourself by focusing on something you're good at or you've been wanting to do. Doing this isn't going to take the pain of rejection away, but you need positive distractions, like finding someone else to like, working out really hard in practice, or working on some intense project inside or outside of school. I know this isn't the perfect answer, but the goal isn't to stop liking the person, it's to not wallow in misery.

DIBS

"Dibs," according to the Urban Dictionary, is "the most powerful force in the universe [and] is used to call possession of a certain object or idea."

> *GUY 1: You can't call dibs on every girl you see! It's ridiculous.*

> *GUY 2: Why not? I don't see you saying anything.*

> *GUY 1: Because it's just stupid. Last Saturday night, you walked into the party and started calling dibs on every girl in the room.*

> *GUY 2: Why not? I'm just saying what I want. Too*

bad for you if you aren't fast enough.

I listened to this conversation between two juniors and burst out laughing at the "dibs" master. What made him so confident that any of these girls he was calling dibs on would like him back? The guy was completely delusional. He had convinced himself that he could see a girl and claim the right to try and hook up with her.

Any guys calling dibs must recognize that the girl's choice trumps any dibs that are called. She has the final call—you can't win if she doesn't like you. Truthfully, dibs isn't about the girl. Instead, dibs is a way for guys to communicate their interest in someone when there's a good possibility that they're competing for the same person with another guy and they want to minimize conflict. Or, your friend is being an ass and doing a power play on you. To further assist you in this effort, here are the Rules of Dibs according to me (and the guys of course).

THE RULES OF DIBS

1. If it's well documented or recognized in the friend group that you liked a girl first or you like her more than the other dibber, than you have the first right to dibs. That means that people know how you feel because you have said something to indicate your feelings.

2. You must follow through with the dibs in a reasonable amount of time, normally defined as about two to three weeks, unless other things come up, like going away for sports or school breaks.

3. If you make no progress or you fail, you must relinquish the dibs and communicate this to the friend in competition with you within one to two weeks.

4. You can't call dibs to spite your friend or be annoying.

5. You can't call dibs if you know you won't succeed.

6. You can't call dibs if you know the girl already likes someone else, especially if that someone is a friend of yours.

7. If the girl you've called dibs on rejects you, graciously bow out.

8. You don't have the right to get mad at another guy for talking (not "talking") to your dibs.

What if the stakes are higher? What if you really like the person your friend has dibs on? That can be even more awkward because it probably means telling the other guy how you actually feel. I don't mean you reveal to him every example of how desperately in love you are. I do mean exchanging at least two sentences (one from him and one from you) that clearly indicate how much each of you honestly cares.

Here's where it gets tough. Because guys can be so reluctant to tell their closest friends how they feel about someone they're interested in, they can be really unclear. Once you're unclear, the other guy can pretend he didn't really get it. Or maybe you were so unclear that he truly didn't get it.

For example, you really like someone and your friend knows. Then you see him flirting with her at school (you think) and then at a party (you're sure). Do you say anything to him? What would you say? Is it better to get another friend to say something to him?

If you really trust a friend to do it for you, go for it, but be clear about what you want the person to communicate. (For example, "Jake likes her, so can you just back off right now?") If you don't trust someone to do it for you, then you need to say something yourself to him, because it's not fair to get mad at the guy if he doesn't know what's going on.

What if your friend asks you if you're okay with him asking out someone you used to like or hooked up with? You say yes because you think you're fine with it, but when you see them together you hate it. Do you have the right to say anything? No.

While you're entitled to your feelings, you need to move on.

Good guys can also violate the dibs terms. Maybe they hook up with someone they really shouldn't have because a friend was into the same person. As a general rule, everyone in that situation should get one asshole pass. If, however, a guy has a pattern of not respecting dibs, then he's showing you that he doesn't respect you, he doesn't respect the definition of friendship, and it's a really good bet that he'll betray you in other things as well.

ARE YOU BEGINNING TO WORRY THAT NO ONE WILL EVER LIKE YOU?

Fact: People come into their own at different times. People physically mature at different times. People become more comfortable talking to people they're attracted to at different times. At some point, all this will come together for you. Meanwhile, the more at peace you can be about the process of getting there, the calmer you'll be, the more confident you'll be and the more people will be attracted to you. If you try to be someone you're not, you'll feel like a fraud. Also, it can help to remember that high school is not the world—there are worlds outside of school right now with people in them. And even if you don't know any girls you really connect with or who share your passions and interests right now, I guarantee you they exist, and as you get older and have more freedom, you'll find it gets much easier to find and connect with people, including girls, who get you.

HOW TO BE A GOOD WINGMAN

Again, from the Urban Dictionary:

The original military term wingman defined a pilot who supports another pilot in a dangerous flying environment. Today we honor that bravery by using the same term to describe a guy who misleads someone into sleeping with you.

And:

Taking one for the team, so your buddy can live the dream.

It really needs to be said that the first definition of a wingman from Urban Dictionary is true. For that reason, I prefer the term "wingman" to describe a friend who backs you up when you really need it—not only when you're trying to hook up with someone. But guys almost exclusively use the term "wingman" when they're trying to hook up, so here are the rules of being a good wingman.

1. Your friend's needs are most important; he comes first.

2. Always instill confidence in your friend—pump him up. He cannot approach this halfheartedly or he'll fail.

3. Predetermine a language/code/signals between the two of you so you can communicate subtly. Like, if you want to go home, or he's not sober enough to make a good decision, or her boyfriend just showed up, you both will know what the other guy is saying.

4. Focus your charm on others (her friends). Don't steal the show. Remember, you're not the nervous

one, so it's easier for you to be naturally charming.

5. Your self-esteem can't come into play. Don't be afraid to make a fool of yourself. (If you do, this only makes your friend look better.)

6. Don't play your friend up too much. He's not perfect, and girls don't buy into that.

7. Keep your friend presentable. Under normal conditions, open pant zippers and something stuck on your friend's face are funny and need to be pointed out. Not here.

8. You can remove yourself from play so long as you communicate this to your friend. He can stay if he wants, but he must be okay knowing he's now on his own.

9. If you don't know beforehand, find out essential information like whether she has a boyfriend.

10. If you discover, for whatever reason, that he is certain to fail, tell him.

11. Make sure at the end of the night that he makes it back somewhere safely

CHAPTER THIRTEEN
PUTTING YOURSELF OUT THERE

Freshman year there was a really cute girl in Spanish class. It was my first time really putting myself out there, asking a girl on a date, and it was homecoming. She said yes, and I was totally pumped. Little did I know I was going to get slapped two weeks later, because a senior also asked her to go and she yes to him too. About a week before the dance, her friend told me the cute girl didn't want to go with me, and I find out at the same time that I was voted by my class as one of the four freshman guys for the homecoming court. That was the worst. I had to go to the dance no matter what, and now I didn't have a date. So my mom fixes me up with a friend's daughter who also didn't have a date for the dance. My first real date ... that I am rejected for and end up going with someone my mom sets me up with. I go with this girl, who's actually great, but she's not the girl I wanted to go with, and we weren't in a group, just two of us. For dinner we don't go to a romantic restaurant, we end up getting burgers at a sports bar—me in my suit and her in a dress. It was so terrible. Then we get to the dance like three hours early because my mom dropped us off. Midway through the dance, they announce that I won "Freshman Prince," so I had to wear this crown that was a spray-painted one from Burger King. I was so embarrassed at wearing the crown, not having the girl that I wanted, oh yeah, and my mom had to pick me up at the end of the night. So of course as soon as I get into the car, she says, "Honey, did you have a good time? How were the decorations? What was the theme?" It was such a roller coaster of bullshit.
—Charlie, 24

PREPARATION

Three weeks before. That's your ideal time to ask someone to a dance like homecoming, prom, or winter formal. Before that, you look desperate. After that, someone may swoop in before you do.

QUESTIONS TO ASK YOURSELF BEFORE ASKING SOMEONE TO BE YOUR DATE

There's this one girl who has a big crush on me, but I have a strong feeling for someone else. To make this girl feel that she isn't neglected or "not enough," I asked her instead, not knowing if I'd be able to ask the girl who I did like to the prom, and her responding yes or no. Now I may think that it was a bad move, because now I'm receiving texts after texts from this girl, trying to get to know me better. It's like she's trying to get me to have feelings for her back, and assuming that we'll get together in the end. Now I'm thinking that it just may be too much for me, and now I have no idea how to stop this without anyone getting hurt. —David, 16

- Do you like the person you've asked out? What I mean is, do you like her personality? Will she be fun to hang out with at an event like this?

- Are you asking someone another guy likes? If you are, have some class and check in with him. He'll probably say something like, "No, dude, go for it," even if it kills him. If you want to be super-classy, you can say, "No really, are you sure?" If he can't be honest, that's on him.

- Are you asking someone as a friend but you know that she likes you as more than a friend? Are you asking someone who likes you as a friend but you like her more? Either way, proceed with caution. Between the limo, dinner, and the one million movies we all see where the girl walks down the stairs and the guy stands there stunned, hopes can be very high.

It feels really scary to ask someone. Some guys do it like nothing, and I applaud them for that. Some guys try and try, get rejected, but just brush it off as if nothing ever happened. I applaud these guys too. For me, I need to be sure that there's a high percent chance of the girl I'm asking saying yes. I couldn't begin to imagine trying to brush off being rejected like some guys do. I'd feel completely embarrassed and horrible. —Ben, 15

If you really don't like anyone well enough to ask out, or the girl you do like is already taken, don't sulk and pine away for her. Go to the event with your friends and have a great stress-free time. Or go with one person who's a friend. Plus, you never know what will happen with a friend. However, if you're willing to throw yourself into the romantic fires, go for it. Put your heart on the line. You may crash and burn. You may have the best night of your life. Who knows? There's only one way to find out....

INTERPRETING THE ANSWERS

Huge smile accompanied by "Yes!": You're good to go. No interpretation necessary.

"I'm not sure": There are two possible explanations. One, she likes you as a friend and is deciding between going with you or with her friends. Two, she's waiting for a better offer. If you're cool being the runner-up, give her three to

four days to give you an answer. Past that time, you don't need to ask, it's an automatic no.

"I may be going out of town, I have a family wedding (graduation, etc.)": Definite no.

"My parents don't know you, so they don't want me to go with you": Definite no.

> *If a girl really likes you, she's going to do anything possible to get there. She's telling you excuses to get you away. And don't get her a gift when you're asking, because it'll put too much pressure on her to say yes if she doesn't want to go with you. —*
> *Sydney, 15*

If a girl asks you, don't stress. You're no less a man, and she's not weird or threatening universal balance by asking you. If you like her, say yes. If you don't, tell her the way you'd want someone to reject you. Straight up but not mean. "Thanks for asking, but I'm planning on going with someone else."

If, halfway through asking her, you realize that she's going to say no, you still have to get through it. You will never again go through this so bluntly. If you keep it to "You want to hang out sometime?" it's much easier to save face when she turns you down.

WHAT IF I MESS UP THE ASKING?

Remember the Friend Zone story? I'm now going to share with you another time when I laughed so hard I cried and couldn't breathe. This time it was during one of my meetings with the juniors and seniors of Bexley High School in Ohio. Like many great stories, our hero, Cody (awesome guy, by the way), faced great adversity, starting from a very understandable mistake.

I asked a girl to prom who I'd been off and on hooking up with the last few months. The last time we hooked up, I had a moment of weakness and asked her to prom. About a week later, I woke up and realized I actually didn't like her. Like I really didn't like her personality. I told my parents that I'd invited her, and I asked what they thought, and they said they didn't really support the idea.

Cody knew it was a mistake to ask someone he didn't like to prom. Asking his parents for their opinion wasn't a mistake. But what Cody did with that information started him down the path of prom drama.

I called the girl and told her my parents didn't really like her and weren't supportive of me taking her.

Who among us hasn't tried to get out of something by blaming it on our parents? On the other hand, kinda lame. But Cody wasn't finished making decisions that would make his life much more difficult.

Now I needed a date. So I asked this pretty, cute freshman that honestly I thought I had no chance with, but she said yes.

Cody had now rejected a junior girl who shared a lot of mutual friends with him for a cute freshman. What happened next was completely predictable. The junior girl's friends told him he was horrible and disinvited him from their prom group. So Cody called the junior girl and apologized.

At this point, I'd left Bexley. When Cody emailed me the following, I responded.

I just got reinvited to the dinner. The girl who planned it told everyone to suck it up even if they're mad. I guess it's a win for me, but in some respect I think it could make things worse, because I'll be going with the freshman and with that entire group with the girl that I blew off. And she doesn't even have a date. I feel like a douchebag. Any tips?

"This is going to explode in your face," I told Cody. "If the rejected girl has to sit there feeling like a loser while you sit next to the cute freshman, she'll blow up by dessert. When she does, no one is coming to your rescue. The other girls won't because even though you're an overall good guy, they have to stand up for a junior girl against a freshman girl. The guys won't back you because then they'll get in trouble with the girls. You'll be hanging all alone with your date. And you better hope that the cute freshman doesn't defend you, because then it will be historic. You're way safer saying to the girl who organized the dinner, 'Thanks so much for saying I could join you all, because I don't really deserve it. I really fucked up and need to deal.' And don't believe the junior girl you rejected when she texts you that she doesn't care if you come with the freshman girl. She does care, but she wants to look like she doesn't. She may even convince herself that she doesn't. Don't trust it. Stay away from the dinner."

Okay. So I just turned in my douchebag card. A guy can screw up one time, I guess. Now we're going in a group of thirty-five to forty people, then I can pretty much stay clear of her. That's what I'm going to do.

Crisis avoided.

DON'T BE MONEY-STUPID.

In some of the schools where I work, guys go all out asking for the date. They fill girls' bedrooms with balloons, they cover themselves in tinfoil, they interrupt a class to get down on one knee with a rose, they give a serenade at the beginning of an all-school assembly, to name a few. If you are willing to put yourself out there and have a sense of humor about it, I think that's great but how you ask someone shouldn't be a competition.

AND don't be stupid when it comes to how much money you spend. Don't do something you can't afford (those balloons are expensive). That includes the night too. Budget how much you can spend on the whole thing and then break it down by category. Limo, dinner, boutonnière for you, corsage for your date, post-event activities if the parents don't organize a post-prom activity. Depending on where you live, the costs will vary, but in general here's a basic budget.

Suit/tuxedo	$100
Tickets to the dance	$25–$40 × 2 = $50–$80
Pictures at the dance	$15–$60
Limo	$300 (split between however many people)
Dinner	$30–$50 × 2 = $60–$100
Flowers for her	$20
Post-prom (optional)	$150
Cigar	2 @$10 per cigar = $20 (for you and a friend)

Total $400–$500

By all means talk to your date about the budget. You can still have a romantic time that night if you talk two weeks beforehand about who's paying for what. I think your obligation is showing up nicely dressed, paying for the tickets, dinner, her flowers, and your share of the limo. You don't have to pay for everything, and you can talk about this with your date. If you're going with a girl who is offended that you even want to have this conversation, I'm not thinking she's going to be very much fun to hang out with.

WHAT DO I DO IF I GET CAUGHT IN A GIRL WORLD COVERT OPERATION?

Two girls who are grade-A Queen Bees started a controversy over before-prom preparations. For some reason, girls find prom to be the pinnacle of all that exists. The group consisted of six of their best friends and their dates. They split the group up and said that the girls, their friends, and their dates are going somewhere else to take pictures and the other group could do what they wanted. Obviously, we want to go with everyone. So my friend and I called one of the girls to see if we could combine the groups, and she flipped out and hung up. Even these girls' dates are on board with me that it isn't right to split the groups. I have multiple classes with these girls, and I do not know what to do. For now I am staying away from the topic in school, but there is a lot of unnecessary drama added from a simple situation. I don't know how to confront them about it. —Kyle, 17

Queen Bees see pre-prom as an important ritual that'll only be special (meaning the exact way they want it) if they only have the people they want to be there. They believe this is their inalienable right. If anyone who isn't part of their group attends, they believe this will destroy their special evening. Therefore, these girls have no choice but to make other plans, which they will do in sneaky ways like what's described above.

These kinds of covert operations are standard stuff when you hang out with girls like this. Unfortunately, it often goes with the territory of hanging out with hot, popular girls who are used to getting their way and really care about getting their way.

If you force the issue so the whole group is together, the girls are going to be extremely snotty and will go out of their way to be obnoxious. You'll either have to take it, confront them, or grab your date and go find some less evil people to hang out with. Saying nothing isn't good because then you aren't doing right by your date. If you confront them, you have to do it face-to-face, alone with the Queen Bee. Your best bet is to say something like this, "I know you don't want X, Y, and Z here, and maybe you think that I'm partially responsible for that. But it's getting pretty tense, and I want the night to be good for everybody. So can you lay off a little and tell the other girls to ease up too? If you're mad at me, can you just hold off until tomorrow and then make my life hell?" If she doesn't think your last line is funny, you can say, "That was a joke, by the way, so thanks for considering it."

Or you can turn the tables on the girls.

> *My senior year my buddies and I were tired of being picked apart by the girls' groups. We decided to make our pre-prom activities together. So all the girls knew when they were asked that they had to be part of our group. They knew we'd take pictures together and have dinner together. It was by far the most awesome dance. — Charlie, 24*

GETTING DITCHED

> *Sophomore year this girl got me to invite her junior friend. I didn't know her well, so at the dance we got our pictures taken and then she disappeared. She starts hanging out with this other guy and then hooked up with him. Then she left with the guy. Actually, it was a relief because it was so awkward. —James, 16*

If you're getting signs at the dance that you're getting ditched—like she's spending way more time with other people or she won't dance with you—ask her one time if she'd rather hang out with those people than you. Don't follow her around hoping that she'll start paying attention to you. Bow out graciously. Then go find some girl friends to dance with (this is precisely why I said you want girls on your side). Don't stare at your now ex-date with a mixture of hate, love, and disbelief that this happened to you.

WHAT IF A GIRL I REALLY LIKE COMES ON TO ME AT PROM?

Don't be douchey—stick with your date. If the other person really likes you, you can get together tomorrow. And if she's obviously making moves on you when she knows you brought a date, keep that in mind. I wouldn't trust someone who did that. You're not that hot.

WHAT IF ANOTHER GUY HITS ON MY DATE?

He's a douchebag. Done. But the real problem is if your date is flirting back. If this happens, let the totally nonclassy date have the douchebag. Again, girl friends are really going to come in handy here. It's not a bad feeling to be a guy dancing with seven girls.

WHAT ARE THE SEXPECTATIONS HERE?

At these kinds of events, everyone has sexpectations at some level, and everyone feels at least a little bit awkward. You don't want to go with someone who has very different sexpectations than you. You're not going to have some really cheesy conversation where you ask your date how far she's gone before and how far she wants to go with you.[20] What you can do is be clear about what you want and be really ready to listen to your date about what she

---

[20] It's worthwhile having the conversation with yourself and your friends about how much drinking or drugs you each plan on doing. You know what I think about that— because stupid shit is inevitable if people are drunk or high, so whatever your particular situation is, plan to take care of one another.

wants or doesn't want. The one and only sexpectation is a goodnight kiss. Everything is bonus if you and your date want it.

PS: If you do hook up with a friend, than read the "Friends With Benefits" section on page 220.

DECLARATIONS OF LOVE

Should you buy flowers, chocolates, or teddy bears when you want to declare your affection? Specifically, should you buy any of these things at your school when it flagrantly uses occasions like Valentine's Day or Christmas to raise money?

Your answer really depends on what stage of the relationship you're in.

If you're in the flirting stage, then this is a great way to find out if the person likes you. You make your statement, you're putting yourself out there, and you live with the consequences.

If you do any of this gift-giving at school, you need to be prepared for the pro and con of having your actions take place in the public eye. The pro is that you're doing something a lot of other people are doing too, so your actions won't stand out. The con is, because you're doing it at school, the chances of your social circle and possibly those beyond it knowing what you did go way up.

If you give her something independently of the above-mentioned school events, you're going to be seen in one of two ways—either as incredibly romantic or as sweet but misguided. If you want to take the chance, I say go for it. In full disclosure, I did it once. Well, I got a friend to do it for me while I hid in my car, peering over the seat to see if she knocked on the right door. The guy never talked to me about it. He just pretended I'd never done it. Not exactly the outcome I'd hoped for.

Looking back, though, as embarrassing as it was, it was really important that I took the chance. That was the first time I'd done something like that, and it was essential for me to realize that I could put myself out there, get rejected, and live. Plus, my friend convinced me he was boring anyway (because that's what friends are for).

Don't give any gifts to a person you're in a Friends With Benefits relationship with unless you want to use this occasion as a way to ask her to be in an exclusive relationship. And if you get a gift from your FWB, you can be absolutely certain that she wants more from your relationship. If you don't, then clearly and compassionately (i.e., don't be a dick about it) communicate that you can't be in the FWB relationship anymore. That's right, I'm saying break it off, because even if she asks to backpedal, she want more.

If you're exclusive or dating someone, you could resent these forced gift-giving occasions because it feels ... forced. Princess girls are going to demand gifts, both as a reflection of your affection for her and as a way to show off to other people how much money you have, how in love you are with her, how she can get you to buy things for her, or a combination of all these things. You'll end up resenting her and even doing things you might otherwise have wanted to do for her only out of obligation or because you want to avoid her anger. If you can relate to what I've just written, you need to either have a direct conversation with her about how you feel and/or get out of the relationship. For me, this would be a very good reason not to be in a relationship.

Giving flowers could come across as This is what I'm supposed to do, so here you go. Now you don't have the right to complain. You need to find out what makes her tick. Flowers may be meaningless to her compared to having an actual conversation. Music may mean nothing or it may mean everything. You're in high school. You're figuring out what is meaningful to other people. Share the things that are meaningful to you.

A gift is about you truly seeing and appreciating another person. It captures the essence of the other person or an experience you had together. It's about recognizing how this person's presence in your life makes things better for you. However, you genuinely express that is the gift.

WHAT DO I SAY IF THE PERSON I'M IN A RELATIONSHIP WITH ASKS WHAT I WANT FOR MY BIRTHDAY?

Reread the last paragraph, apply it to yourself, and then tell her what you want.

CHAPTER FOURTEEN

HOOKING UP AND SEXPECTATIONS

Hooking up: any form of getting some type of action. Vagueness is its hallmark. "A guy can say, 'I hooked up with so-and-so,' and no one knows what he did. It protects you and makes you a player at the same time" (Urban Dictionary)

Obviously, hooking up means different things to different people. It could range from kissing to having sex to anything in between. But in the moment when a guy tells other people he hooked up with someone, there's an assumption that everyone is in agreement about what exactly he means. This is one of the ways untrue gossip spreads.

The other reality of hooking up in high school is that whoever you hooked up with may have previously hooked up with someone you know, or has wanted to, or still wants to. That someone may be an inner-circle friend, a guy in your larger group, or someone on your team. For all these reasons, hookups often have larger consequences for your social life beyond any relationship you have with the person.

You need to handle this with class and some personal standards. To help you with this, the guys and I have created a hookup ethics chart. As you can see, it explains your rights and how long you have to wait to hook up with someone who is somehow connected to another guy. Like what if you like someone your best friend or someone on your team used to like? How long are you supposed to wait before you can go for it? This chart will make it clear.

If you want the best chance of reducing post-hookup drama, believe the following truths to be self-evident:

• You can't depend on privacy: You have to go in

with the mind-set that anyone who wants to find out about your hookup can and will. That means that you can't get away with hooking up behind someone's back. If you try to do that, you'll have about thirty minutes after you're done to tell the person who's going to be upset or else that person will find out from someone else.

- Keeping a hookup a secret is too hard: Even if you get away with hooking up behind someone's back, keeping what you did private would take way too much effort for the hookup to be worthwhile in the first place.

- Don't make excuses: If caught, don't say, "It's not my fault, she likes me better," or "I was drunk."

- Be considerate: Under no circumstances are you within your rights to be completely obvious in front of the other guy. No in-your-face flirting, like having her sit on your lap, or picking her up so she shrieks and laughs.

If your relationship is officially over, then you don't have the right to demand any say so about who can hook up with your ex. She's moving on, and so should you. If she's hooking up with a friend, then the only thing you can ask is that your ex or your friend refrain from rubbing it in your face. Other than that, if it really bothers you, don't torture yourself. If you see them at a party, distract yourself with something else. Just don't do something stupid like get really drunk, get into a fight, or hook up with someone you'll regret.

LYING ABOUT HOOKUPS

You just make shit up all the time. You say things about what you've done with girls who go to other

schools. So when people question you about it, you just say, "She doesn't go here. You don't know her."
—Javier, 15

I was trying to fit in with a new group of guys in eighth grade, and they're all talking about blow jobs. So I said I hooked up with this girl and I fingered her. Then I made the mistake of using the girl's name, and she found out. It was not good. She came up to me screaming, "Stop telling lies!" I never talked to her again. —Raye, 18

Facebook is the worst when you lie. I wrote this stuff on my wall about this girl, and of course she saw it. I didn't lie about her ever again. —James, 16

The problem with lying about what you've done with a girl isn't that you may get caught by your guy friends. If that happens, your friends will laugh at you, but you can accuse them of doing the same thing or give them shit about something else. But for the girl you're lying about, it's a whole different level of problem. If a girl says she hooked up with you when she didn't, unless there's something really wrong with her, your reputation won't suffer. The opposite is true for her. It's a total double standard and something I'd love people to stop tolerating or supporting.

Think of it this way: If a girl says she hooked up with a guy when she didn't, the only thing that happens is that the guy looks good. But when the roles are reversed, it's likely that the girl will be worried that people think she's a slut. She's more careful about what she says and how she acts around people. And no matter what she does, people don't congratulate her; instead, they talk behind her back, they're rude to her face, and guys will try to get her to do the same thing that the gossip said she did. That's why she flips out on the guy after she finds out what he said about her.

WHY PORN IS SCREWING WITH YOUR HEAD

Porn is a crutch. You can see anything you want, and it's all at your fingertips. But I think it makes you lazy. Why do I have to go through the effort of actually putting myself out there and meeting someone when I can just download porn at home? —Mike, 16

Talking about porn with you made me laugh, because it is a topic so right field that I never expected you to ask me something like this. It's also funny because it's actually true. I've always thought of it as a "I can't get any so why not watch this" kinda thing. But now I realize how its skews the thoughts of people who watch, and like everything else, it's troubling and successfully doing its job. — Carl, 16

I'm not going to get into how often or what kind of porn you and your friends watch. I'm not getting into the morality of it. I understand that some of you may have older guys in your lives who think this is a great way to introduce you to sex. And I get how insulting it is to your intelligence if adults talk to you about porn and try to come across as if they've never watched it themselves.

This is what I think. You want to be good at hooking up, right? You want your partner not only to think you know what you're doing but for it to be so good that even if you stop hooking up with this person she will look back fondly on your "interaction?" Or maybe she'll even tell other people how good you are? None of this is going to happen if you watch a lot of porn.

Even though it may seem as if porn is showing you how to be good, it's actually doing the opposite. The majority of porn is set up to fulfill men's fantasies that are directly connected to the ALMB. Most Internet porn is especially focused on getting the guy off. Particularly the "money shot" where a guy is coming on a girl's face and the girl couldn't be happier about it. There's no effort on the guy's part to get the woman off because it looks like she's having orgasms no matter what's happening. Of course, if this actually happened in real life, no guy would ever have to worry about his sexual performance. You'd always be guaranteed that you were awesome.

There's zero percent connection between your real life and what you watch in porn. It's like watching WWE and believing that's what will happen if you get into a fight. To refuse to accept this reality or to expect otherwise is naive. For example, the girls you hook up with aren't necessarily going to look like the girls in the video (probably for the better), and you don't have the right to demand that they do. You may see completely hairless women in the videos, but that doesn't give you the right to freak out when you're hooking up with someone because she has pubic hair.

What complicates this even more is that girls are growing up in the same culture and, believe it or not, watching some of the same porn you are. What they're seeing becomes the "new normal" for them too. Even if they wouldn't be turned on doing what they're seeing, they're going to pretend otherwise.

> *I can't even count the number of times I've hooked up with a boy and convinced myself to do something I didn't really want to do because I thought, Well, that's how this works, right? You give some and you take some. I realize now nine times out of ten I was doing all of the giving. I think the other thing about porn is it sort of gives guys the idea that if they ask for something they're going to get it. —Maureen, 18*

Combine that with the fact that girls have been receiving super-sexualized messages since they were young (remember those Monster High Dolls), and they often have an entirely new image of how they should be sexual with you. Unless they're incredibly self-confident and have adults in their lives with whom they can have honest conversations about sex and relationships, they're also vulnerable to porn influencing them in the same way it can influence you.

Porn may also give you unrealistic expectations for your own performance as well. You may not actually say to yourself, I should be able to have sex for hours, but when you watch porn, that message gets into your brain and sticks there. Remember—it's fake.

> Not only should guys not expect girls to act like porn actresses, they shouldn't expect themselves to live up to these completely unrealistic examples of sex. Ha ha, I don't even know if guys sit around depressed about not being able to please girls.... But if they do, they shouldn't really. At least personally I think they get points for effort. — Sofi, 18

> I know plenty of guys who didn't have sex with their girlfriends because they were afraid they wouldn't last like the guys in porn . . . which is stupid. —Rick, 17

Most guys want relationships where there's give-and-take. Most guys want the person they're having any kind of sex with to truly enjoy herself as well. Guys want romance. Don't roll your eyes and pretend you don't. If you're watching porn to the point where it influences your understanding of how relationships are supposed to go, you're going to have disappointing sexual interactions and even worse relationships.

I'm not telling you this to get up and announce how degrading porn is to women. What I am saying is this: the next time you watch porn, ask yourself what you're learning from it. You deserve to have better sexual experiences than what porn portrays. You deserve to have your sexual partner actually tell you what they want and be genuinely attracted to you. You should be into giving another person pleasure. If you do that, no matter what it is you're technically doing, it's going to be great.

CROTCH SHOTS VS. KISSY LIPS

From the classic pouty kissy lips in a bra to full frontal nudity, why the hell are girls sending guys these pictures and then being completely shocked when guys show them to other people? Doesn't a girl forfeit her right to be upset the second she presses Send? What did she expect to happen?

Some of these reasons why girls send these pictures may seem really stupid to you. But not so fast. Don't guys send inappropriate pictures of themselves? How about sneaking your friend's phone out of his backpack, sticking it down your pants, taking a picture, and then sneaking it back into his backpack so he sees your dick the next time he uses his phone? Hilarious. Or your friend takes a picture of his balls and asks another guy, "Do you want to see my brain?" When the other guy is stupid enough to say, "What?" he shows him the picture and … you both laugh your ass off.

The fact is, guys have a serious advantage over girls in the stupid inappropriate pictures department. Because it's almost always a close-up of some guy's genitals, it's much harder, shall we say, to confirm the identity of the guy attached to those genitals.

Plus, if you get a picture of a guy's penis, you're ALMB status isn't going up if you show the picture to every guy you know. Quite the contrary. When you're a girl and you get a picture like this, your reaction is, "That's disgusting. Why is that immature jerk sending me this? And if I'm telling anyone it's my parents, because I'm a little freaked out." For all these reasons, when guys send sexually inappropriate pictures, the viewing public is limited—not everyone in every school in the general vicinity, plus your grandma in Iowa, will see the picture.

But you know that's not the same for girls at all. Girls send inappropriate pictures for completely different reasons and have insanely different consequences as a result. And frankly, taking the picture isn't always inappropriate. The problem is the tsunami of shit that happens to her when that picture goes viral.

WHY GIRLS SEND SEXUALLY EXPLICIT PICTURES

Reason 1: *Non-skanky flirting*. People your age have lived their lives online, so it only makes sense that you flirt online. There's nothing wrong with that. Sometimes that flirting looks like sexy texts or pictures between people that aren't intended for public display. If you get one from a girl in this situation, it's intended for your eyes only.

Reason 2: *Getting your attention*. There are girls who are so insecure that getting Girl World attention is like a quick drug fix. These girls will spontaneously send you pictures that mimic the porn look I described earlier. These girls are train wrecks. Don't take advantage of their massive insecurities. Maybe you're reading this and thinking, But she loves the attention. Those pics give her exactly the attention she wants, and that's not my fault. Check yourself. That line of reasoning is like justifying giving meth to a meth addict. Sure, they want it, but you're contributing to their sickness. So don't take advantage of a girl sending you this kind of picture. It's a really douchey thing to do.

Reason 3: *Being manipulated*. When a guy asks a girl to send him a picture because she's so sexy and hot or to prove how much she loves him, and then he forwards it to all his friends, the whole school knows in two hours. Yes, she was stupid for doing it, but it wouldn't have happened if some guy hadn't taken advantage of her feelings for him.

Reason 4: *Revenge*. A girl might have sent a picture to a guy that he kept private until they broke up. It's super-douchey to take old private pictures of your ex and spread them around.

Reason 5: *Blackmail*. In rare circumstances, a guy tells a girl that she has to send him a picture or else he'll somehow make her life miserable. A guy could also use pictures to stop a girl from breaking up with him. For example, he could tell her, "If we break up, I'm sending the pics to people." In one school I worked in, a girl sent a topless picture to her boyfriend, who forwarded it to one of his friends. When the friend got it, he told her he'd share it with everyone unless she sent him another picture. Thankfully, she finally got over her embarrassment and told the principal, who handled the situation well. The girl had to meet with a counselor, the now-ex-boyfriend was suspended for the day for violation of the school's tech policy, and the friend was expelled.

WHAT DO I DO IF I GET THESE PICTURES?

You don't forward them under any conditions. Ever. If you do, you're contributing to the problem. You give yourself one minute to look at them (I get it, you're human), and then you delete them. I want you to delete them because if you don't do it right away, you're going to forget you have them on your phone. When you forget, then there's some kind of weird universal magnetic pull that will make you leave your phone in your pants pocket and put your pants in the laundry. Then your mom will take out the phone before she puts your pants in the washing machine and check it to make sure you're not being bullied or texting during class, and somehow this picture will come up on your screen. And then you will have one of the more horrible, uncomfortable conversations with your mother you've ever had, and it will go something like this: "Is this what your girlfriends are doing these days? Sending pictures of themselves to you? Is that why you're friends with these girls? I don't know who you are anymore. I can't believe I raised a son who would do this."

> *Having your parents find a pic like this is the worst. Worse than if they find drugs and alcohol. If my mom found it, it'd be like a ten out of ten. If my dad found it, he'd say, "Get that off your phone," and then walk away, but it'd still be pretty bad. Like eight and a half out of ten. — Will P., 20*

You also want to delete pictures from starved-for-attention girls for this reason:

> *This girl I'd recently broken up with decided to get drunk at her house and send pictures of herself topless. I deleted it, and then the worst thing possible happens. Her father looks at her phone records and sees that she sent pictures. Instead of talking to his daughter, he decided to call my parents. My parents called me in a fury, and I told them I'd deleted the picture. But her dad took it to the school and told them to kick me out for harassing his child. I was afraid I was going to lose my scholarship and get kicked out of school. — Winston, 16*

If you delete pictures, you can prove it on your phone records and therefore won't be punished. But if you store a picture in your phone, even if you never send it to anyone, you're still liable if it's found in your stored photos.

The whole thing with pics is fairness. I know "life isn't fair," but we don't have to make it worse by just accepting crappy situations. When you send a picture of your dick to your friends, they laugh and forget about it. Or even if you send a picture like that to freak someone out, it's really hard to prove it was you. A girl sends a topless picture to a guy she stupidly falls in love with, and she's humiliated in her entire community.

WHAT IF I'M THE ONE TEMPTED TO HOOK UP BEHIND ANOTHER GUY'S BACK?

One of my good friends has liked this girl for a while, and she and I were hanging out today. The subject of him came up, and she said things along the line of, "Oh, I don't like him really, and we're just friends." But she mentioned that she thought I was "cute," and before I left I asked her out on a date and she said yeah. What's the rule on being interested in or hooking up with a girl that a guy has had eyes on but

the girl doesn't like him back? Not sure what I should do here. —Rafael, 16

Our editor Jake lays it on the line:

1. He says they're good friends, but how good of friends are they?

2. How much does the friend like her? If it's more like, Oh yeah, she's kind of hot, I think I want to try to get with her, then that would make it more acceptable. But if it's, I really like this girl, and I think I'm going to try to get into a relationship with her, then no way.

3. How much does he like the girl? If all he plans on doing is hooking up with her, then is it worth potentially making his friend really mad at him? But if he thinks it could turn into a relationship and he really likes her too, then maybe it might be worth it.

4. The friend's personality plays a big role too. Some guys would be like, She's not into me, so it's not my place to tell her what to do. Go ahead. But

others won't be so easygoing and willing to let her go.

5. Talk to the friend about it, no matter what about it. He has already gone through enough since the girl he likes has rejected him and picked his good friend over him. If he says don't do it, say why you really want to and why you think you should be able to without attacking him. Also remember that it's just high school, and so it's not worth losing a very good friend who you could be friends with for life over a girl who you will probably never see again after high school except for a few reunions.

FRIENDS WITH BENEFITS

The Urban Dictionary gives us two definitions of "friends with benefits":

> *Typically two good friends who have casual sex without a monogamous relationship or any kind of commitment.*

> *A healthy, fun sexual relationship between two people.... Until one falls for the other, the friendship blows to pieces. And those two people find themselves worse off than they were before.*

It looks so easy. A sexual relationship with no time requirements or obligations. But it's easy appearance is exactly why it's so confusing. It's absolutely true that two people can maintain a friendship that sometimes has a sexual component without it disintegrating. There can even be positives to it. Hooking up with people you actually know and have to talk to the next day is a good thing. But when people don't know how to communicate their feelings or are willing to manipulate someone else's feelings for their sexual satisfaction, that's when things run off the rails.

In addition, when you tell someone explicitly that you want to have a Friends With Benefits (FWB) relationship, there's an implicit understanding that neither party wants or will ever want more in the relationship. Which is totally different than hooking up with a friend and not knowing where it's going. There are girls who are comfortable having a sexual relationship without commitment. But then there are also girls who say they want, or agree to have, a FWB relationship but really want more. They just don't want to admit it. In those situations, girls try to convince themselves they're okay with it. But what's not cool is to know that about the person you're hooking up with, or have a pretty good suspicion that's in fact what's going on, and use her anyway. Why? Because you can claim that she has no right to be upset about what you do with someone else if she said she was fine with it. If she complains or has any feelings about it, then you're likely to tell her she's "too emotional." Look back at the rules of anger in the beginning of this chapter and you can see how this will play out. The girl sits on her anger and then explodes when it feels like you're rejecting her. In the end she's left being mad at herself because you can say, "What did you expect? You told me you were fine with this. You're being totally irrational." No, she's not. She's on the receiving end of psychological warfare.

It's really not cool to use people's baggage like this. But I do understand that it can be very difficult to read between the lines when a girl says she's cool with it, or even suggesting it herself in the first place. Use the following three questions to determine if a girl is being truthful about whether she's really fine with your FWB relationship:

1. Does she say, "It's fine"? If so, it's probably not fine. If she was actually okay with it, she would give an answer with more substance.

2. Does she get upset when you can't hang out? If

so, she's emotionally invested.

3. Will she ditch other things or friends to hang out? If so, she's emotionally invested.

Of course, if you actually like a girl, even if she's your friend, you could always not be a wimp and take the risk of going for the relationship. Just an idea to consider....

Guys ask: Do girls think about sex like guys do?

The girls and I say: Some do, some don't. It depends on the girl. But the reason it's hard to know is if girls went around making comments about sex like some guys often do, they'd get a reputation for being a slut. Again, it's an unfair double standard.

Girls ask: Why do guys think about sex all the time?

Guys say: Because we're obsessed.

I say: Like girls, some do, some don't. And like girls, guys have hormones, and sexuality is new and exciting. Unlike girls, society more readily accepts sexually aggressive behavior in guys, so they have more freedom to express it and are often encouraged and rewarded for expressing it—which of course is a double standard and would probably
annoy you too if you were a girl.

WHAT DO I DO IF A GIRL PLAYS GAMES WITH ME?

The reasons I don't trust [high school] chicks is they don't know what they want. A lot are manipulative

*liars, a lot of them have unstable personalities, and
the freaking games—there's no end to them. —
Victor, 18*

Imagine yourself in the following situation. You're a
junior and have recently hooked up (as in made out) with a
girl in your school. You like her and are interested in seeing
where the relationship goes. A week after the initial hookup
she texts you this message, "Want to hang out? Parents
not home." You interpret this text as direct communication
that she wants to hook up again (which is a reasonable
assumption). You drive out to her house (which isn't
nearby), and you ring the doorbell. When she opens the
door, she's wearing sweatpants, and her hair is in a
ponytail. The sweatpants confuse you. They aren't yoga
pants. You're not expecting her to dress up for the
occasion, but it's not exactly what you had in mind, and
you begin to doubt if she wants to hook up. You go in the
house, and you proceed to talk. There's no sexual activity
or any possibility of some on your horizon. As you talk to
her on the couch, she eats a bowl of cereal. You become
increasingly confused. Why did she want you to come
over? Why did she tell you that her parents weren't home?
After a while, you give up trying to figure it out and drive
home.

What happened? There are two possible answers.
Either she's a girl who likes to mess with guys' heads (this
is the minority of girls, but they tend to be very cute, so a
lot of guys like them and therefore have this experience) or
she's testing you to see if you really like her. I totally
understand if you see the second explanation as still
playing games. But the reason a girl does this is actually
understandable. Girls are often, and for good reason,
worried that a boy they just hooked up with is only
interested in them for future easy hookups. Your behavior
after this experience is crucial. If you're still nice to her
during and after the situation at her house, then she knows
you like her as more than just a hookup. This may look to

you like she's playing games with you, which I guess technically she is. But some girls want to know if you're just interested in using them or if you actually like them (which, again, is reasonable).

Could Will M., our guy editor who had this situation, have foreseen this happening? Based on the text and his prior interaction with the girl in question, no. That's why I'm telling you not to jump to conclusions. If you find yourself in this type of situation, you need to be able to see it for what it is and change your game plan. If you like her, try to turn off the part of your brain that's angling for the hookup. Because you don't want to be or come across as that guy who makes snide comments or tries to force the hookup because you feel like it's owed to you.

And the truth is, you may really like this girl—even if you think she's playing with you. What if you want a chance to see if this girl is worth hanging out with? What if you want more? The next chapter will navigate all of that.

CHAPTER FIFTEEN
OUTWARD BOUND

Before we go on . . . something I really wanted to do when writing this book was make it inclusive to all guys—regardless of their sexual orientation and how they want to present themselves to the world. What I first tried to do, unsuccessfully, was write "them" instead of "she" whenever I wrote about hooking up, dating, and relationships, but it ended up being grammatically confusing and making it hard to figure out who or what I was talking about. But the fact is, gay guys experience the same insecurities and fears in their romantic lives that straight guys do, except for one thing—it's worse. Not only do gay guys have to come to terms with their sexuality, but they also are doing it in an environment where they're uncertain at best about how people are going to accept them, and there will always be people who really believe they have the right to make gay guys miserable. Even more annoying and potentially dangerous is when adults who are supposed to protect all kids' well-being and safety back up the homophobic kids or do nothing about it (which is the same thing).

Public attitudes about homosexuality are changing rapidly, and your generation is leading the way. But there are still huge obstacles to acceptance. I've asked a few of the guys who have helped me on this book and who also happen to be gay and have a lot of straight guy friends to share what they think is most important for you to know. Ian, a junior from Bexley, Ohio, is out with his family and in school.

I'm tired of the stigma that comes with being gay, like the feeling that I'm a typical "girls' gay best friend." It's just not who I am. Of course I have lots of friends who are girls, but I'm not begging them to go

shopping and cry over The Notebook. . . . I hate how
people expect me to know everything about
musicals and Broadway.

In addition, I've asked Matt, also a junior, who's only
out to his best friend and dad, to share with you what it
was like for him to realize that he was gay.

The fear starts when you realize that feeling, no
matter how small, that you're attracted to the same
sex. You can't shake it off. You try to convince
yourself that it's silly. I'm just confused, I told myself.
I couldn't be gay; I couldn't be what many around
me regarded as being wrong and perverse. And
since countless people use "gay," "homo," and "fag"
as insults and as a substitute for "stupid" or "lame,"
it seemed like everyone hated who I was. I was
scared of being myself around my closest friends,
my own family, my parents, the most important
people in my life.

This is why it matters when people carelessly use the
word "gay" or any word like it to put someone down or
when they use it for "stupid" and then assure everyone
else that "It doesn't matter, it's just what we say." As Matt
said, the callous use of these words makes guys like him
feel like they're hated for just being themselves. And then
they have to put up with the people who say it and refuse
to take responsibility for what they're doing.

As a straight guy, you need to know what this is like for
your in-the-closet gay friends, which of course you may
have, even if you don't know it. You may have close
friends, guys who you may deeply respect and like, who
are also terrified to reveal this truth to you. So as you read
Ian's and Matt's words, imagine that someone you care
about is going through what they describe.

I just couldn't hold it in anymore. One night I texted one

of my best friends. I took about ten minutes to type the words and send them. "I'm gay." Send. She wrote me back telling me that she loved me no matter what. The weight that was lifted off of my shoulders was incredible. After a week, I told my dad. We both sat down, and I just couldn't get the words out. Finally, I counted to three and told him. His face turned into one of deep understanding, and he hugged me tighter than he ever had before. I realize that my case is different than most. I've heard of people who have gotten kicked out after telling their parents, which was one of the reasons I was so terrified to come out to my dad. But telling those two people made the biggest difference in the world. It helped me believe that I might be able to live a regular life. But coming out is a personal choice. I came out to two people in the space of a week, but haven't come out to anyone else since then, and it has been six months.

I also asked Ian to write this letter.

Dear (Possibly) Gay High Schooler,

I don't know whether or not you're out, but we must acknowledge that other people may see us as inferior to them. If you come out, you may lose a couple friends, and on top of that, people who weren't your friends before may use you as a target for attack.

If you have straight, male friends, and you're afraid to tell them that you're gay, you're not crazy. I was terrified to come out to my straight friends. I prepared by deeply thinking about what would I do if they decided that they couldn't be my friends anymore. My first male friend I came out to looked at me as if I was about to pounce on him and force him to make out with me. For the next month he didn't answer any of my calls or texts and wouldn't talk to me at school. After a month I finally got a hold of him and asked him if he wasn't responding because I was gay, and bluntly he said, "Kinda ... yeah." But now, three years later, we're just as good of friends as before I told him, and the experience gave me ideas on how to come out to other straight friends.

You should go into it knowing there's a possibility of losing a friend after the talk. Be as calm as you can, and tell them in private. Also, don't take anything he says right after you tell him to heart, because he will be surprised, like, "So ... you like dick?" or, "I'm straight ... just to let you know." After this exchange, give him space and let him come back to you. He will probably need time to register what just happened before he can develop thoughts on it, so it may take a day, a month, a year, or he may never get over it.

In the case of losing a friend, you must trudge on and roll with the punches. There's no clock ticking down the time until things get better, so you must make it better for yourself. Embrace who you are and absorb the attacks, because that makes you more masculine than them. Now, when embracing who you are, you don't have to swing your hips when you walk and go shopping every weekend if that's not your thing. Be whatever gay you want to be; you should be the one defining how "gay" applies to you, because the moment where you're defined by your sexual orientation is when people see you as "that gay kid." If you're miserable, hang in there, because I guarantee that someone loves you. You're worth something, and don't let anyone tell you otherwise.

I wish you the best, Ian

I hope you can see from these guys that being gay isn't a "preference." No one, especially in their teen years, prefers to be something that could possibly make their parents and friends reject them. No one would choose to be something that puts a bull's-eye on their back. And just because you're a gay guy doesn't mean you want to hit on every guy you know. As Jason Collins said when he came out, Believe me, I've taken plenty of showers in twelve seasons. My behavior wasn't an issue before, and it won't be one now.[21]

In response to people who say being gay is against their religion, if that's how you interpret your religion, then there's no arguing with that. I've had students get Bibles from their lockers to show me where it says homosexuality is a sin. But that's not the issue. Freedom of religion, your belief that something is a sin or not, doesn't give you the freedom to take away the rights of others. That's what the problem really is—using religion to excuse people who degrade or abuse gay kids. Unfortunately, religious teachings and values have been used to discriminate against people of races, ethnicities, and other religions for generations. I know there's nothing new there. I know you know that. But that fact doesn't make it right or mean that we should just accept it.

So while the adults around you struggle to do the right thing, I'm asking you to uphold the basic dignity of all guys—and I'm asking you to do it as a defining point of what it means to you to be a man.

---

[21] Collins, Jason. "Why NBA Center Jason Collins Is Coming out Now." SI.com, Sports Illustrated, 29 Apr. 2013, www.si.com/magazine/news/20130429/jason-collins-gay-nba-player.

CHAPTER SIXTEEN

PRINCESSES, PARENTS, AND OTHER RELATIONSHIP PITFALLS

A whole relationship doesn't happen because someone is afraid to say, "Hey, I kind of really like you." —Aaron, 16

I haven't asked a lot of girls on dates or to be my girlfriend because I'm afraid of rejection. But I can tell you this, when asking the girl you truly like, it's an amazing feeling when she says yes. However, those few seconds or minutes you wait in an accelerated heartbeat are horrible. Your mind will be out of control and thinking a million thoughts at once, and you'll barely be able to speak, and those scenes you see in movies on how the guy walks up to the hot popular girl and tells her smoothly how he wants to go out with her is not even a close depiction of how asking girls out goes! (Unless you are super-smooth and naturally gifted, of course.) I guess what I'm trying to say is, asking girls out is hard, your hands sweat, and it can be very embarrassing at times, but the moment that special girl says yes, you'll know it was worth it all. —Luke, 15

After you've hooked up with someone more than once, you may wonder what you're doing, or the other person may have an opinion about what you're doing. As in, exactly what is the arrangement between us? And no matter what you officially call it, once your relationship gets to a certain level, you need to be prepared to have some intense experiences and conversations.

But first, let's just admit it right now that behind all the denials, a lot of guys are incredibly romantic and fall hard when they fall in love. There is nothing wrong with that! You'll fall in love. There are going to be great moments, crushing moments, incredible frustration, joy, anger, fear. It's just a mess of an experience.

What complicates this even more is how rarely guys are given good advice about relationships, if anyone even says anything to them at all. Even the good, intelligent dads, uncles, grandfathers, and friend's dads limit their wisdom to things like, "Don't think with your little head. Think with your big head!" As if the only relationship advice you need is about not getting a girl pregnant or contracting an STD.

Another common piece of advice that is usually well intentioned but patronizing and wrong is when people tell you, "You're too young to seriously be in love. Your feelings aren't real. It's not like you're going to get married." Or, if you break up, they respond with, "Don't let it bother you, there are always other fish in the sea" (a comment, by the way, that adults rarely make to girls). Remember that, unless you have evidence to the contrary, they mean well, but you need to let their comments roll off your back. You have the right to your feelings whenever you have them. Just because you're young doesn't mean your intense feelings are superficial and immature. The relationships you have now are important because it's these experiences that enable you to define your personal standards and how you effectively communicate those standards to others. To say it another way, you want to keep your dysfunctional, highly irritating relationships to a minimum. Everyone is probably going to have a relationship like that, but you want to learn from it so you don't develop patterns of dating crazy.

Your experiences matter. Don't forget that.

But you may be getting other kinds of advice about relationships that is worse than just ineffective, annoying, and dismissive of your experiences. One of the most frustrating things about writing this book for you has been listening to my guy editors tell me some of the truly messed-up things that men and older guys say to them about relationships with girls. Here are a few of my non-favorites:

> *"Treat them like dirt and they'll stick to you like mud."*

> *"Have fun on Saturday and abort by Sunday."*

> *"Always control women. That's what they want even if they won't admit it." "Just let them think you agree and then do whatever you want."*

WHAT GUY SHOULD I GO TO FOR RELATIONSHIP ADVICE?

Someone who has a track record of good relationships, including breaking up well, or who has strong bonds with his sisters or mom.

WHAT GUY SHOULD I AVOID FOR RELATIONSHIP ADVICE?

Someone who has hooked up a lot but usually ends relationships badly.

Someone who doesn't respect his mom or other women. Someone who cheats or plays with people's feelings.

Someone whose advice sounds like the bad advice mentioned above.

If you take this kind of advice to heart, you're guaranteed to have train-wreck relationships and to look like and then eventually become a complete douchebag. No matter how hot the person is, how good you look together, or how sexually attracted you are in the beginning, your relationship (of whatever intensity, duration, or title) will be superficial and eventually unsatisfying and highly irritating. If you aren't honest or smart enough to demand more from yourself and therefore the people closest to you, then you'll become that guy who only talks about women in clichés, talks in sports metaphors, and has no core self. You don't want to be that guy. You aren't someone with limited emotional intelligence and therefore limited emotional needs—which is exactly what that advice assumes you to be.

> *My dad has the worst relationships with women,*
> *including my mom. He constantly tells me, "The man*
> *always has to have the upper hand. Women never*
> *know what they want. You have to show them who's*
> *boss." There's no reason why I'd ever listen to him.*
> *—Anthony, 16*

While it's unfortunate that Anthony is dealing with a dad like this, at least he's intelligent enough to know that his dad isn't a good role model. But clearly, not all guys in Anthony's position react this way. Instead, they take the negative advice about women they get from their dad, uncle, or older brother and adopt it as their own. What's so sad and annoying is how arrogant these guys are. They think they have relationships all figured out and believe they give great advice to their friends. And it does look like they have it all figured out, because there's always at least one pretty enough, insecure wreck of a girl who will hook up with them and then allow them to continually use her, hoping whatever they have will turn into some great relationship.

Even if it looks good on the outside, trust me, you don't want this.

Let's get clarity on some terms. Most guys I work with define "dating" as having some kind of regular sexual interaction and meaningful emotional connection that's in the public eye. Dating includes having social obligations to the other person. Being "exclusive" is defined as being in a sexual relationship with only one person, but it's private and hidden. This is usually because one or both of the people involved aren't ready to deal with commentary and opinion from their friends, and or don't want the stress of the expectations and obligations that come along with dating. Like a FWB relationship, being exclusive is ripe for someone to be seriously taken advantage of, with one person pretending to be fine with the arrangement but really not feeling that way at all.

What qualities do most people say they value in a boyfriend? Here are the most common answers to that question:

> *"Someone who pays attention to me."*

> *"Someone who treats me the same no matter who's around."*

> *"Someone who's cute and funny but not perverted all the time."*

> *"Someone I can talk to without worrying about my looks or how I sound."*

Of course, talking and writing in the abstract about good boyfriend qualities is easy. Here's a dose of reality.

> *I've [had] girls say to me that they have a "nice guy" who wants to go out with them but they don't know what to do 'cause her asshole ex is trying to get back with her and she leaves the nice guy hanging while she gives the other guy another chance 'cause "maybe it'll work this time." It's freaking ridiculous.*
> *—Victor R., 17*

It's fair to say that Victor speaks for most guys your age. Why do so many girls like arrogant guys? I asked girls to answer Victor's question, and this is what they said:

> *we like those guys because they're hot and can be really cool alone. Here's what I think: guys who look confident are attractive. Some girls mistake*

*arrogance for confidence and are drawn to these
guys because it makes them feel better about
themselves. Also, arrogant ALMB guys often have
high social status and look like they're in control.
What these girls really love is being in some kind of
defined relationship (either in their own minds,
privately between the two of them, or publicly) where
everyone sees the guy's persona but the girl is the
only one who sees his "softer" side. By the way, this
is the reason girls can so easily rationalize when the
guy treats them badly. So if you've heard a girl say,
"You just don't know him like I do. When we're
alone, he's not like that, he's really sweet," you're
talking to a girl who's deluding herself.*

A slight variation on this question is when guys ask,
"Why do girls say they're looking for someone who listens
and respects them, and then they put up with it when guys
don't?" Girls admit that sometimes they can get blinded by
their feelings. In most relationships, there's good and bad.
When things go bad, it's easy to trick yourself into putting
up with it. You convince yourself that either the other
person didn't mean to be hurtful, he was having a bad day,
or you did something that caused it, etc., and you believe
the good parts of the relationship will return. This is true for
guys who are friends as well as with boyfriends.

IS BEING IN A RELATIONSHIP AS AMAZING AS EVERYONE SEEMS TO THINK IT IS?

A lot of girls and guys believe that once they get a
relationship their lives will automatically be better. Once
you're in a relationship, one of the first things you'll
probably realize is that it's harder to be in one than not. It's
true that boyfriends and girlfriends can make life better. It
definitely feels great when someone likes you and is
attracted to you. If you're having problems at home, it's
comforting to have someone comfort you. But no matter

how in love you are or how great your relationship is, you're in a relationship. That means the two of you will have different opinions, and you'll get upset, frustrated, and really angry with the other person. Most of these conflicts, taken by themselves, aren't automatic deal-breakers. In fact, usually what breaks people up isn't the conflict itself but how they treat each other as they get through the conflict.

For example, there are couples who never outwardly fight, so it looks like things are fine, but at least one person in the couple isn't saying what he or she really feels because of a fear of getting shot down. Not good. That's the kind of relationship where the quiet person sacrifices so much of himself that he neglects what's important to him and forgets that he has rights in the relationship.

Then there are relationships in which the two occasionally get into conflicts, hopefully where both of them can express what they think and feel, believe that the other person is truly listening, and vice versa. On the other extreme are people who fight a lot. That means they're not listening to each other. It's a power struggle. This relationship is exhausting and way way more trouble than it's worth.

But the problem is that once you're in a relationship it can be really hard to see what you've got. Your feelings get jumbled. That's okay, because relationships are messy, but a little bit of clarity is always good.

THE PRINCESS PROBLEM

I once had a girlfriend who went totally nuts and crazy because I wasn't reaching her "expectations." For some reason she thought that the idea of having a boyfriend would be a true Cinderella story come true. And she was so pissed off that she just ignored me, avoided eye contact, everything, all for some test to see if I really cared for her! Like where is the logic in that?!? If I didn't care for her, I would of never asked her out! —Ben, 16

This princess thing has to end. It teaches girls that guys should treat them as delicate and weak. But here's the irony. If the princess doesn't get what she wants, she's entitled to turn into an angry, spoiled brat who can bully the guy into letting her get her way. Or in Ben's case, who gives him the silent treatment.

Ben's isn't alone. Other guys have talked about this princess thing. Read Jake's problem later in the chapter about arguing with his girlfriend and you'll see what I mean. So ... if you want to be in a relationship where you're going to trust each other, depend on each other, have fun, and feel comfortable being yourselves (including sharing the bad things), the princess thing must end.

For those of you who are reading this and arguing with me about how you want to be polite and you were raised to treat girls as special delicate flowers, I'm not saying I want you to stop being polite. I'm saying there's a fine line between being polite and encouraging the idea that girls aren't as capable as you so they constantly need someone to take care of and protect them. So hold doors and pay for the first couple of dates. You can even be her hero—as in standing up to guys (including your friends) who are disrespectful to her. But once you get to a place where you insist on paying for everything (and by the way, going into serious debt to cover these things is just stupid) or treating her as anything less than a fully competent person, you're encouraging girls to be incompetent, spoiled, and superficial.

For your part, it's not so great either. Guys who take care of princesses aren't supposed to experience or admit any weakness or failure. But that's not reality. Being the knight in shining armor may look good, but it's impossible to keep up all the time. Once in a while, sure. Just not all the time.

"DO I LOOK GOOD IN THIS?"

When a girl asks this question, you never say, "I don't know. Sure. It looks fine. It looks like everything else you wear/are trying on." Instead, while looking at her, you say, "You look amazing." If she responds by saying, "Are you sure my butt/stomach/thighs don't look huge?" don't roll your eyes and sigh. Just repeat that she looks great.
If, however, you think she'd look better in something else and you're a guy who can focus on details, then you say, "You look amazing, but I think something else may complement your figure better, like [insert example of a dress she already has that looks great on her]."

HOW DO I DEAL WITH MY JEALOUSY?

*For about two and a half months, I've been worried about spring break. I'm going on college visits, and my girlfriend's going to Florida. I wouldn't be that worried, but I just found out she's going to the same place where the guy that she tried to have a long-distance relationship with lives. He's a junior too, and they had a little thing over winter break, and I'm worried it might happen again. How can I talk to her about it without sounding too overprotective? —
Gus, 17*

Jealousy is a natural feeling to have in a relationship, especially in the beginning when things seem so unsure. However, you really want to avoid coming across as a possessive crazy stalker. Here's my advice if you find yourself in a situation like Gus's.

You have the right to be nervous, and you're entitled to your feelings. That said, you have to walk a fine line between telling her what you feel and want from her and coming across as not trusting her or not "allowing" her to hang out with the other guy, which will backfire. Either she'll lie to you and see him anyway, get angry with you for being too possessive, or won't see him only out of concern about you getting angry. If she tends toward drama, you're setting up the dynamic where she'll want to hang out with him more because he's "forbidden."

You want her to not hook up with him because she respects your relationship and she'd rather be with you than anyone else. So you really have to be genuine about how you feel without giving her ultimatums and telling her what to do. So I'd say something like: "I'm not sure if you know this, but I really like you for (X) reasons. I know you're going to be near [whatever his name is], and obviously I can't control what you do, but I really hope you don't hook up with him, because it would make me feel like crap. I'm not asking you to make any promises, I just want you to know where I stand."

I guarantee this will work better than making her promise that she won't see him or checking her Snapchat or Instagram posts. There are some girls who really need attention. If they get attention from someone else while they're dating you, they're going to want you to know because your jealousy makes them get more attention. If you get insanely possessive about it, it's going to feed the attention she needs. If she sees him anyway, you don't want to date someone who acts this way after you've been so cool about it. No matter how cute she is or how much you love her. I know, it's hard to cut off the relationship, but being in love with someone who consistently does things to make you unsure about the relationship can make you miserable.

HOW DO I DEAL WHEN THE OTHER PERSON IS JEALOUS?

First, you have to honestly assess your own behavior. When you're in public with this person, is it clear that you're together? If it is, and if you check in with the other person periodically, you're allowed to freely socialize. That means you're allowed to talk to other people. You're allowed to have a good time with other people. You're allowed to think other people are attractive. If you're flirty by personality, once you're in a relationship you can still be this way, but just be cautious about how the other person feels. What you're not allowed to do is flirt exclusively with someone else. You're not allowed to make any comparisons between the person you're with and the other people you've dated.

> *Don't just say they're being crazy. If they didn't think their feelings were true, they wouldn't talk to you about them. And they thought it over many times before telling you, so it isn't just an impulse. —Matt, 17*

You really have to be honest, for both your sakes. If you're making the other person feel insecure, the meanest thing you can do is dismiss those feelings by saying that person is seeing things and is insecure. If you believe you're treating the other person well but you feel like they won't allow you to have other relationships or socialize, then that's being possessive. Just because you're in a relationship doesn't mean you own each other.

ARGUING IN RELATIONSHIPS

> *My girlfriend and I have a really great relationship. I'm being kinda nitpicky with this, but it gets to me sometimes. I never say anything concerning any of her faults. I really try to treat her like a princess. But it's more that she's my best friend, and I would never want to say anything that would upset her. But occasionally she has no problem pointing out what she perceives as my flaws. She openly says things with no remorse, like, "You have a huge ego," or, "Nobody is as smart as you," in that sarcastic tone we all love. The other day I told her I didn't like when she said stuff like that, and it was maybe the first fight we really had. She thought I was being just a little too touchy. Am I? It's definitely a possibility,*

which I accept. But she (like many girls) doesn't even try to accept any part of what I say really, probably feeling that if she did it would be like I "won" the argument. Is there an appropriate way to deal with this? Am I being ridiculous? —Jake, 17

Here's this princess problem again. Strong relationships depend on being able to say things to each other when you aren't happy about something the other person is doing. But you do it in a way that is straightforward and kind. If there are things that are bothering you about your girlfriend, you have the right to say something to her about it. Here's the SEAL.

> *Stop and Set Up by talking to her privately and in person, or at least over the phone: Look, I want to tell you about something that's bothering me. Is now a good time for you?*

> *Explain: I don't like how sarcastic you can be in (X) situations ... and you won't admit that it really bothers me.*

> *Affirm and Acknowledge: I want you to tell me if I'm doing something annoying, but you have to tell me in a better way.*

> *Lock In: I'm telling you because I always want to tell you the truth.*

The big push-back is when she tells you that you're being "too touchy." You're always entitled your feelings, just like she is. Turn the tables and ask yourself, If she was really upset about something and I said she was being overdramatic, how would she feel?

The two of you need to have a quiet sit-down with no distractions. You may get mad at each other, and it may get very uncomfortable, but every relationship has to go through this.

PROBLEM: YOUR FRIENDS DON'T LIKE THE PERSON YOU'RE DATING

If your girlfriend doesn't like your friends, or vice versa, it can easily feel like you have to choose between them. Actually, you don't—they have to respect that you have the right to have deep relationships beyond the one they have with you. Neither side has the right to make nasty comments about the other. But if your friends are worried about you and believe the other relationship is dragging you down, that's another story.

If there's a possibility that this is what's going on, step back, listen to your friends, and determine their motivation. On the one hand, they could be jealous that you have a relationship. If this is their motivation, their comments will mostly revolve around ridiculing you for being controlled by your girlfriend, and it'll be a constant theme of their conversation with you. If your friends are really looking out for you, they'll make comments that may even come across like a joke. So ask them, "Is there a specific reason you don't like her? Is there something I need to know?"

On the other hand, it is true that being in a relationship means you won't have the same amount of time for your friends that you used to. If, like a lot of guys, you've had a tight core of friends who have all hung out together since you were little, it's going to shake things up. Even if they get along with your girlfriend, there's a good chance they'll have different interests, and finding ways for them to hang out together doing something they all enjoy can be tricky. For example, inviting your girlfriend to your friends' marathon Xbox sessions is, if she isn't a gamer herself, the sort of thing that can lead to her awkwardly sitting there, bored out of her mind. She won't thank you for that, and neither will your friends.

The key in this situation is to be fair about budgeting your time. You owe your girlfriend a real relationship, which means spending time with her consistently (and not just when you happen to feel like it). At the same time, if you just bail on your friends completely, they're going to be justifiably pissed off—and alienating your friends for the sake of a relationship can backfire, because if the relationship ends, then you can be left without any support.

Think hard about what your most essential shared activities with your friends are, and try to preserve those. But also be willing to give up some of the other time you might have spent with them, in favor of your girlfriend. The important thing is to be open and up-front about it. Don't be shady or inconsistent or make plans you can't keep. If there's something it's important for you to do with your friends, tell your girlfriend that, and do the same with your friends.

WHAT IF MY PARENTS DON'T APPROVE OF MY RELATIONSHIP?

Many, many people have written me for advice when their parents don't like their boyfriend or girlfriend. Sometimes it's because of the way the person looks, like her hair is in her eyes, or she mumbles, or she wears all black. Sometimes parents don't trust kids who are super-polite and preppy. Or parents think you're too young to be this seriously involved. And sometimes parents don't approve because the girlfriend or boyfriend is a different race or religion or comes from a different country.

Let's tackle the easiest issue: they think you're too young. It's not wrong to be in a relationship, but some can get so intense that they pull you away from doing things you really like or hanging out with other people you care about. If a relationship is truly strong, it can withstand each person in the relationship having strong ties with other people. So if you're constantly hiding in your room so you can talk to this person when you're not seeing them every second of the day, you need to take a step back and evaluate for yourself what's a good balance between being with this person and any of the other good things that are going on in your life.

Next, what if your parents don't like the person based on how they look or act? If your parents make unfair assumptions about your girlfriend take a step back and see it from their perspective. For example, if your girlfriend comes into your house and mumbles, doesn't look your parents in the eye, or acts like she isn't that smart or interesting, that's all your parents have to go by. It's not their faulty if they think you're dating a wet dishrag with no personality or a superficial flake. They don't see her in other contexts and situations where she may be more comfortable being herself. That means you need to give your parents the opportunity to get to know this person better. Invite your girlfriend to watch one of your sister's or brother's games so she can hang out with you all. More high pressure, but a possibility, is to invite her over to have dinner and watch a movie—but no PDA!

Sometimes people get together with someone to piss their parents off. If you're doing that, then at least admit to yourself that's what you're doing. Under the circumstances, it's not insanely illogical that your parents are acting the way they are. They're doing exactly what you knew they would do, and apparently wanted them to do. The important question to ask yourself here is, why are you doing this? Because the fact is, you're old enough to differentiate between making decisions that are good for you that your parents may not approve of and making decisions to spite them. If you're doing something to spite them, then they have just as much control over you as if you were dating someone they'd love.

If your parents are prejudiced, you're not going to change their minds overnight, or possibly ever. I don't want you to lie to them or sneak behind their backs, because when they catch you they can use the fact that you lied and deceived them to deflect taking responsibility for their own behavior and possibly blame the person you're dating for making you do it. I understand if you feel that you have no choice, but ideally you need to be up-front.

How do you do that? By being more mature than they are. You're going to say to them something like, "Mom, Dad, I love you and respect you" (even if you're not feeling that way, trust me, just say it). "I need to be honest with you because that's how you've raised me" (again, just say it). "I'm dating Katya." If they don't know Katya, then say, "She's Mexican. I don't want to sneak behind your back because I'm dating someone who's different than we are, but I also want to make sure if I bring her to the house that she's treated with respect."

If your parents push back by denying that they're racist (or homophobic)—"We just want what's best for you"—your answer is, "What's best for me is that we have an honest, respectful relationship." If they can't handle that, then go ahead and date Katya, but don't bring her around—keep your personal life separate from your home life. Don't lie, but keep your parents on a need-to-know basis. As in, they have the right to know where you are, and you must obey curfew and other family rules regarding your safety.

No matter what anyone else thinks, remember that any relationship is going to come with some serious highs and serious lows. While you may be lucky enough to be with someone who really makes your life better, it probably won't always be that way. You may have no idea why you've fallen for someone, you may know the relationship isn't good for you, but you still can't shake how you feel. One of the weirdest things about being in love is that sometimes that's not a good enough reason to be in a relationship with someone. It seems like that should be enough, but it's not. What's equally important is that you aren't making each other crazy or miserable. That's what it really comes down to. No matter what you're officially calling your relationship, how do you make each other feel? Is it worth it?

CHAPTER SEVENTEEN

BETRAYAL, BREAKUPS, AND REVENGE

A couple of months ago I broke up with my girlfriend. She was the first girl I had ever fallen in love with. I had always told myself that love wasn't possible in high school and it was simply infatuation with this girl. We immediately hit it off, and after a month and a half, I knew that I loved her. We kept going until I found out she cheated on me. But she didn't just cheat on me once. She cheated on me with three people. I ended it with her, without ever cursing or yelling at her. I simply ended it and haven't talked to her since. To this day I never understood why she did it. I treated her like a princess. I was a junior, and she was a freshman (not tooting my own horn), but I'm a good-looking guy, and frankly, people didn't even know why I went for her because I could have done better. But yet I loved her. I still can't fall asleep many nights just thinking about it. I've done what most guys try to do to get over the past girlfriend and hooked up with a couple of other girls, and that hasn't helped at all. I try to forget her or push her out of my head, but that doesn't work. I feel empty, and that sounds so lame and stupid, but it's true. I honestly feel like I'm missing something. Don't get me wrong. I don't love her anymore. Actually, I despise her with every fiber of my body, but for some reason it won't stop hurting when I think about it. How do I get over this girl? —Dylan, 17

How was Dylan going to get over his ex? My answer to him applies to anyone who has been betrayed.

1. You can't control who you fall for or why. Honestly, it could be pheromones (the way the person

smells).

2. You can't force yourself to stop having feelings for someone, even if that person did something really shitty to you. This isn't because you're stupid or blinded by love or lust. Most likely, it's because the person had some really good qualities and that was the reason you fell for him or her. It just so happens that this person also has some other qualities that can really bring you down.

3. You can love someone who doesn't deserve it.

4. The more you deny (1), (2), and (3), the longer it will take you to get over the person.

5. When you see this person, remind yourself of (1), (2), (3), and (4). Say them in your head and then repeat them.

Any guy in this situation also needs two more things: backup and an understanding of the dynamics between you so you'll be more likely to recognize the danger signs if you ever fall for someone like this again. It's like a hugely extended SEAL.

1. Backup (as in a Wingman consistent with the original definition): You need one friend you can tell how you feel. This person is a friend who will listen to you especially when you're feeling bad about it or weak. He won't make fun of you, tell you to just get over it, or ever talk about it in public. This person will also protect you from making bad decisions. For example, he'll stop you from doing something stupid like getting back together with her or getting into a fight with a guy she's flirting with at a party. If you're determined to drink (which obviously isn't a good idea), your backup will at

least make sure you get home safely.

2. Understanding the dynamics so it's less likely to happen again: One of the reasons Dylan struggled with all these emotions and couldn't get over his ex-girlfriend was because he never told her how angry he was. I understand why he didn't—he didn't want to give her the satisfaction of knowing he was angry and hurt—but the problem with this strategy is that it doesn't take into account that emotions can't just be told to behave and go away. Instead, they fester. All the anger, the feeling of betrayal, and the positive feelings too. Of course he's still thinking about it all the time. That's why the backup and the mantra are so important.

One more thing about the girl if you're ever in Dylan's position. I don't want you to feel sorry for her, but at least understand why she acted this way. A girl who hooks up with three guys while she's technically with someone, especially as a freshman, usually has some significant issues. Like she needs validation from guys and no matter how much she gets it'll never be enough. That also means she's pretty good at getting and holding a guy's attention. I don't just mean the way she looks. I mean I wouldn't be surprised if she was very good at making you feel like you were the most important person in the world. A girl who struggles with self-esteem can do that almost on autopilot.

Oh yeah, and get over the princess thing. I know ... I'm a broken record.

CHEATING AND MAKING AMENDS

I cheated on my girlfriend. She confronted me about it, and I owned up to what I did. I feel that SEAL could help me. But what should I tell her? I want to let her know that I really like her and that I screwed up and have no excuse. What would you want to hear in her position, and how could I make it clear that I want to be with her right now? — Tom, 16

Cheating is lying with your actions. Anyone in this girl's position wants to hear that you're sorry and that you actually mean what you say. You also understand that her trust is something you'll need to win back with your actions over time. Some girls are going to be very skeptical, like Sofi:

No matter how much I liked or loved a guy, I would never go back to him if he cheated. It may be because of my history of my dad cheating on my mom, so I have a bias, but I just would rather hurt alone than hurt more with someone who cheated. But for other girls out there that would go back, the guy would need to start all over with her. He can't try to go straight back to a relationship, he's gotta start at the beginning as friends, build trust. Then the ball is in the girl's court as to whether or not she'll give you another chance. Most likely, if she lets you be friends with her after the cheating and the breakup and lets you try and rebuild the "bridge of trust," then she's been thinking about trying again for a while and you've got a shot. —Sofi, 16

But there are a lot of girls who want to know why a guy cheated. This may seem strange, but many girls who read this chapter said something very similar to what Natalie and Lara said:

I think it's vital that the guy explain why he cheated. If my boyfriend cheated on me, I would be up all night figuring out why he did it, if something's wrong with me, what I did wrong, etc. People cheat for a reason, and that particular reason could cause problems later on. —Natalie, 15

When I got cheated on, I was mostly concerned about whether it was something I did (or didn't do) that was bothering him. Even if it had been "I don't find you attractive" or "You wouldn't have sex with me," it would have felt better than being in doubt about why it happened all the time. —Lara, 16

ARE THERE DIFFERENT LEVELS OF BEING A CHEATING SCUMBAG?

In fact, there are. While cheating is never right, there are gradations to it. So we've come up with a structure to give some sort of order and rank to the severity of cheating. The basic rule is this: the more emotions the cheating brings up, the more wrongdoing there is on the guy's part.

Level One: While any guy cheating on level one is still being unfaithful, he carries the least blame. To fall into this category, the guy must not have an actual relationship with either girl, and the girls can't know one another. (The douchebag will excuse his behavior by saying he's just dating.) Guys who cheat on this level are more careless than anything else: they are not consciously toying with the emotions of two girls, they just want to get some. If he works hard to stop the girls from meeting, then he's playing the girls. For example, you go to a party, all the girls you are currently hooking up with are there, and this causes you a great deal of stress. The majority of cheating attempts never make it past this level.

Level Two: Any guy who's in a relationship with one of the girls he is cheating on is cheating at this level. Still, the girls must not know about one another; if they do, the guy has moved to level three. Essentially, level two is for guys who are consciously choosing to deceive two girls but are not malicious enough to do it at level three.
Level Three: It doesn't get worse than level three; guys at

this level are fully aware that what they are doing is wrong, deceitful, and even cruel. If any guy is cheating with more than two girls, he's at level three, regardless of how involved he is with each girl. Also on level three are any guys who maintain two separate relationships with two separate girls. Last is the guy who two-times despite the fact that the girls know one another and are aware of each other's relationship with him. Many guys think that this isn't their fault because, if the girls know about one another, then he isn't to blame because they're consciously getting played. However, this is false. If a guy is aware that this is the case and still continues two-timing, he's acting out of line and manipulating the significant self-esteem issues of one or both of these girls to maintain the relationship.

IT'S NOT ALL ABOUT YOU

Obviously, you're not going to marry every person you date or fall in love with. So you might as well treat her well so the next guy she dates doesn't have to deal with a lot of crazy baggage because she dated you. Likewise, when you date crazy girls, wouldn't it be better if the guy she was with before you treated her well so she wouldn't be insane now?

BREAKING UP

> My girlfriend and I have been dating since the beginning of last summer, but I'm not feeling the same way I did in the beginning of our relationship. I want to break up with her, but she's so innocent, and I know it would kill her because she thinks we are going to get married eventually. I was wondering what the best approach to this is that will result in her being the least sad. —Kevin, 16

There's no way around it. Most relationships will end.

Someone's going to get dumped. If you're the one doing the breaking up, you have to be man enough to handle it honorably. Most guys don't want to do it honorably because it's a hugely stressful situation. It seems better to just run away, ignore the whole situation, and hope the other person somehow just gets the message and leaves you alone.

That's never how it happens. If you break up with someone, that person wants to know why. When you're on that side of things, you're going to want the same thing.

So you have to handle it well. If you don't, you're being cowardly and you're making the situation worse because at some point you're having the conversation.

The general reasons why guys want to break up are usually as follows:

- They have no idea why. They just woke up one morning and didn't like the other person like they did the day before.

- They realize they like someone else more.

- The other person wants to have sex or do more things sexually and they don't.

- They want to have sex or do more things sexually and the other person doesn't.

- One person is drinking, smoking, etc., and the other person doesn't approve and is becoming the parent in the relationship.

- The two of you are growing apart because you have different interests, you have different friend groups, you're leaving for another school, or you're going to college.

HORRIBLY IMMATURE WAYS TO BREAK UP

1. Changing your relationship status on any social

network from "In a Relationship" to "Single": No one should find out they got dumped by having their ex (who they don't even know is an ex yet) change their relationship status from "In a Relationship" to "Single." It's just cowardly and mean. Adding to the humiliation is the likelihood that five minutes later all the "friends" are going to see it and then post things on the rejected person's wall like "I'm soooooo sorry!" "When did it happen???????" and "WHATTTTTTT!!!!! U MADE THE CUTEST COUPLE!!!!!"

2. Breaking up by text: Too impersonal and disrespectful.

3. Breaking up through any form of instant-messaging: Instant-messaging isn't much better then texting and has a higher risk for sketchy behavior. You don't even know if you're really talking to the person you think you are, and even if they're there, they can leave you hanging. So there you are at your computer typing, "Hello? Are you still there?" right after saying, "I hope we can still be friends." Another big negative is that instant-messages are easy to copy, paste, and forward. Lastly, there's little personal investment on the part of the person doing the rejection because he or she could be doing ten other things at the same time.

4. Leaving a voice-mail on the other person's cell phone: At least with voice mail you've taken the risk that the other person may pick up, unless you deliberately call when you know that's unlikely. If that's what you're doing, then using voice-mail is like texting: your rejection lacks respect because you're not giving the other person a chance to have a conversation. The only good thing about

leaving a voice-mail message is that the other person can hear your voice and hear your emotions.

5. Sending an email: Email's benefit is that it can give the person being dumped the opportunity to read it on his or her own time and decide when to contact you back. However, email still isn't that great an option because people are more than capable of dumping someone meanly and then forwarding any part of the exchange to other people. Also remember that email can be misinterpreted, even at its best.

BREAKING UP LIKE A MAN

The best way to dump someone is to do it face to face, without other people around. A good time to break up is before a school-break so you don't have to see the person. A bad time to break up is on the person's birthday or Valentine's Day.

> *They [the person who gets dumped] are going to trash you no matter what, so timing is important here. Don't do this when you're about to see them in the next few hours, so don't do it in the middle of school. After school, like when they can go to practice and run out their frustration, is good. —Alex, 15*

You need to reject another person in a clear and direct manner. I know that's hard to do, but nothing about this situation is easy. By the very nature of what you're doing, you'll hurt the other person's feelings (unless that person didn't like you and was hoping, being too chicken, that you'd break up with him or her first).

WHAT IS THE BEST WAY TO TELL SOMEONE THAT A "FRIENDS WITH BENEFITS" RELATIONSHIP IS OVER?

You owe the other person a face-to-face conversation, but you have to pick your location carefully so you don't accidently hook up again. That means you're looking for a public yet private place. Talking in a private part of the library at school is good, or while walking home after practice. For those of you who go to schools with private music practice rooms, don't go there for this conversation because you know you're not getting out of there without hooking up. Once there, keep it short with something like, "Our relationship is too complicated for me, so I'd like to back off the hooking-up part."

GETTING DUMPED

When you get dumped, it's going to be painful on many levels. There are the actual feelings you have about the person, how the breakup occurred, and how things go in the immediate aftermath. Because in high school it can feel like everything is played out on a public stage.

Even if you don't like the person, it's still going to hurt your ego, you'll feel rejected, you'll be embarrassed when you see people for the first time after the breakup, and you'll think everyone knows. You'll be sitting at home and your relationship status has changed and people will ask you about it and/or have an opinion about it. You may fantasize about getting revenge or getting back together.

Having all of these feelings is completely fine. If you don't process the feelings you have, then various things can happen. You won't learn to recognize the warning signs the next time you're in a relationship. You can get so frustrated and cynical about being in intimate relationships that you close yourself off from the possibility of having good ones. You want to avoid being a stalker. You want to avoid making an ass of yourself. And with the public nature of the breakup—since social media now makes everything public—it's really understandable to feel like everyone knows your business.

WANTING TO GET REVENGE

It's completely, 100 percent understandable to want to get revenge on someone who broke your heart. Here are the three ways I usually see guys do it—and the reasons why none of them is a good idea.

1. Spread rumors: Guys who do this always talk about what she did or didn't do sexually or they disclose an embarrassing physical characteristic of hers that she wouldn't want anyone to know.

2. Publicize private communication: Guys who resort to this tactic forward any pictures of the girl in a bra or less that they've saved from the better times, spread secrets about her, so that she's humiliated or gets in trouble with her friends.

Pros for strategies 1 and 2: Feels good in the short term.

Cons for strategies 1 and 2: At some point you get the sinking feeling that you just did something that'll completely get out of your control and make her and her friends incredibly angry with you. Then you're stuck with the consequences—usually a group of high school girls publicly humiliating you as only a group of high school girls know how to do and/or getting in trouble with the school for cyberbullying your ex-girlfriend because you sent that pic of her in her bra. You decide which is worse.

3. Hook up with someone else.

Pros of strategy 3: Sometimes feels good and gives you a few moments to reaffirm that you're hot enough to get someone else.

Cons of strategy 3: So many. Sometimes even the actual hooking up is really weird and awkward. But that's just the beginning. Say you go out to a party and you're determined to hook up with someone else so you can throw it in your ex's face. If you're that determined (meaning desperate), this means your standards for who you get together with won't be stringent. And which girl is going to be the most receptive to your advances? Don't kid yourself. It's always going to be the girl who also has the lowest standards (Solo Cup Girl?) or is the least socially intelligent girl in the group. Remember, nothing is private in your life. Everyone knows what you're doing, including the girl you're hooking up with. This doesn't look cool to other people. It looks obvious. And one of those people who think you're being pathetic is going to text (possibly with photos) your ex with that exact commentary.

What if you're really going for maximum damage? What if you deliberately hook up with the one person who'll really bother your ex? Like someone she hates or a friend of hers? First, this will probably take significant effort on your part. Second, if you're successful, think about what happens. You just got rejected or dumped. Right now you hate your ex, but that may not always be the case. If you do this, you lose almost any chance of ever being friends with her again. But that's not all. Her other friends will hate you. If you're friends with these girls too, they're going to give you relentless crap. And forget about the possibility of hooking up with any of them in the near future. Plus, your guy friends aren't going to back you up if it means getting into trouble with these girls (which would reduce their chances of hooking up with any of them). Now, I could be wrong. It's possible the girls won't back each other up like I think they will—but do you want to take the chance?

WHEN YOU HAVE A STALKER

Change your password on your phone ASAP. That way, she can't find your phone "accidentally" (like when she gets it out of your backpack) and look through all your texts.

WHEN YOU NEED TO GET OUT OF THE RELATIONSHIP

Have you ever been attracted to someone who you didn't really like? Gone to a party and stayed later than you wanted to because a friend didn't want to leave? Gotten into a car with someone you knew you shouldn't be with but did it anyway? Most people have. It's not because people are weak or stupid. It's because, in the moment we make the decision, we come up with a logical reason to explain to ourselves that what we're doing makes sense.

This is pretty much the same reason why people find themselves in really messed-up relationships. In the moment, you want it to work out. No one's relationship deteriorates overnight. It happens gradually, after you've become invested in the relationship and the person. After you know the good sides of the person as well as the bad.

Think about it in your own life. By the time you're a sophomore, you usually know of at least one relationship that is so screwed up that it makes no sense to you why the person who's treated like dirt doesn't leave. You've seen someone have to check in with a girlfriend or boyfriend all the time, a relationship where the jealousy and possessiveness are out of control, where the abuser can put the abused person down by saying unbelievably mean things and then the abused person accepts it and even makes excuses for the abuser.

Everyone, no matter what their age, can get into a seriously messed-up relationship. Everyone includes guys your age. I know you most often hear that girls are the victims in abusive relationships and guys are the perpetrators, but here are some recent statistics that show a very different picture.[22]

- 44 percent of perpetrators of psychological teen dating violence (TVD) are male (56 percent are female).

- 76 percent of perpetrators of sexual TDV are male (24 percent are female).

The guys represented in these statistics are in an even more complicated situation than girls in their position. As I said in the beginning of this chapter, adults talk to girls about relationships. They give them books, the girls often read those books, and each book usually has a section on how to recognize and get out of abusive relationships. While it's really difficult for girls to talk about being abused, they don't feel stripped of their femininity when they do. Compare this to guys. As I've said, adults don't usually talk to them beyond cautioning them not to get girls pregnant and to avoid STDs. They don't usually give guys books on relationships, and even if they did, a lot of guys wouldn't read them. Unless they're in a class at school that covers relationship abuse and is taught by a teacher they think has a clue, guys are operating from a significant information deficit.

But all of that is nothing compared to the challenge of admitting in the first place that they're being abused: to a guy, this admission feels like literally being stripped of his manhood. It doesn't help that his friends are probably giving him shit about his girlfriend all the time.

_____

[22] Josephine Korchmaros, Michele Ybarra, Jennifer Langhinrichsen--- Rohling, Danah
Boyd, and Amanda Lenhart, "Perpetration of Teen Dating Violence in a Networked Society," Journal of Cyberpsychology, Behavior, and Social Networking, 2013.

If you ever find yourself with this problem, I want you to remember the following, no matter what:

1   Just because you're in love with someone doesn't mean you should be in a relationship with that person.

2   People who are abusive, no matter what their sex or age, are usually highly socially intelligent and manipulative. That means they know exactly what to say and do to control you and keep you in the relationship.

3   You're always entitled to your feelings and perspective. Abusers are amazingly good at getting you to question yourself. They'll literally make you doubt your sanity or grind you down so that you give in.

If you're on the outside looking in and getting increasingly frustrated at your friend because he won't leave an abusive relationship, or he keeps getting back together, I get it, but I want you to just consider the following. It's impossible to fall out of love overnight, even when the person you love treats you like dirt. Abusers can make you feel like the most special person in the world, so you tend to focus on their good qualities and minimize the bad, screwed-up, manipulating parts.

So guys can be both the abused and the abusers, and it doesn't do any good to argue about who is abused more, girls or guys. What matters is to remember that, when people are in these relationships, they need help. If you're in a relationship, do yourself the favor of checking whether you're over the line on either side. Here's a list of things to ask yourself either way to make sure you're not in an abusive relationship:

•   Are you consistently made to feel guilty if you want

to hang out with friends or family?

- Do you feel like you have to check in throughout the day about where you are and whom you've talked to?

- If you don't get back to the person right away, do you worry that he or she will get angry with you?

- Do you feel like your decisions are questioned to the point where you feel stupid?

- Have your friends tried to talk to you about their concern about your relationship not being good for you?

- After you've been made to feel really bad, does the other person tell you he or she loves you?

- Do you get angry if the other person doesn't consistently check in with you?

- Do you make negative comments about the other person's appearance or abilities?

- Do you feel like the other person's friends don't like you and are constantly trying to break you up the two of you?

- Have you expressed your feelings to those friends? How do you think those friends would describe your behavior during that communication?

- Did you answer yes to these questions and then immediately come up with logical explanations for your behavior?

GETTING INVOLVED

I have a friend who has been dating this girl for about a year. It's like they're married—the really f——ed-up kind. I like him, but he has a temper, and when he's angry, he can be pretty mean. But he's never mean to me like that. We're all in this group of friends of guys and girls, and the girls now hate him, and they aren't friends with her either. It's so complicated. He never hits her, but it's like she's his slave and he can do anything to her. I don't really get why she stays with him. He makes fun of her all the time, he puts her down. She has to tell him where she is all the time. It's crazy, but if you ever bring it up with him he just blows you off. Once in a while she tries to break up with him, but then she always goes back to him.
—Brent, 16

If you're friends with someone in an abusive relationship, it can feel like it's none of your business. So when do you get involved?

If you're friends with the abuser and it's a guy, what you're probably going to see is him saying something rude to his girlfriend. He's going to question her intelligence, he's going to say little cutting things to humiliate her in public. If you bring it up, he's going to minimize it ("Don't worry about it, we're just having a fight," "She's having her period," "She's insane, she's totally overreacting," "You know how she gets"), or he'll tell you it's none of your business. The way the guy abuser reacts pretty much depends on who's bringing it up—a girl or a guy. If it's a guy, he'll almost always take the minimizing approach, which is an attempt to get you on his side.

But if a girl speaks to him, that's when you'll usually see the guy abuser get incredibly angry at her (or at the group of girls who are bringing it up).

If you're friends with both the guy and the girls who want him to stop treating his girlfriend so badly, this can get to be a very tricky situation for you, because you may not want to come across as "siding" with the girls, who by this point can be pretty angry about the whole thing. Except it's not a matter of "siding with the girls," it's a matter of doing the right thing. If you have a friend who's like this, he's got serious issues with women and is never (or at least not in the near future) going to listen to a girl who is telling him to stop abusing his girlfriend.

What does make people change their behavior is their connection to each other. If you have a friend who's being abused, you can use SEAL to frame your words. If you have a friend who's doing the abusing, you can use SEAL to frame your words here as well.

Time to man up.

YOU (Explain): I really don't want to bring this up, but things with Carrie are out of hand.

FRIEND (Push-Back): I know, she's insane.

YOU (Explain): That's not the way I see it. You're not treating her like you should treat anyone, but especially a girlfriend.
FRIEND (Push-Back): Come on, you know how she is.

YOU (Explain): Making her feel stupid and checking up on her all the time isn't her fault.
FRIEND (Push-Back): This is ridiculous, and it's none of your business.

YOU (Affirm): You know we've been friends for years and I'd never say this to you unless I really believed it. And you're better than this. You're not that kind of guy.

FRIEND (Push-Back): Maybe I am.

YOU (Lock In): No, you're not. Look, this wasn't the easiest thing to bring up. I want you to be happy, but I'm also telling you that you need to treat Carrie better. For both of your sakes.

Abusers aren't out of control when they're mean. Even if they're drunk or high or if they're having a really bad day, they only unleash on people they can get away with abusing. They have complete control over who they go after and how. That's why you may never see this part of your friend's personality. But just because you don't see it doesn't mean it's not happening. Remember back in chapter two when I talked about situations where guys keep quiet even if their friend is totally making their life hell? The same thing is going on here, but it's even more intense. Things have to be bad enough to make you get over your embarrassment. If someone admits to being in an abusive relationship, believe that person. Even on the off-chance that the person is making the whole thing up and you end up feeling like a fool for being tricked, believing the person is still better than it is if he or she is telling the truth and you turn away and refuse to believe it.

WHAT CAN I SAY TO CONVINCE SOMEONE IN AN ABUSIVE RELATIONSHIP TO LEAVE?

Whenever someone is in an abusive relationship, it usually takes an extreme that opens up the person's eyes and makes them realize that they have to get out. My mother was in one, my aunt was in one, and I think my grandmother was in one too. If someone close to me is in an abusive relationship, like a sister or cousin, should I take the initiative and get her/him out of that situation? And if I see the abuser, should I try to make sure he never seeks out her/him again?
—*Victor, 17*

The problem with the strategy Victor proposes is that he actually would have no control over the situation. He can't force the abused person to stop seeing the abuser, and he can't stop the abuser from seeking out the victim.

Even if he could a particular guy, chances are excellent that if the abused person doesn't get help to figure out why she's getting into abusive relationships in the first place, she's going to find another relationship just like it. So will the abuser. If you need more help, go to the National Domestic Violence Hotline at thehotline.org.

THE DARK SIDE

You probably know guys who enjoy ruining people. Guys who will go out of their way to take advantage of someone's insecurity and inability to defend themselves and crush them. It doesn't matter who their victim is, whether it's an insecure girl who drinks too much or a guy on their team they want to mess with.

I'm not saying it's a guarantee that you'll walk into a room at some party one night and see a girl who is passed out and being passed around by a bunch of guys. I'm not saying it's an absolute certainty that you'll walk into a locker room and see some guy doing something really twisted to someone else (I've dealt with situations involving brooms, coke bottles, and keys). But these things happen. And if you aren't minimally prepared, you will be powerless. So here's what you should know.

If you walk into a terrible situation, you may have an unbelievable urge to do an about-face and walk away. One of the reasons why this happens is that your brain goes into autopilot. It doesn't want to deal with what it's seeing, so it commands your body to deny the reality that you just experienced. Another common response is to immediately convince yourself that whatever you're seeing isn't that bad and therefore there's nothing you need to do about it. For example, if you're accustomed to seeing people drunk or high at parties, when you see a really drunk girl being taken somewhere by a group of guys, it's easier to not take the situation seriously. Plus, no one takes anything seriously when they're drunk themselves. But the reality is, she may need your help. It doesn't matter what you think about her—whether you like her, whether she's annoying, what she looks like, her reputation, or whether she made a complete fool of herself earlier in the night. None of that matters. Your opinion of this person does not matter. The bottom line? This is a person in a bad situation. She isn't in a position to consent to what is happening to her. She needs help, and unfortunately for you, you're the chosen one. That doesn't mean you have to do it all by yourself, but you can't stand there and do nothing or go along with it.

No one wants to be in this position, but don't be mad at her. The only person you should be mad at is the asshole (or assholes) who put everyone in this situation.

So what do you do? If you really feel that you can't straight up say to him, "You have to stop," you can trick him. You figure out who the Mastermind is in the group and say something like, "Hey, the girl's friends are downstairs and have been looking for her. They're saying her dad is looking for her." This takes the focus away from the immediate circumstance and gets the job done without you having to say something like, "Gee, it looks like you're about to sexually assault this girl, and you need to stop!" Then help the girl get her away from these guys. By the way, you know it's not enough to say, "What if that was your mom or sister?" These guys don't care, plus think about that question for a moment. Is the only reason a person shouldn't be raped is because they're some guy's mother or sister? Don't girls and women, regardless of who they're related to, have the right to not be raped? Don't guys have the right not to be sexually assaulted or raped? And they're no one's mothers or sisters.

I also know that some of these guys could be your friends. They aren't horrible all the time. But why should being cool with you give them a pass to go after someone else? And if you have friends who are sending you pictures of doing any of this, and it looks like it's still happening, you need to communicate however you think is most effective,

"Stop what you're doing now." And then do whatever you think is best to stop what they're doing.

AFTER THE FACT

By the time you graduate from high school, you will probably know someone who has been sexually assaulted. It could be a friend, the girl sitting next to you in class, the guy on your team, or someone in your neighborhood. This is true for everyone. It doesn't matter how rich or poor you are, where you live, or what kind of school you go to. Chances are also pretty good that at some point you'll find out after the fact that someone you care about was involved in some way—either as a perpetrator, bystander, or victim. So, no matter how you look at it, you're going to have to deal with this.

If you know that someone (male or female) has been sexually assaulted in any way (as in, the person who participated in the assault used any part of their body or any kind of object)—this is what you do: Immediately, tell that person you believe him or her and you're so sorry this happened. Don't encourage revenge, but keep in mind that the person may want to report the assault later, even if not right now. If the person doesn't want to report the assault right away and is still wearing the clothes he or she had on during the assault but now wants to change, suggest that the clothes be put in a bag. They may contain important evidence.

Someone who has been assaulted also usually wants to take a shower. Like really wants to take a shower. They feel dirty and they want to do anything to feel clean and literally wash away what just happened to them. If there's any way to convince the person to report the assault first and then take a shower, that's very helpful if he or she decides to press charges later, because a shower would destroy important evidence.

If someone tells you a few weeks later about having been assaulted, you will still say something like, "I'm so sorry and I believe you." This person needs help processing what happened and what he or she wants to do about it, so this is absolutely the time when you figure out who is the adult in your life who can be entrusted with this information and who will get the right kind of help.

But again, there are a lot of adults who don't want to deal with this kind of problem. There are adults who will accuse the victim of always wanting attention, being drunk, or being stupid for being there. Other adults will try to convince the victim to "move on" or "put it behind you." These responses are about trying to convince the victim not to come forward so the adults don't have to hold the perpetrator accountable.

This is one of the reasons why there's so much pressure on the victim to not come forward in the first place, to minimize what happened, or to take back the report after making it. I've seen this happen so many times that I've lost count. A boy or a girl is assaulted by one of the guys no one wants to hold accountable. Within a few days, the kids at school are turning on the victim and anyone who supports the victim. The parents are saying, "It's just a fluke." And then everyone pretends it never happened.

You can be a part of stopping these completely messed-up situations from occurring. You can stop it if you walk into it like I described above. You can support the victim's rights, and you can hold the adults accountable if they blow off the problem by working with the one or two adults you can depend on. It may not work out perfectly, but at least the parents and administrators can't keep denying that the assault happened.

I'm asking you to think about this. I'm not accusing all guys of being rapists. But some are. One day you may find yourself in a position to do something about it. You are powerful. You may feel really nervous. Your other friends may not back you up. But the hero's moment is about realizing when something is wrong and then having the courage to try to stop it.

If you have any other questions, go to rainn.org. RAINN—which stands for Rape, Abuse, and Incest National Network—has a twenty-four-hour hotline that's private and anonymous.

CHAPTER EIGHTEEN

EXILE

My two friends and I were suspended for five days for drawing offensive things on a school map that was hanging in a school hallway. I'm not sure how it happened. I remember sitting with my friends and telling all these jokes, then someone just went up to the map and wrote "cocaine" on Colombia. I drew a fence on the border of Mexico and the US and a calculator under South Korea. I think part of the problem is that I didn't think about doing it, I just did it. I deeply regret what I did. But my parents are very upset. I haven't had a conversation with my parents for a week, and they won't look me in the eyes. My older brother is mocking me and making the whole thing more miserable. My friends say that my parents will eventually forget it and all will go back to normal. But it's the present, not the future, and it quite frankly sucks. I've been reading a lot of novels because it makes time go by quicker. — Evan, 14

Sometimes you mess up and your life changes in an instant. Overnight you don't feel welcome in places that were your home away from home, like school or your team. The life you had seems to have been forever taken from you, and you have no idea how to get it back. You've been exiled.

We've already spent a lot of time on what to do if you screw up with your friends. This chapter is specifically focused on what to do if you screw up with adults (like your parents, coaches, teachers, and school administrators) and your actions damage your public reputation. It'll show you how to go through a process that will make you feel better.

There are two different types of mistakes we'll address. One, you did something incredibly stupid but didn't realize it at the time. Two, you knew exactly what you were doing and your cover-up failed. The benefit of being ignorant until the ax comes down is that you spend no time dreading getting caught. The drawback is that you'll probably have a very unpleasant conversation with your parents, who'll ask, "What the hell were you thinking?!" and feeling like an idiot, all you'll be able to say is, "I don't know."

On the other hand, when you know what you did was wrong, there's no period of blissful ignorance. You'll be such an anxious mess that your performance in all aspects of your life will suffer, you won't sleep well, and the most innocent comment by anyone will throw you into paranoid delusions. It's truly a horrible way to live.[23]

Ignorant or not, the moment you find out you're in trouble the most common reaction is to go into cover-your-ass mode. Any smart parent or school administrator knows this. That's why they ask you some variation of the following, "Can you tell me why you think I asked you to meet with me today?" (administrator) or, "I just talked to Brian's dad. What do you think he told me?" (parent). You, on the other hand, are trying to figure out how much they know so you can do damage control. While it's totally understandable to cling to the illusion that you can limit what they know, it's not worth it. Don't lie. Haven't you seen enough stupid politicians try that and make things so much worse for themselves? Don't be that guy. Even on the off chance that you do successfully conceal what you did from everyone else forever, you'll always carry around the fear of discovery.

---

[23] The only person who does something wrong and really doesn't worry about it is either a sociopath or someone who feels that he's entitled to be above the law (either the law of the land or the law of his school or family). I'm going to assume that this kind of offender won't be reading this chapter anyway.

The most important thing to remember is that the way you respond determines if and when people will regain their respect for you. If you refuse to take responsibility for your actions, if you blame other people, if you get your punishment but make a point of telling other guys how stupid the person is who disciplined you, you're being a spoiled brat. If you try to get revenge on the person you believe to be responsible for your getting caught, you're being an immature, vindictive bully.

If you do admit what you did and how it hurt people around you, you will regain the good reputation you once had or even build a better reputation. But that's not easy to do because it requires a lot on your part that you may be reluctant to do.

Before I go any further, I want to discuss an assumption I'm making, and it's a big one. I'm referring here to mistakes that hurt or offend other people. Obviously, there are other things that can get you into trouble with adults. For example, if you cheat on a test because you're overwhelmed, it's true that you're breaking a rule, but it needs to be addressed in a way that considers why you felt so desperate. If you cheat because you're lazy and you get caught, don't play the overwhelmed card and manipulate people into feeling sorry for you. Either get off your butt and do the work or admit to yourself that you aren't interested right now in challenging yourself.

If you get caught violating a technology or alcohol and drug policy, you may think the rules are stupid or unfairly applied, but you agreed to those rules when you became a participating member of that community. That means that if you violate those rules, you accept the punishment and you don't try to get your mom or dad to get you off. By the way, if you're showing up to school high or drunk or carrying alcohol or drugs in school, you have bigger problems than getting suspended.

When you're told your punishment, don't protest and don't lie. All you need to say is, "I'm really sorry I [did whatever you did], and I need to apologize for it. I'm going to take responsibility for my actions. May I be excused?" Under no circumstances should you walk out of that meeting and pretend that you're blowing off what just happened in that room. If you do, the administrator will know and it will come back to bite you in the butt. Your behavior will convince her that you're not "getting it," which can increase your punishment.

When you get home or when you see your parents, repeat exactly what you said to the administrator and then tell them you'd like to be left alone to think about what happened. Then go upstairs, put your headphones on, and allow yourself to feel everything you've been keeping inside.

Your feelings could be so jumbled together that it's hard to sort them all out. Here are some of the most common in this situation: embarrassment, anger that you got caught, fury at someone else for somehow getting you involved or selling you out, shame, denial, and paranoia that everyone is talking about you behind your back or that this one mistake will forever damage your future. These are all understandable feelings to have.

Now, as unpleasant as it is, you have to be honest. First with yourself and then with the people who were impacted by what you did. The best way I know to do that is to write it down. Writing it down forces you to reflect on what you really, truly feel. So write it down and then look at what you've written. Do you believe what you've written, or are you coming up with excuses? Reading what you wrote, you might see that you're really angry with yourself for something like getting manipulated by a friend or not seeing that your actions would hurt others. So take your time. (You probably have that time anyway.) Sleep, read books, listen to music (if that hasn't been taken away from you), and stare at the walls. Then read what you wrote again and change whatever you need to so that whatever is on that paper best reflects your truth.

Now it's time to make amends. Ironically, the sooner you publicly hold yourself accountable the sooner you'll feel better. First, you have to say something to your mom and dad. If you want to, you can write a letter to your parents. Here are the basic concepts this letter should include:

- You're really sorry for [whatever you did].

- You recognize what you did that was wrong and you're not making excuses for it.

- You realize that your future actions have to reflect your words now.

- You will make your parents proud in how you handle it.

WHAT IF MY PARENTS FREAK OUT?

I've talked to a lot of guys whose parents make the problem worse by freaking out when they find out their son messed up. Variations on these reactions are pretty common:

"I have failed as a parent."

"I can't believe my child would do something like this. I'd totally understand if Sally's kids did this, but not you, not my kids."

I know this comes across as your mom or dad saying that this one thing you did cancels out every good thing you've ever done. It can also be really hard to take when a parent says that all of their years of parenting have led to this "failure," meaning you. Part of you may feel rejected or angry at them for being so dramatic.

The reasons parents flip out like this is because they're overwhelmed by their embarrassment, anger, and anxiety. They probably feel really worried and confused about you.

It's also possible that you've been giving them pretty obvious signs that things were running off the rails before but they chose to ignore them. So when they do have to face the problem, they're dealing not only with what's happening right now but with all the factors that led up to it — like their own denial. They also could be angry that you aren't representing the family well, which doesn't necessarily mean they're being superficial. Instead, it really could be that they're upset that you didn't act according to their values.

Without excusing the really bad and ineffective things parents can do, just recognize why this situation is so painful for them as well as for you. The whole thing makes them feel like they've been bad parents, makes them worry about what people think about your family, and makes them worry that maybe they don't know you as well as they thought they did. It rocks their world.

Or they could miss the opportunity to be self-reflective. Let's go back to Evan's family.

> *My brother and parents would make jokes at every possibility, but the worst time was dinner because I can't text, listen to music, or do anything other than stare at the table and wait for it to pass. They'd joke about how "I'm on vacation, and what we need is a map around the house. Oh wait, Evan will be tempted to draw on it."*

To be clear, what Evan did was wrong. It was racist, and insensitive. But what his family did was worse in one very important way. They were intentionally humiliating him by ridiculing him. It's ironic, but their response provides some explanation (not a justification) for Evan's actions. Nevertheless, this is a critical life crossroad for Evan. Sometimes you learn values in your family that are wrong and don't serve you well in the larger community. The challenge any guy in Evan's situation has is learning to accept the family you were born into but sometimes decides to conduct yourself differently.

Evan isn't alone by any stretch. Many of the guys who've helped with this book are in similar situations. It's painful because it's your family, and some part of you really loves them or at least wants them to be good people. Remember, people are messy. Just like we're talking about with guys, no one should be defined by one thing they do. If you repeat disrespectful or dishonest actions, however, at what point do you become a dishonest person?

By the way, if someone close to you (a sibling, a best friend) is rubbing your mistake in your face, take note that this person is going through a phase of being horrible. Hopefully it will pass soon. But in the meantime, don't let that person bring you down even more than you already are. You may want to say something like, "This is hard enough as it is without you making it worse. Obviously, I can't control if you're going to be a dick about this or not, but this is actually hard for me, so it would make it a little easier if you laid off. If you were in my situation, I'd never do this to you. Not just because it's wrong but because you're my brother."

WHAT ABOUT THE FOLKS AT SCHOOL?

Here's a sample letter you can use when you write your own letter to the school administrator. I'm giving this to you only to help you get started. You have to make it your own to mean anything to you or the people you're addressing.

> *I'm really sorry for writing those things on the school map. I can imagine it's hard for you to believe that I couldn't figure out that it was wrong before I did it, but for some reason that I don't understand right now, I didn't. I know the rules of the school, and I also know what the school stands for, and what I did was against that. I know it's not just about what I say*

but about what I do from now on. I'd like to take responsibility for my actions by apologizing to the class. I hope to gain your trust back one day, but I know it will take time.

Sincerely,
You

HAVE I RUINED MY FUTURE?

In the United States, being disciplined in high school can be included on your college or university application. In other countries, it's almost never done. So if your applying to schools in the United States, this could be an issue for you. I've had countless conversations with school administrators about this issue. I promise you, if you truly take responsibility for your actions, your teachers and administrators will explain to college admissions offices what happened by mentioning the positive things you've done and what you learned after the event. Maybe this was the wake-up call you needed to get your head on straight.

Sometimes a college will defer acceptance until a student has a chance to prove that he's learned from an experience. If this happens to you, it can feel like you've failed. I know parents can sometimes flip out in these situations and not see the larger picture. I promise you that you're better off taking a step back, figuring out what course of action is right for you, enrolling in the school later, after you've taken some time to think and get yourself together. Yes, I know this is easy to say when you're not in the middle of all your friends getting into school or you're facing the wall of your parents' disappointment, but if you don't stop and figure out how you got into this situation, you're doomed to repeat it, and each time the stakes get higher.

These experiences are hard. "Excruciating" is a better word. This is truly one of the moments when you learn what kind of person you are. You get to decide what that means. No one else. But one thing I know for certain. The moment you decide to face what you did and make amends is the moment you begin to transform the experience into one that helps you regain your sense of honor.

CHAPTER NINETEEN

PROBLEMS WITH AUTHORITY

At some point in a guy's life, his mother will get mad at him. I'm not talking about the kind of mad like when she yells at you for the tenth time to stop playing video games and do your homework. I mean mad like you think it would be a good idea if you moved to another planet for a while until she calms down. If you have this experience, here are some suggestions to follow.

1   Pick up all the dirty clothes off your floor and put it in a laundry basket (not under your bed or in the closet, that doesn't count).

2   Go through all the rooms of the house and pick up all your dirty socks and put them in the same laundry basket or laundry room (whichever is closer).

3   Set the table. Without being asked.

4   Spray your shoes with shoe deodorant spray or powder.

5   Take the dog for a walk and give her food and water. Without being asked.

6   Don't fight in the car with your brother or sister and don't scream, "Shotgun!"

7   Don't play music in your room at the highest volume it can take without breaking. When you're in the car with your mom, ask her what she wants to listen to. Don't make a face or complain when it's not your station.

8　Tell her she looks pretty.

9　Admit when you lied.

10　(To be used in extreme circumstances) Write any thank-you notes you owe to any grandparents, aunts, or uncles. On paper. Not by email.[24] It doesn't have to be pages long. A few lines are all you need to write. After you're done, casually ask her for the addresses you need. You can also ask your dad, because as soon as you leave the room he'll tell your mom. If she asks you why you want your grandmother's address, you say, "I realized I never thanked her for my birthday present." Then immediately walk out the door and go put your letters in the mailbox. Just turn around and pick her up if you hear her fall down in shock.

Note: Don't do all of these things at one time! It's important to space them out. Otherwise, your mother may become so suspicious that she'll think you've done something really really wrong, and then she'll completely freak out.

SPEAKING OUT WHEN YOU'RE BEING SHUT DOWN

When I was angry at my dad, it felt like my head was ten times bigger than my mouth could move. There was no way I could consolidate everything into one sentence. There was so much pressure to make that one all-meaningful sentence that would change his mind or [make him] listen to me. But there's no way to do that, so I just shut down. — Charlie, 24

---

[24] At the least, thank the person by phone, but the thank---you note is the gold standard.

I'm not sure why so many dads forget what it was like to be a guy your age. It's especially strange because so many of them like to start conversations with you like this:

"When I was your age ..."

"When I played football (soccer, etc.) ..."

"When I was applying to colleges ..."

And do these conversations sound familiar?

DAD: Did you put out the trash?

YOU: Yes, I did.

DAD: Is the lid on the trash can?

YOU: Yes.

DAD: Is it on the right side of the driveway? Is it off the curb?

DAD: Did you mow the lawn?

YOU: I'm getting to it.

DAD: ???????? ... Did you weed-whack? Did you wrap the hose the right way? Did you put the gas cap back on when you refilled the mower?

Some parents don't seem to stop until they catch you falling down on the job. Then they tell you you're lazy, unfocused, or immature. Sure, you're probably some of those things occasionally, but not all the time. In my experience, it's much more likely that you have a lot going on, it's hard to keep up with everything, and in many ways you're under a lot of pressure. What's so weird about this dynamic is that most parents don't seem to have any idea how irritating they are or to realize that you stopped listening to them a long time ago. What's even weirder is that almost all parents really want a good relationship with their son. But that desire gets lost if they forget or doesn't believe there needs to be overall mutual respect between the two of you. Combine that with the fact that you live under their roof and understandably wants you to do your part, and you're going to have major power struggles.

The power struggle can be about anything. Big things. Little things. Things you can anticipate, things you can't. Not all of you have a controlling parents, but for those of you who do, it's really important to know how to handle yourself the best way possible. Instead, what usually happens is that you get angry and bottle up your rage. When it finally comes out and explodes, you look stupid or immature, and that feeds into their image of you. You need to be more strategic here: how do you formulate an argument and avoid either being accused of talking back or shutting down because you don't know how to talk to him?

> *I came home from practice, and I had tons of homework to do. So then my dad tells me to take out the trash. I say, "Fine," but I ask if my brother can help out by taking out the recycling. My dad's response is, "Fine, you can take out the garbage for a month." It's just so stupid. Everything is a power trip with him, and I can't say anything without him doing something to make my life worse. —Mark, 18*

This taking-out-the-trash example is great because even though it was technically a small issue, it created a buildup where Mark felt like his father was relentlessly beating him down. If you're in this position, your resentment builds, your anger builds, and the next thing you know you want to beat the crap out of your dad. If you can manage yourself well in this situation, I think you'll be pretty much set for handling yourself with anyone. I'm serious. No one gets under your skin the way a family member does.

I'd met Mark after an evening parent presentation at his school. Earlier in the day, he had attended my student presentation and come back so he could ask me how to get his dad to listen to him. For the next twenty minutes, Mark, two other boys, and I hung out and strategized how to SEAL it with his dad. Here's what we came up with:

Stop and Set Up: There's absolutely no point in trying to argue with your dad in the moment. Anything you say will be taken as you being lazy, uncooperative, and ungrateful. So stop your work, take out the trash, and go back to your work. While you're taking out the trash, instead of focusing on how much you hate your dad, focus on when is the best time to talk to him. Some of the guys I talked to said it's when their dad is watching TV. Your Setup is to wait until he's watching TV and then mute it during the ads. That means you have approximately three minutes and thirty seconds to talk to him.

Another part of your Setup is deciding if your mom should be there when you do this. What are the pros and cons of your mom being there? Usually, the pro is that she can see that you're handling this maturely. The con is that she may defend your dad or make excuses for him, and then you'll get really angry at your mom. You need to decide what you think is best. My bet is that it's usually better without your mom.

Last thing in your preparation. You have to be willing to admit your part in it. On the face of it, taking out the trash is a reasonable request. And it's possible that you've occasionally said you'd do it, had every intention of doing it, but forgot. Or you and your parent have very different definitions of "soon" and "in a minute." Be honest too: if you have a history of not following up, then you have to acknowledge that this is part of the problem. Here's the rest of the SEAL:

YOU (Explain): Dad, I want to do my part around the house, but when you asked me to take out the trash, I was in the middle of trying to figure something out with my homework. I wasn't trying to be disrespectful when I asked you if it could wait [or if your younger brother could help you].

DAD (Push-Back): Well, I need you to do your part around the house, and I'm not going to take any excuses.
YOU (Acknowledge): Dad, I realize that I've been forgetting to do things, so I'm working on it.

(Or, if you've been making a conscious effort to be more on top of things before you talk to him): I realize I've been slacking, so I've been trying to do better. That's why I waited to talk to you until I'd done that.[25]

A few days later, Mark wrote back:

> *I had the talk with my dad just like you said I should, and it worked out really well. That one sentence made my week. I wish I could show you a picture of Mark, but suffice it to say he's a big guy and I'm guessing his dad is about his size. Clearly, any kid who waits for hours to ask an adult he's only met in a student assembly really cares about how he's getting along with his dad. But look, I know you may try this with your dad (or whoever is coming down on you like Mark describes or worse), and the person may not be cool about it. Your biggest challenge in this situation is that this kind of dad often believes that the way to teach you responsibility is to relentlessly ride you. It's his justification for acting like a dick and bullying you. Here's the thing. He's wrong. It's*

---

[25] You can do this two times max. After that, you're going to lose credibility.

actually possible to raise a son into a responsible
man without being a raving asshole. Having said
that, don't expect him to change. For whatever
reason, he's invested in being the way he is.

But one day you'll get out from under his roof, and
obviously this isn't the legacy you'd like to carry on. When
you're in a situation where you have power and authority,
you have to watch how you exercise both, especially when
you perceive that someone is challenging you. If you don't
get some self-awareness on this, you'll easily fall back on
being like your dad, because that's what you grew up with.
It takes effort to be a different kind of man. You have to
pay attention to the way you're reacting and be honest
with yourself. You have to have the courage to be a
different man because it's easy to be a bully who lashes
out whenever he thinks his authority is questioned.

YES, OFFICER, IS THERE SOMETHING WRONG?

You're driving with your friends, having a great time.
You're only going a little over the speed limit. Or your town
has a curfew, and you didn't leave your friend's house in
time, so you get in your car to drive home and start rushing
because you don't want to get into trouble with your
parents. Or you desperately want to see your girlfriend, so
you wait until your parents are asleep and then sneak out
the back door. It's awesome to be outside enjoying the
night air—until a police car slowly pulls up beside you . . .

As a guy, you inevitably at some point will be stopped
or pulled over by a police officer. Your experience is going
to vary a great deal based on what community you live in,
your race, your socio-economic class, and how well known
your family is known in the community (for better or worse).
To help you manage the situation most effectively and
minimize the problems you'll get yourself into, I've asked
Officer Lindsey Wilson of Virginia, a police officer with over
sixteen years of experience, to explain the dos and don'ts

when interacting with law enforcement officers (LEO) and what to do if you run into an officer who's a bully or a racist.

TOP FIVE THINGS NOT TO DO WHEN SPEAKING WITH A LAW-ENFORCEMENT OFFICER

1. Don't tell the officer what he/she must do. LEOs are trained to take charge of the situation, restore calm, and fix the initial problem . . . then leave. LEOs are controlling by nature, and they're also human beings with egos and faults. They don't like being told what they must do. Officer Wilson says, "If you tell me I have to let you go on your way because you know someone important, I guarantee I'm giving you a ticket after I take my sweet time writing it."

2. Don't tell the officer what he/she can't do. On the flip side, a big and common mistake is telling a LEO, "You can't arrest me." You're practically placing yourself in handcuffs and ensuring yourself a ride to the pokey when you make this statement.

3. Don't insult the officer. "Don't you have anything better to do?!" This classic statement always leads to a negative experience. Officer Wilson's response to this question is usually, "No, this is what I do. I write tickets, I stop you from parking in the handicapped space, and I interact with the public while enforcing the law. No, there are no unclosed murder cases I'm working on, and no, I'm not assigned any drug kingpin cases . . . so pretty-please-with-sugar-on-top move your car out of the fire lane in front of the grocery store and park it in the vast empty parking lot like everyone else."

4. Don't assume a LEO is uneducated. Many LEOs attended college and earned degrees. Many more are prior military with years of public service. Some people think that LEOs aren't intelligent and that it's important to remind the LEO that he/she is a public servant and that, in a figurative or perhaps literal sense, "I pay your salary!" Trying to make yourself feel better by degrading others is never a winning hand.

5. Don't be physically aggressive. Never become physically aggressive in posture, gesture, or movement when dealing with a LEO. As Officer Wilson explains, "Don't stand behind me. Don't point to my gun or reach your hand toward it. If I step back, don't continue to step forward toward me. Don't become angry and try to fight me. The more you win the more you lose. I have a pretty good idea how many LEOs are in my sector, my county, and the county next to me. If I press a button on my radio, they will all come to help me. ...plus some guys and girls alike are happy to say, 'You can't make me . . . I don't have to . . . my parents pays your salary . . . and don't you have anything better to do?' I recall one sixteen-year-old who puffed up his chest and came at me when I wouldn't allow him to enter a high school basketball game. Luckily for him and me, his mother tackled him before he reached me. The bottom line is a reality that we all knew at one point but may have forgotten somewhere along the way. LEOs are empowered to use force to achieve their objectives. 'You can't touch me!'. . . Well, actually I can . . . and I will if I must."

TOP FIVE THINGS TO DO/SAY WHEN YOU ENCOUNTER A LAW ENFORCEMENT OFFICER

"Every fight, drunk in public, domestic abuse, loud noise complaint, accident in the home, dissolved friendship, and tragic occurrence seems to start with a can of beer or a margarita," Officer Wilson observes. "And it's not that you have to be drunk to say something stupid. Maybe your girlfriend only had one twenty-two-ounce beer when she blurted out that your best friend was hot. Perhaps you asked, 'Do you want to dance?' but her ears heard, 'You look fat in those pants!' The fog of her vodka-and-cranberry can be blurry indeed. I've never broken up a fight where intoxicated people started arguing over the Higgs-Boson particle versus Jesus Christ, or the dangers versus the benefits of nuclear proliferation. People get drunk and stupid. A lot."

It should hardly come as a surprise, then, that Officer Wilson's first rule for speaking to law enforcement is:

1   Be sober. "Really. You would be surprised at how many people end up talking to LEOs when they're drunk. Including the people who call to complain about something and have an officer respond to their home." In Officer Wilson's experience, these people "are oftentimes drunk themselves. The number-one rule when dealing with a cop is to be sober, and act sober."

2   Be polite even if it's hard. "Your perception of the police often depends on where you live," Officer Wilson notes. "Just saying the words 'New Jersey State Trooper' sends a wave of fear through many people's body. Or perhaps 'Fulton County, Georgia, Sheriff's Office' bothers another. Immigrants new to the United States bring their

own fears when the specter of blue lights flashing in the rearview mirror becomes reality. But no matter what, be polite. It seems easy enough, but when you're stopped and speaking to a LEO, there's often a film reel of thoughts, fears, and prejudices going through your mind as the officer is standing in front of you. It's important to put all of your thoughts behind you and simply be polite."

3   Be direct. "If you're asked a direct question," says Officer Wilson, "answer the direct question. LEOs generally get frustrated when they have to sift through a lot of meaningless backstory that isn't relevant to the case at hand. Stick to the facts. Politely."

4   Stay put. Officer Wilson asks that you "appear calm and refrain from sudden movement. A LEO doesn't need you to reenact the crime or wave your arms like you're a signal officer on an aircraft carrier. Keep your hands out of your pockets. A LEO will appreciate your hands on the steering wheel where he/she can see them, or your feet firmly planted on the ground with your hands by your waist. Motionless."

5   Be honest. "We all lie to ourselves a little bit. I'm bald," Officer Wilson admits, "but I still brush my hair. Much to my wife's horror, I rinse and repeat with the shampoo in the shower. Sure it's a waste of soap, but I like the way the $20 bottle of Biolage shampoo smells. So what? I'm not hurting anybody, and if my follicles are trying to regenerate on my thirty-nine-year-old pate, then more fragrant power to them! Lying is common, and for most people it's a problem we live with and keep under control."

It's a different matter if you're talking to a law enforcement officer. "When a LEO's standing before you," Officer Wilson advises, "be honest. Don't lie or you're cooked. Don't think they won't find out. You don't have to vomit out a crazy story that runs around the truth. Tell the facts as you know them and purge yourself of fear and uncertainty. LEOs won't judge you … at least not immediately … in your presence. LEOs place a very high value on honesty, so play into their value system."

WHAT IF I'M DEALING WITH A RACIST OR GENERALLY HORRIBLE POLICE OFFICER?

In Officer Wilson's opinion, "Racist cops are inexcusable. If you do encounter a racist cop or a cop who behaves inappropriately, deal with it later. Don't get caught up in the moment and fight the authority. Later. Complain later!"

WHAT IF ONE COP PULLS ME OVER AND THEN SUDDENLY THERE ARE TWO MORE CARS SURROUNDING MY CAR?

Officer Wilson explains what's generally happening in this situation. "One cop marks out on the radio with a suspicious person. Two other cops in the same sector aren't doing anything, so they swing by to check it out. No big deal to the cops. For the juvenile, however, it's a really big deal. One cop with a uniform and flashing blue lights is huge … but two or three?!! Something wild must really be going on. Well, not really. Not usually. The right reason is for officer safety purposes, but it could be that the other cops are often bored on a slow Tuesday evening." But if you follow the guidelines Officer Wilson provided earlier in this section, "you'll get through with the least amount of problems."

CONCLUSION

Writing this book in some ways has been similar to what I've been asking of you: do things that scare the crap out of you where there's a high probability of failure and maybe even public embarrassment. I can't say for sure that this book will be a success, but I wrote it because I believe that you deserve to reach your potential—whatever that happens to be. You need to give yourself permission to admit what you really feel and think. Because if you say, "It's fine, don't worry about it, it doesn't matter," often enough, you start to buy what you're selling. It becomes your identity and creeps into your soul.

You have the right to be passionate about the things you care about. Being passionate is the key to being successful. I'm not defining this as going to a particular college or university, getting a certain degree, or making a lot of money. It's about working for what you want, apart from other people's expectations, baggage, and opinions about what they think you should be doing. You have to care enough about your future to take the steps now to actually give yourself a choice. So it's not, what do you do? Instead, it's, what do you contribute? What do you create? Who are you connected to? When you can answer these questions in real ways, you've broken out of the box and you are the man you want to be.

ACKNOWLEDGMENTS

Ryan: Rosalind, are you going to put our names in the book?

Me: Yes, you'll be in the acknowledgments.

Ryan: All of us? You promise?

Me: Of course. But we need to talk about what I sent you last week to review. What did you think?

Will: It's OK.

Me: What does OK mean? Charlie: It's fine.

Me: Really, what does that mean? Connor: Well...

Awkward silence filled the room, which was really odd because up to that point these guys wouldn't stop talking.

Me: Guys...come on. Tell me what you think.

Will: We don't really use the term "wingman" like you do. We only use it when we want to hook up with a girl and our buddy helps us out.

Me: Why didn't you tell me this before? That's all I've been writing for the last two weeks. I've sent you so many emails, and no one said anything.

Fifteen pairs of shoulders shrugged.

Me: Let me explain something to you. As Ryan just asked, your name will now be in this book. My name is going to be on the cover of this book. You're now a part of this, and if I get this wrong because you won't tell me what you really think, then I'll look like an asshole and you'll look like an asshole.

Jordan: Well...the whole chapter was sort of boring. Kennedy: Yeah, I didn't really get it.

Me: Thank you. Now we're getting somewhere.

I doubt many writers threaten to publicly embarrass the people who are helping them. And I realized shortly after this conversation that the boys had to trust me to tell me when I was wrong. Once we got over this hurdle, they never held back again. And for that, I am immensely grateful. So... to each and every one of you, thank you. Thank you for trusting me to do a good job and share what you really thought. Thank you for reaching out to each other. Thank you for taking the leap of faith that we could do this. Thank you for going to parties on a Saturday night and taking my questions with you and reporting back. Thank you for dragging other guys to meet with me. Thank you for meeting me early on a Saturday morning at the beginning of your summer holiday. Thank you for sharing aspects of yourself that you have always kept private. Thank you for making me laugh, learn, and remember why this book was so important to write. There were times writing this book that I never wanted it to end, and that was because of you all.

The Editors: Andrew Seide, Aaron Hutchinson, Aaron Wilson, Abram Blau, Al Hernandez, Andrew Steggman, Anthony Conselatore, Anthony Kuhnriech, Antoine Oates, Antonio Guanes Gomes, Auguste Boova, Austin Howard, Ayon Basu, Blair Jones, Brian Firshing, Brian Tien---Street, Brian Wolfson, Bryan Devlieg, Byron Schaeffer, Case Van der Velde, Johnathan Calderson, Calvin Phillips, Carol Krell, Charlie Schubert, Christopher Hall, Cody Phillips, Connor White, Corey Campbell, David Colvey, Duncan Harvey, Emily Munch, Erik Overdyk, Ethan Pacifico, Evan O'Leary, Graham Dick, Grant Wolf, Haris Ghayas, Hunter Gofus, Ian Brennan, Ian Davis, Ian Dumas, Ian Tasiopulos, Jack Zwemer, Jackson Crispin, Jacob Freund, Jake Stein, Jason Benedict, JD Birks, Jordan Noble, Justin Meyer, Joshua Klein, Kennedy Kommor, Kevin Kopervas, Kevin Bengtsson, Kris Craiger, Lachlan Moore, Luuk Kuiper, Najee Booker, Mathias Tucunduva, Matt Dias, Max Guidry, Mendel Schwarz, Michael Birks, Ned Oliver, Noah Hackman, Ondre Johnson, Owen Yaeger, Pedro Quirino, Raffaele Saposhnik, Ricky Coston, Riley Jamison, Robert Chen, Ryan Perry, Sam Fishel, Samuel Burge, Sam Paplow, Sebastian Luna, Sebastian Medina---Teyac, Seondre Gambrell, Stanley Feeney, Stephen Goodly, Tristan Anderson, Troy Washington, Trevor Riley, Tyler Wells, Tucker Stas, Victor Chang, Victor Ruiz Fierro, Vincent Santos, Will Llewellyn, Will Melley, Will O'Malley, Grace Ishime, Will McAnulty, William Davis, Will Oldham, Winston Robinson, Alejandra Charrabe, Anna---Rogers Daub, Sarah Nugent, Corrine Asher, Natania Lipp, Annie Hall, Annie McCall, Antonia Smith, Carrie Anderson, Claire Sleigh, Crista Butler, Crystal Staebell, Emily Callahan, Molly Oliver, Emily Munch, Claire Dickinson, Emma Merrill, Georgina Eaton, Diana Perkins, Barbara Lannert, Grace Ohaus, Hannah Schmelzer, Melissa Vaz---Ayes, Hannah Scott, Anisha Datta, Izzy Gwozdz, Julia Sidman, Morgan Rogers---Daub, Adrienne Gallus, Teresa Davis, Kate Maguire, Elizabeth Beckman, Lenna Soltau, Ryley Van der Velde, Sarah Farnsworth, Alicia Furlan, Ellie Jay, Victoria

Karem, Lizzie Dollar, Kasey Hemeon, David Keyer, Kimber Ludovico, Maddy Lyons, Mary Oliver, Maureen Lei, Gracie Parrish, Melody Estevez, Mia Henkebein, Michelle Dange, Paige McClellan, Pascale Bronder, Sam Westrum, Samantha Schweickhardt, Sarah Bode, Sofi Sinozich, Jack Twomey, Matthew Disilva, Chris Baker, Chris Doyle, Christopher Esselman, George Isaacs, Isaac Keuber, Jack Tiedman, Jacob Hoffman, John Villanueva, Michael Borger, Nick Christensen, Noah Tuell, Parker Duff, Preston Luniewski, Tyler Lolla, Will Stern, Michael Webb, Coley Sullivan, Tyler Lolla, Alicia Furlan, Camden Donner, Farrah Staebell, Kacey Wheeler, Katie Hillebrand, Molly Speth, Paige MccLellan, Sarah Camp, Tori Smith, Wambui Watene, Nico Adamo, Zack Anderson, Dante Chavez, Ryan Choi, Cole Emry, Saijai Kaushal, Brooks Lebow, Michael Maragakis, Wayne Nelms, Dylan Patel, Bennet Speicher, Essex Thayer, Jack Tortolani, and Jack Witherspoon.

The Parent Editors:

Andy Meyer, David Horn, Sean Britt, Tim Katz, Christine Tiedemann, Heather McCubbin, Jennifer Zwember, Melissa Moore, Johanna Olson, Kyle Esh, Melissa Smith, Sharon Ney, Amy Hewitt, Christine Buchberger, Lynn Devlieg, Maria Grat, Mark Frega, Rana Clarke, Steve Shapiro

The generational bridge editors (guys in their twenties): Max Neely Cohen, who literally made this book something I can be proud of. Will Pierce, who started out not at all sure if this was a good idea but stuck with me. And Charlie Kuhn, who joined this project at the exact right moment.

The initial outreach to the editors wouldn't have been possible without incredible teachers, administrators, coaches, and community leaders connecting me to the boys and, in some cases, girls. Thanks to my partner schools: Walden, Louisville Collegiate, Sophie B. Wright High School, Hynes Middle School, Moorestown Friends School, The Hill School, Millbrook, Haverford School, Gilman School, Bexley High School, Graded School Sao Paulo, Brazil, Potomac Falls High School, Montgomery Blair, and Sidwell Friends. Thank you to the other schools where I presented to your students and they came forward to help. Thank you also to educational colleagues: Carey Faversham Goldstein, Susan Steinman, Linda Van Houten, Andre Perry, Sharon Clark, Margo Johnson, Katie LuBrant, Michelle Douglas, Kirk Dolson, Officer Lindsey Wilson, Dan Feigin, David Swaney, Laura Morgan, Patty Manning and her staff at Cincinnati Children's Hospital, Janet Seide, and Eugenia Brady. Thank you also to my publisher, Crown; my editor, Rick Horgan; Nathan Roberson; my uber--- editor Tina Constable; and Jim Levine and everyone at Levine Greenberg Literary Agency.

Thank you to my husband, James Edwards, who again made it possible for me to go into the writing cave. And thank you to my sons, Elijah and Roane Edwards, who showed absolutely no interest in the book—except for the chapter on video games. I completely respect their honesty and constant ability to give me so many opportunities to put my advice into practice.